Talking Business.

Strategies for
Successful Presentations

Ava Cross
Ryerson Polytechnic University

Prentice Hall Canada Career & Technology
Scarborough, Ontario

To my mother
And to the memory of my father and my sister

Canadian Cataloguing in Publication Data

Cross, Ava, Date
Talking business : strategies for successful presentations

Includes index.
ISBN 0-13-081071-1

1. Business presentations.   I. Title.

HF5718.22.C76 2000   658.4'52   C99-930393-7

Prentice-Hall, Inc., Upper Saddle River, New Jersey
Prentice-Hall International (UK) Limited, London
Prentice-Hall of Australia, Pty. Limited, Sydney
Prentice-Hall Hispanoamericana, S.A., Mexico City
Prentice-Hall of India Private Limited, New Delhi
Prentice-Hall of Japan, Inc., Tokyo
Simon & Schuster Asia Private Limited, Singapore
Editora Prentice-Hall do Brasil, Ltda., Rio de Janeiro

ISBN 0-13-081071-1

Vice President, Editorial Director: Laura Pearson
Acquisitions Editor: David Stover
Art Director: Mary Opper
Associate Editor: Susan Ratkaj
Production Editor: Matthew Christian
Copy Editor: Lisa Berland
Production Coordinator: Peggy Brown
Marketing Manager: Sophia Fortier
Cover Image: PhotoDisc
Cover Design: Alex Li

  2 3 4 5   03 02 01 00

Printed and bound in Canada.

Visit the Prentice Hall Canada web site! Send us your comments, browse our catalogues, and
more at **www.phcanada.com**. Or reach us through e-mail at **phabinfo_pubcanada@prenhall.com**

Contents

Preface xi

**Chapter 1 Business Speaking Skills:
The Basis of Success 1**

What the Market Wants 2

What Research Shows 4

The Modern World of Work 5

    Teamwork 5
    Technical Support 5
    Downsizing 6
    The Service Attitude 6
    Open Communication 6
    Diversity 7

Business Speaking and Public Speaking 7

    It's the Same 7
    But It's Different 7

Professionalism and the Business Speaker 9

    What Does Professionalism Mean to a Business Speaker? 9
    The Issue of Ethics 10

The Benefits of Effective Business Speaking 10

    Business Benefits 10
    Personal Benefits 10

Chapter Summary 11

Applications 11

References 13

**Chapter 2 Preparing to Speak:
Purpose, Audience, and Time 14**

Organizing Yourself 15

Know Your Audience 17

Defining Your Audience 17

Some Special Audience-Related Problems 20

The Shadow Audience 21

Noise 22

Formulating Your Objective 23

Determining Your Key Points 25

Developing Your Key Points 26

Managing Time 29

Determining Your Time Limit 29

Correlating Content to Time 30

Chapter Summary 30

Applications 31

References 31

Chapter 3 Making It Accessible: Openings, Closings, and In-Between 32

The Opening 32

Keep It General 32

State Your Purpose and Preview Your Key Ideas 33

Examples from the Real World 34

The Closing 38

Summarize, But Do More 38

Avoid These Mistakes 40

The Speech Body 40

Transitions 41

Internal Previews 43

Internal Summaries 44

Signposting 44

Language and Style 45

The Mechanics 45

Words 46

Sentences 49

Pulling It Together   50

Chapter Summary   53

Applications   53

References   54

Chapter 4 Establishing Rapport: Platform Manner, Vocal Delivery, and Note Management   56

Developing Effective Platform Manner   57

    How to Control Public Speaking Anxiety   57
    How to Energize Your Speech   61
    How to Present with Partners   65
    How to Deal with Question-Answer Sessions   66

Improving Vocal Delivery   67

    Controlling Pace   67
    Preventing Needless Fillers   69
    Injecting Variety   70
    Maintaining Volume   71
    Enunciating   71

Managing Notes Sensibly   72

    Scripts   72
    Outlines   74
    Handling Your Notes   76

Chapter Summary   79

Applications   80

References   80

Chapter 5 Presentations I: Reporting and Training   82

Oral Reporting   83

    Reporting on Written Documents   83
    Presenting Detail   85
    Using Supporting Evidence   88
    Two Common Types of Informational Reports   90

Training   93

    The Learning Organization   93
    Preparing to Train   94
    Clarifying Technical Terminology   101
    Delivering Training   104

Chapter Summary   107

Applications   107

References   108

Chapter 6 Presentations II: The Strategies of Persuasion   110

Preparing to Persuade   111

    Your Audience for Persuasive Speaking   111
    Approaches to Persuasive Speaking   112

Building Persuasion   116

    Questions of Personal Value   116
    Questions of Evidence   119
    Questions of Argument   120

Three Types of Persuasive Business Speaking   122

    Motivational Speaking   122
    Oral Proposals   125
    Speeches That Justify Decisions and Actions   127

Chapter Summary   129

Applications   130

References   131

Chapter 7 Visual Support: Planning, Preparing, and Presenting   132

The Need for Visual Support   132

    How Visual Support Helps Your Audience   133
    How Visuals Help You as a Business Speaker   133

Planning Your Visuals   134

    Using Your Outline for Placing Visuals   135
    Calculating the Number of Visuals   135

Types of Visual Aids   136

    Design Considerations   136
    Charts   138
    Tables   149
    Illustrations and Videotapes   149
    Objects   150
    Some Cautionary Words about Visual Aids   151

Presentation Media   154

    Manual Presentation Methods   154
    High-Tech Presentation Media   157

Chapter Summary   158

Applications   159

References   160

Chapter 8 Groupwork: Meetings and Telemeetings   161

The Team Culture and the Canadian Workplace   161

    The Benefits of Teamwork   162
    The Problems of Teamwork   164

Meetings: A Primer   164

    Planning for Meetings   165
    Managing the Discussion   167
    Two Elements of Problem-Solving   168

Telemeetings   172

    Electronic Meeting Systems: Some Mechanics   173
    Tips for Electronic Meetings   174
    Teleconferencing Choices   175

Chapter Summary   176

Applications   177

References   177

Chapter 9 Interpersonal Communication on the Job: Listening, Interviewing, and Dealing with Disagreement   179

Listening   180

The Two Types of Listening   180

Informational Interviewing   184

Targeting Questions   184
Arranging the Meeting: Some Practical Considerations   184
Introducing the Interview   185
Concluding the Interview   185
Types of Questions   186
Nonverbal and Vocal Cues in Informational Interviews   188

Dealing with Disagreement   188

Conflict at Work   188
Maintaining Interpersonal Relationships   189

Chapter Summary   192

Applications   192

References   193

Chapter 10 Employment Interviewing: Expectations and Performance   194

Pre-Interview Planning   195

Step One: Self-Analysis   195
Step Two: Document Preparation   198
Step Three: Company Research   198
Step Four: Interview Rehearsal   199

Interview Formats   200

The One-on-One Interview   200
The Panel Interview   201
Electronic Interviews   201

Interview Behaviour   202

Those First Moments   202
During the Interview   203

Departure   203
Controlling Nervousness   204

Interview Questions   204

Questions about Technical Skills and Workplace Knowledge   205
Questions about Communication Skills   206
Questions about Interpersonal Skills   206
Questions about Integrity   207
Questions about Personal Strengths   207

Chapter Summary   208

Applications   208

References   209

Chapter 11 Ceremonial Speaking: Mixing Business and Pleasure   210

Some Basic Rules for Ceremonial Business Speaking   210

1. Lean Toward Brevity   211
2. Make It Positive   211
3. Make It Personal   212

Types of Ceremonial Business Speeches   213

Speeches Celebrating Employee Achievement   213
Speeches Marking Retirement and Departure   214
Speeches Marking Company Milestones and Achievements   214
Speeches Announcing Community Service Programs   216

Chapter Summary   218

Applications   218

References   219

Preface

Talking Business is a practical, hands-on book for speaking in the workplace. The focus is on analyzing your audience and your purpose, and on applying the strategies that will help you communicate successfully when presenting information to small or large groups, participating in meetings, and interacting one-to-one. Business people at all levels can use this book as a resource for honing their business-speaking skills. Students will learn the basics of oral communication at work, and gain a firm footing for fulfilling many business-speaking tasks. Without a doubt, speaking skills are a highly valued job qualification. I hope that *Talking Business* will help you develop this competence.

While *Talking Business* offers guidelines for speaking successfully on the job, it avoids a formulaic approach. A running theme in this book is adaptation: you must be sensitive to the distinct needs and knowledge level of your audiences in order to create successful presentations and to interact with groups and individuals effectively. *Talking Business* encourages you to analyze your listeners carefully and to focus your purpose for each separate speaking event, because no two audiences are alike.

This oral communication book uses examples and advice from business people at all levels, from Canada's leading executives to managers and support staff. *Talking Business* also employs three fictional characters, one a computer programmer, another a bank's mutual funds advisor, and a third an independent marketing consultant, to portray the challenges facing many business people when preparing and delivering presentations, attending meetings and job interviews, and speaking one-to-one. The choices these characters face and the decisions they make to communicate in a clear and meaningful manner to their specific audiences will help you apply the many ideas in this book.

You will learn:

- why it is necessary to develop oral communication skills, the many forms of business speaking in the modern workplace, and the benefits of speaking effectively, both professionally and personally;

- how to build presentations through thorough planning and preparation;

- how to focus your purpose and adapt your speech to your time limit;

- how to use language to guide your audience through your speech and to communicate with non-experts;

- how to project confidence through platform manner and vocal delivery;

- strategies for organizing and delivering reports and training sessions;

- strategies for persuasive speaking, including how to select the right strategy for your audience, and how to build your argument to gain the support and commitment of your listeners;

- the importance of ethics: why you must be scrupulous about the integrity of your argument and how to integrate your evidence into your presentations;

- how to plan and prepare your visual support: guidance for selecting the right graphic aid for your purpose and the right media to communicate your visual information;

- group and interpersonal skills to help you maintain productive work relationships;

- strategies for performing well at the all-important job interview, including advice for dealing with common interview questions; and

- strategies for preparing a variety of social business presentations.

Special features of *Talking Business* include exercises for practicing the principles I present, and the book's thoroughly Canadian content. The excerpts from speeches delivered by Canadian executives not only serve as examples of good business speaking, but also examine many timely issues concerning Canadian business and Canadian society, such as the changing nature of the workplace, the impact of technology, and the importance of lifelong learning. I hope you enjoy learning what Canadian business leaders have to say about Canada and the place of business in it.

Acknowledgments

As a teacher of business and technical communication at Ryerson Polytechnic University, I have had the pleasure of learning from my students. I would like to thank them, and in particular Janice Simms, Brian Greenwood, and Suzana Neves, for sharing material with me. Radhika McDoom granted me permission to use a speech outline prepared for an oral communication class.

I interviewed business people, professionals, and teachers to learn about their business speaking activities and their thoughts on effective communication. I thank Lisa Carter; Kenneth Chapman; Pam Ellis, B.P.H.E., A.C.E., certified personal trainer; Professor M. Gillian Mothersill of Ryerson Polytechnic University; Christopher Jackson, CFP; Cal Smiley; Bill Stevens; and Mark Swartz, career consultant, speaker, and author, for patiently responding to my questions.

The following executives and organizations graciously granted me permission to use material: Don Calder, president and CEO, BC Telecom, Inc.; Shahid Hussain, director, Marketing, BCT. Telus; Bank of Montreal; Bell Canada; Carol Stephenson, president and COO, Bell Satellite Services; Cameco Corporation; Canadian Centre for

Occupational Health and Safety; Canadian National Railway Company; Dofasco, Inc.; Noranda, Inc.; Nortel Networks; Royal Bank of Canada; Scotiabank; Spar Aerospace, Ltd.; Suncor Energy, Inc.; TD Bank Financial Group.

The people who reviewed parts of the manuscript's first draft saw where I was heading, and their insights helped to guide me there. I would like to thank:

Jennifer MacLennan, D.K. Seaman Chair in Technical and Professional Writing, College of Engineering, University of Saskatchewan

David McCarthy, Centennial College

Maryrose O'Neill, Seneca College

Leslie Savage, Capilano College.

David Stover at Prentice Hall Canada was interested in my idea for a Canadian business-speaking text, and I am grateful to him for giving me the opportunity to write this book, my first. I also want to thank Susan Ratkaj, Matthew Christian, Lisa Berland, and Pat Thorvaldson for their expertise in shepherding the manuscript through production.

I was very fortunate to receive the encouragement of my family, in Canada and the U.S., throughout the writing of this book. John Cross read every word of the first and second drafts. His honest criticisms and his unfailing and humourous support were invaluable. Miriam and David were always patient and loving. Leslie Gordon Politzer and Sharon Barbanel Geier gave me the benefit of their own experience. Bill and Eleanor Cross keenly followed my progress; Eleanor would have liked to see my work in print. The dedication honours my parents and my sister for what they gave me.

CHAPTER 1

Business Speaking Skills: The Basis of Success

I want you to look at the career progress of two people, one in a technical field and the other in business.

After completing a 12-month college-level computer programming course, Françoise was hired by an Alberta health care agency as a junior programmer. Her first duties were to write specifications and design computer programs under supervision. Two years later she was promoted to programmer analyst. She now delegated and tracked the work of junior programmers and summer students, and served on committees deciding on software purchases. She also collaborated on program design with her project team and delivered status reports at monthly meetings. The head of information systems invited her to attend a major computer conference, and upon her return she delivered a presentation on the sessions she had attended. After four years as a programmer analyst, she became a systems analyst. Her supervisory duties expanded to include the additional task of training end-users on new software.

Quan joined the human resources department of a Manitoba printing firm upon completion of his degree in business management. Focusing on benefits and compensation, his duties involved keeping up to date on benefit plans, listening to the concerns of employees, and answering their questions. After a year on the job, he gave lunchtime seminars to employee groups on benefit changes. As time went on, he became a specialist in his area—he provided written reports to the vice-president of human resources that evaluated insurance programs and he reported orally on his findings and recommendations to committees. As Quan progressed, he trained new members of his department.

What do such work histories tell us?

1. People rarely work in isolation. They have to communicate with their colleagues as well as with individuals outside of their organization.

2. Oral communication activities are varied. They include interpersonal communication, presentations to groups of different sizes, training sessions, meetings, and interviews.

3. As employees prove themselves, they are presented with new challenges.

4. If employees accept challenges, inevitably they will be required to communicate orally with more people, often in more formal and complex ways.

The examples of Françoise and Quan represent stories I listened to while doing research for this book. While many of my sources, like Françoise and Quan, have college and university degrees, and some have graduate degrees and professional designations, a number have not earned any formal credentials. Some of the business people and technicians who gave me the wisdom of their experience entered the workplace as clerks or shop-floor workers, with a secondary-school education, and took opportunities as they appeared. As these people advanced, they upgraded their communication skills through self-study, workshops, and continuing education classes. Some have returned to university as part-time degree students. A running theme through our conversations was that when they began their careers they had no idea that they would progress to their current positions involving supervisory and decision-making responsibilities. Nor did they suspect that a variety of oral communication activities would form such a large part of their duties.

In this chapter we will examine the importance of effective business speaking skills and their benefits.

What the Market Wants

I know I don't really have to justify the need for effective business speaking skills. Anyone already working or looking for work knows these skills are important. But for the sake of reinforcement, let's examine some Canadian job advertisements. If you look in your local newspaper, chances are you'll find several positions that require some competence in oral communication. Another source of job postings is the World Wide Web. It's interesting to see how pervasive the need for effective oral communication skills is.

The telecommunications company Nortel includes proficiency in oral communication under the heading "valued skills and abilities" in their technical job postings.[1] What does the word "valued" imply? It does not necessarily mean that the skill is required to get the job. Instead, "valued" suggests that the skill is an asset—it can set one applicant apart from others, and can be a deciding factor in securing a job at Nortel. Nortel separates the category "valued skills and abilities" from "relevant technical skills and interests": these assets require background in such areas as "real-time systems" and "microwave radio systems"—in other words, the technical knowledge applicants must have to do the job. But "valued skills" are a distinct plus. They are sought for positions in software design and development, business information systems, and information technology, for example, and include the following traits:

- excellent interpersonal and teamwork skills
- excellent oral and written communication skills
- teamwork orientation
- high level of interpersonal skills and service orientation

Similar phrases appear under the heading "relevant," rather than "valued," skills and interests in Nortel's business openings, such as human resources and marketing. These qualifications are deemed essential where communicating with people is the main part of the job.

Nortel is but one example of a Canadian company valuing communication skills. The Alberta oil producer Syncrude seeks engineers and designers with "excellent written and verbal communication skills."[2] The Royal Bank Financial Group seeks customer service professionals who "possess strong leadership and communication skills ... and enjoy the challenge of working with both staff and customers."[3] The Royal Bank's job posting for programmer/analysts says, "proven oral, written and interpersonal skills are essential for success in this exciting and technically challenging position."[4] Look at Figure 1-1 for typical business and technical speaking tasks.

Figure 1-1   Typical Business and Technical Presentations

Providing technical information

Discussing marketing plans

Discussing project status

Reviewing a design

Presenting technical aspects of a system design

Giving computer demonstrations using computer displays

Reviewing and assessing other organizations' plans and products

Analyzing budget submissions

Source: H.J. Scheiber and Peter J. Hager, "Oral Communication in Business and Industry: Results of a Survey on Scientific, Technical, and Managerial Presentations," *Journal of Technical Writing and Communication* 24, no. 2, 161-179.

Not only employers seek effective oral communication skills. Professional associations sponsoring training for certification require communication courses in their programs of study. The syllabus of the Certified General Accountant program, for example, claims that a "high standard of written and oral communication is expected of the professional accountant."[5] Prospective CGAs must take an oral and written communications course to earn their designation. Many technical and industry associations also support speaking courses. The Aluminum Extruders Council, for example (many professional associations *are* highly specialized), sponsors a joint Canadian–U.S. "Effective Presentation Skills Workshop" for improving the presentation skills of technical experts.[6]

What Research Shows

We've just seen that the real world wants workers to have speaking skills—it's part of their job, be it technical or business. Studies reveal how employers rank the importance of oral communication skills. A survey of systems analysts shows that, after analytical skills, communication skills were tied with technical skills for second place.[7] A 1995 U.S. study of the communication needs of business people shows that 84 per cent of survey respondents believe the ability to speak to a small audience is either "important" or "very important." One respondent remarked that in his organization oral communication on a one-on-one basis or in small groups was "far more important than writing skills."[8] According to a 1997 study, managers believe that "oral communication is more important than written communication for entry-level positions." This study also reveals that competency in oral communication ranks first in hiring criteria.[9]

A common comment in the 1995 study mentioned above was that communication skills of staff members were weak. It was noted that "language skills are vitally important (and frequently lacking) in anyone who pursues a career in business."[10] Another workplace study shows a paradox. We have just seen that oral communication skills are ranked high in the search for qualified job candidates. Yet when the candidate becomes an employee, and is evaluated at the annual or semi-annual performance appraisal, supervisors often recommended that these skills be improved.[11] In other words, workers aren't well equipped for communicating orally in the workplace, even though effective speaking is a qualification for the job.

While such studies are often U.S.-based, what applies south of the border also holds true in Canada. There is a great need for improving business speaking skills. Without a doubt, the abundance of in-house and external communication workshops offered to business people testifies to it. And a foundation for future professionals is being formed through Junior Achievement Programs. In Vancouver, for example, as many as four thousand business people have volunteered their time to help high-school students improve their interpersonal and public speaking skills.[12]

The Modern World of Work

As I said at the beginning of this chapter, people do not work in isolation: communicating with co-workers, clients, customers, and suppliers is part of the job. Let's briefly consider the nature of the modern workplace.

Teamwork

This term often appears in job descriptions. Numerous positions Nortel had available as this chapter was written sought applicants with a "teamwork orientation." The 1996 annual report from Noranda, a Toronto-based mining company, discusses the "flattening" of the organization by grouping employees into self-managing teams.[13] In a speech about the future of the steel industry in Canada, John Mayberry, president and CEO of Hamilton-based Dofasco, discussed the "delayering of management" in the company. "We now have 5 layers where once we had as many as 13," Mayberry said. "We're trying to push decision-making down to where it belongs—with the people actually doing the job every day ...."[14]

In many jobs today, an employee is a member of a team. He or she has specific duties that must be accomplished individually, but they all contribute to the completion of the group project. The outcome of the group effort is the product of the team, not of one person. Being a team member requires a number of skills: good interpersonal skills that help complete the project efficiently and maintain a friendly atmosphere, good meeting skills that facilitate problem-solving, and good oral reporting skills that clearly keep colleagues up to date on the progress of your contribution to the team effort. Without these oral communication skills, workplace teams cannot function productively.

Teams may be composed of people who are experts in the same field or who have expertise in different fields. Imagine a scenario, for example, in which an engineer works on the same team with a marketing expert—perhaps the group is responsible for designing a product and analyzing competing products. The technical expert will need to explain ideas and processes in a way that the business person can understand. Oral communication skills needed here involve the ability to speak to the nonexpert in accessible terms.

Technical Support

The ever-growing applications of technology form another characteristic of the modern workplace, and one that also requires special communication skills. Many specialists are involved in technical support. This may mean training people on new software or computer systems, or trouble-shooting problems and explaining to the customer what they are. As with the situation of the engineer and the marketing expert, the ability to translate technical terms into those the nontechnician can understand is a vital business speaking skill.

Downsizing

Another feature of the modern workplace is an outcome of the "downsizing" of the last thirty years when many large and small organizations laid off workers and restructured. Downsizing often resulted in new job descriptions and the consolidation of duties. Circumstances compelled employees who kept their jobs to take on responsibilities they did not previously have. Someone who once worked exclusively on the shop floor may now have managerial duties and be expected to supervise employees, chair meetings, and report to superiors. The key quality for the modern worker is versatility, the ability to learn new skills along with their exclusive forms of business speaking.

Many people who lost their jobs retrained and entered new careers. Many started their own businesses, as entrepreneurs or consultants. In these roles, people were required to promote their special abilities. Business speaking skills needed to grow your own business involve persuasion—convincing a financial institution to give you a business loan, for example, or demonstrating to potential clients the value of the service you can offer them.

The Service Attitude

The service attitude is another key term that characterizes the modern workplace. This phrase not only embraces an organization's customers, but often fellow workers as well. The concept of customer service means that people are treated with respect and courtesy. With customers, the goal is to increase business. With colleagues, the goal is to maintain a positive workplace environment. Good interpersonal skill is the central attribute of a service philosophy.

Open Communication

Many modern organizations nurture an environment of open communication. This practice means that employees are encouraged to question management about the organization's strategies and goals, operations, problems, and dealings with employees, for example. Often such communication is conducted through a company newsletter—print or electronic—via a question-answer column, or an intranet, an internal e-mail system. Sometimes open communication is practised orally. Four times a year Aetna Life Insurance Co. of Canada holds a forum where employees question senior executives on company and employee issues. A different employee conducts each session—someone who may not be accustomed to speaking in public. Part of the moderator's job is to encourage the timid to speak up. Such open forums are beneficial for the company: Aetna says that their forums permit management to keep employees up to date on the ever-changing insurance industry, and to be aware of employee concerns.[15] These sessions are also good experience for the moderator, giving him or her practice in conducting a large meeting.

Diversity

Diversity in its broadest sense characterizes Canadian business. Any presentation or one-to-one communication is also an exercise in intercultural communication. The need for relevant information and clear presentation unites all members of your business audience. But this audience is composed of individuals from different cultural backgrounds. Effective business speakers respect their audiences and adapt to any special requirements—inevitably, sensitivity to your diverse audience helps to cultivate a productive and pleasant work atmosphere.

As you can see, the modern workplace requires versatile communicators. It is not just executives and managers who must prepare presentations, conduct and participate in meetings, and deal with customers, clients, and colleagues. It is virtually anyone in today's world of work.

Business Speaking and Public Speaking

I have used the term "business speaking" frequently in this chapter. You may be asking yourself, how is it different from public speaking? Like me, you may have been forced to take a speech class in secondary school, college, or university (or all three) as a part of your curriculum. The experience was perhaps painful, but certainly useful. A public speaking class gave you the opportunity to develop a level of comfort when speaking to a group of strangers. It also gave you practice in two basic forms of oral communication: informative and persuasive. But is public speaking any different from business speaking?

It's the Same

In general, business speaking isn't different from public speaking. Both forms require you to speak before a group of people. Both forms require you to focus your topic and to organize your thoughts. Both forms require you to present your ideas clearly. Both forms require you to understand your audience.

But It's Different

But business speaking is somewhat different from public speaking: we can best think of it as a more focused form of public speaking.

The Business Purpose

First and foremost, business speaking has a business purpose. In any business setting, the purpose of a business presentation—or any business speaking task—influences a business decision: for example, whether to enter a new venture or to continue with a project. The task may also be to train employees or clients so that not only is their knowledge enhanced, but business goals are advanced, resulting in an improved customer relationship or a market for a new product. Public speaking, as we have practised it in school, tends to be politically, culturally, or socially motivated. Business speaking almost always has a business motivation.

Respect For Time Limits

Second, when delivering business presentations, business speakers have a heightened awareness of the time limit, probably because violation tends to be penalized in a business environment. Typically, your business presentation is just one segment of your audience's full, often hectic and pressured day. Speakers who take more than their allotted share of their audience's time may experience a decline in their image and reputation, and, possibly, in their business relationship with their listeners.

The Straight and Simple

Third, business speakers often reject the rhetorical devices of public speaking. By rhetorical devices, I mean the use of metaphors, visual imagery, attention-grabbing introductions, stirring conclusions—the flowery stuff. Business speaking tends to be more straightforward and to the point—it tends to be businesslike and economical.

The Inspirers

Now, you are probably wondering about motivational and inspirational speeches delivered by Canadian business leaders. It is not unusual to find motivational speeches by business people that are meant to inspire employees or the general public. This book includes addresses by such business leaders as Matthew Barrett, former CEO of the Bank of Montreal, and Carol Stephenson, president and COO of Bell Satellite Services. When venturing into the public forum, Canadian business leaders display some of the stirring techniques of public speaking. But typically, either directly or indirectly, these leaders use the public forum for business purposes: to communicate a vision of business in Canadian society, or to promote their own organization or industry. Often, though not always, a business purpose underlies the business person's public effort.

So as you read this book you will be reminded of your public speaking classes. Yet you will see that the types of business speaking tasks and the nature of the business audience require skills and ways of thinking that evolve from those used for public speaking. Some business speaking activities, such as training, will be quite different.

Professionalism and the Business Speaker

Although you may never be asked to deliver a speech at an MBA conference or to a group of business leaders at a stock exchange luncheon, a professional attitude and behaviour should always govern your business-speaking activities.

What Does Professionalism Mean to a Business Speaker?

What professionalism means to a business speaker is a question I asked my sources for this book, people who have risen from entry-level to positions of greater responsibility. This question received serious and impassioned responses. I'd like you to look at some of them.

Gillian Mothersill, a former training manager who is now a university teacher, remarks,

Little things that I think are signs of professionalism are not to panic if things don't go well. Over the last 15 years I've been in countless technical seminars where someone has been introducing a new product or trying to sell a product and invariably there has been some kind of a technical hiccup. I think it's a sign of real professionalism not to panic about this because most of us in the technical field have been there. You need to be prepared for these things when they happen, that is, have some kind of a backup plan. But sooner or later it will happen to even the best presenters so you need to develop a strategy for dealing with that.[16]

Mark Swartz, a career consultant, speaker, and author, lists the following requirements for professional business speaking:

- adhering to the agenda and time limits set
- taking into account the needs of the audience
- satisfying the objectives set out by management and achieving pre-defined goals that the audience has agreed to in advance
- dressing, speaking, and behaving appropriately with regard to the audience[17]

To Christopher Jackson, a Certified Financial Planner, speakers with a professional attitude are ones who are "well-prepared, who have made it their business to know what they are speaking about, who are sensitive to the unique concerns of the audience, who do research on the audience." Chris says that speakers with a professional presence also display "that extra X factor—credibility."[18]

Lisa Carter, who has worked as network administrator and support for a major North American property management company, uses the terms "decorum," "respect of others' views," and "preparation" to describe a competent business speaker.[19]

The Issue of Ethics

Another dimension of professionalism and business speaking deals with ethics. Many Canadian companies, and divisions of international companies operating in Canada, have written codes of ethics guiding the behaviour of all employees. In its document "Core Values," Nortel outlines the ethical standards for its workers.[20] The guidelines say that an employee's manner of communication—at any level—affects "the integrity and credibility of the company as a whole." They also urge employees "to communicate our ideas and concerns in an honest and clear manner" and state that "'acting with integrity' also means that while we may not always be sure of every answer, we will not say one thing and then do another."

The damage for violating an organizational code of ethics is often irreversible. The repercussions of unethical behaviour described in the Nortel code apply to any business, large or small: "When individuals choose to disregard the Code, we could all suffer from damage to the corporate reputation and the ensuing loss of customers, community and employee goodwill, and profitability." As a business speaker, you have a commitment to present your information truthfully and accurately—ethical behaviour is critical to a speaker's and an organization's credibility.

The Benefits of Effective Business Speaking

I'm sure by now you realize that effective business speaking skills have all sorts of implications—organizational, personal, and ethical. Let's consider the benefits of effective speaking.

Business Benefits

The most obvious benefits are those to your organization. As you communicate effectively, be it one-to-one, in a meeting, or through a presentation, your clear, straightforward, and well-organized expression of ideas will help your listener make a decision or solve a problem. The company itself will run more smoothly, because you are fulfilling your part in a productive way. If you deal with suppliers or clients outside of your organization, your manner of communicating will enhance your company's reputation. Obviously, communicating well to your external audience also builds goodwill and business.

Personal Benefits

It is apparent that effective communicators advance at work. Communicating well earns high marks in performance appraisals and the recognition of your colleagues and superiors. As we have seen earlier in this chapter, effective oral communication is to many employers the most important business skill.

But there are other kinds of personal benefits; these can be grouped under the heading "the intangibles." The intangibles are psychological: feeling good about yourself, knowing you've achieved something, such as overcoming the fear of giving a presentation or leading a meeting or open forum. You may be familiar with the saying, "success breeds success." It's true—overcoming anxiety and performing well develops self-confidence and raises your self-esteem. These intangible qualities are important personal outcomes of effective speaking, and your new self-image can bring opportunities you've never predicted, in your work as well as in your life.

Chapter Summary

This chapter ended on a high note. I hope I gave you some confidence to continue onto Chapter 2 and beyond, to apply the concepts and skills I will discuss to your work lives. As we have seen, employers rank effective speaking skills as a prime criterion for hiring. Oral communication informs virtually every business activity, and affects the work environment as well as the balance sheet. Your personal approach to speaking at work determines not only the success of the business, but also your success as an employee.

Oral communication, despite being vital to a business's productivity and reputation, is a requirement that causes people anxiety and apprehension. Many seasoned executives, as well as entry-level employees, experience dread when delivering a speech or presentation to a group, be it large or small. The awareness that at any level, in any interaction, how you present yourself and your subject matter can influence your organization's well-being, as well as your own, can be unnerving.

Business speaking is something people in junior, intermediate, and senior levels have to do, and do well. Chapter 2 will get you on your way by discussing how to prepare for business speaking tasks.

Applications

1. Create a definition of professionalism as related to business speaking. Apply it to business speakers you have heard. To what extent have they surpassed those standards? How much do they need to improve?

2. Apply your definition of professionalism to yourself. To what extent do you consider yourself "professional" as a business speaker? In what areas would you like to improve?

3. What are the ethical requirements of a business speaker? Why it is important that a business speaker be ethical?

4. Self-analysis: What are your on-the-job speaking tasks? Have they changed? Fill out the following worksheets to determine the nature of your oral communication activities at work. You may be surprised at how varied they are.

A. Speaking Activity Worksheet

Activity	Frequency					
	Daily	3/week	1–2/week	2/month	Monthly	Other
phone conversations	_____	_____	_____	_____	_____	_____
training individuals	_____	_____	_____	_____	_____	_____
training groups	_____	_____	_____	_____	_____	_____
interviewing job applicants	_____	_____	_____	_____	_____	_____
interviewing for information	_____	_____	_____	_____	_____	_____
live meetings	_____	_____	_____	_____	_____	_____
phone conferences	_____	_____	_____	_____	_____	_____
videoconferences	_____	_____	_____	_____	_____	_____
industry/business conferences	_____	_____	_____	_____	_____	_____

B. Frequency of Speaking Activity Related to Career Advancement

Complete the following worksheet based on the course of your entire work experience.

Activity	Less frequent	1	2	3	4	5	More frequent
Phone conversations		1	2	3	4	5	
Training individuals		1	2	3	4	5	
Training groups		1	2	3	4	5	
Interviewing job applicants		1	2	3	4	5	
Interviewing for information		1	2	3	4	5	
Live meetings		1	2	3	4	5	
Phone conferences		1	2	3	4	5	
Videoconferences		1	2	3	4	5	
Industry/business conferences		1	2	3	4	5	

References

1. Nortel, "Students and Graduates." [www.careermosaic.com/cm/nortel8.html#H], July 2, 1997.

2. Syncrude, "Jobs." [www.syncrude.com/u125/jobspecs.htm], June 20, 1997.

3. Royal Bank Financial Group, News and Community Centre. [www.royalbank.com/english/hr/hr/custserv.html], June 16, 1997.

4. Ibid.

5. Certified General Accountants of Canada, "Becoming a CGA: Guide to Syllabus." [www.cga-canada.org/education/C/syllabus/intro.htm#Written], May 29, 1997.

6. Robert O. Hirsch, "Turning Technical Experts into Expert Speakers: Aluminum Extruders Council Sponsoring Workshops," *Association Management* 45 (July 1993), 108.

7. Mark Misic, "The Skills Needed by Today's Systems Analysts," *Journal of Systems Management* 47, no. 3 (May 1, 1996), 38.

8. Frederick K. Moss, "Perceptions of Communication in the Corporate Community," *Journal of Business and Technical Communication* 9, no. 1 (January 1995), 63–76. See also S. Clay Willmington, "Oral Communication for a Career in Business," *The Bulletin of the Association for Business Communication* 52, no. 2 (June 1989), 8–12.

9. Jeanne D. Maes, Teresa G. Weldy, and Marjorie L. Icenogle, "A Managerial Perspective: Oral Communication Competency Is Most Important for Business Students in the Workplace," *Journal of Business Communication* 34, no. 1 (January 1997), 76.

10. Moss, 68

11. Roberta Bhasin, "Improving Communication Skills," *Pulp and Paper* 69 (October 1995), 37.

12. Melinda Montgomery, "Canadian Accountant J. W. Trask's Volunteer Work with Junior Achievement," *CA Magazine* 124 (August 1991), 6–7.

13. Noranda Inc., 1996 *Annual Report*, 23.

14. John Mayberry, "Steel Industry Focus on the Future" (delivered to the Canadian Club Breakfast Meeting, Hamilton, Ontario, May 6, 1996). [www.dofasco.ca/news/news_speeches.html#Voyage], August 11, 1997.

15. Margot Gibb-Clark, "How to Keep Employees Informed," *Globe and Mail* (November 1, 1996), B12.

16. Gillian Mothersill, interview with author, Toronto, Ontario (June 5, 1997).

17. Mark Swartz, e-mail to author (June 11, 1997).

18. Christopher Jackson, interview with author, Toronto, Ontario (June 5, 1997).

19. Lisa Carter, interview with author, Toronto, Ontario (June 12, 1997).

20. Nortel, "Core Values: A Guide to Ethical Business Practice," and "Living the Commitments: Guidelines for Ethical Decision Making." [www.nortel.com/ethics], July 8, 1997.

CHAPTER 2

Preparing to Speak: Purpose, Audience, and Time

Let's consider the following scenarios:

- Mahima, a technical specialist at a large pharmaceutical firm, is asked to give a presentation to upper management recommending a notebook computer to be volume-purchased for sales and marketing staff.

- Lyndon, a consultant, is to present the results of a marketing study for a product manufactured by a small business owned by recent immigrants to Canada.

- Andrew, a bank's customer service representative who has recently been certified to sell mutual funds, will give his first presentation to bank customers on mutual fund investing.

Although Mahima, Lyndon, and Andrew are speaking on different topics to different audiences, they can follow a common strategy when preparing their formal business presentations. By "formal," I mean a presentation with a scheduled time and place to which members of the audience are invited; the speech is prepared ahead of time, not delivered spontaneously. At this event listeners are deliberately seeking information that will influence a business decision or help them understand a concept or process. Without a doubt, preparation is the single most important element in the success of a business presentation. The highest expectation of an audience is that the speaker be well prepared.

Preparing for a presentation can be fraught with indecision, uncertainty, and confusion. What do I say? What does my audience need to know? Who is my audience? Will I be able to fit everything I need to say into my time limit? Will the projector work? As you can see, preparation goes beyond developing the content for a speech. It also means understanding your audience, investigating the venue, and preparing visual aids.

Perhaps you already give presentations in your job, either on a regular basis or occasionally. If you are beginning your career, rest assured that, in the modern Canadian workplace as described in Chapter 1, it is likely you will eventually be called upon to deliver a presentation. I'm sure you believe that speakers who plan and prepare their presentations perform better and feel less nervous than those who don't. Subsequent chapters will discuss organizational approaches and speaker-audience concerns for specific business speaking situations; however, the basic concepts explained here can be applied to any business speaking activity—job interviews, interpersonal communications, and participating in meetings. This chapter covers audience analysis, focusing your purpose to meet your audience's needs, and time considerations: the three essentials of planning a presentation.

Organizing Yourself

Before we consider these essentials, I want to discuss managing your own time. This too is an important element to the success of your presentation.

Before you actually begin outlining or scripting your material, it is useful to sit back and obtain an overview of the entire process, from preparation to delivery. Many business people have a strategy for planning a presentation. The following steps constitute a logical method, one, perhaps, that may mirror your own.

1. Determine the purpose of the meeting.

2. Determine who, if anyone, will also be presenting, your place in the order of speakers, and how much time you are allotted.

3. Think thoroughly about your topic and purpose.

4. Analyze your audience.

5. Create a preliminary outline of your key points.

6. Do your research.

7. Create a detailed outline of your presentation.

8. Refine your outline; perhaps write a script.

9. Prepare visual aids and handouts.

10. Rehearse and revise.

11. Rehearse and revise.

12. Visit the venue to ensure that it suits you and that all equipment is functional.

13. Rehearse and revise.

These steps suggest that it takes considerable effort to prepare an effective presentation. You may know through experience that the process is time-consuming. When you are assigned the task and the date you are to speak, you should begin thinking seriously about the event. Don't procrastinate! You need to incorporate this assignment into your already full schedule.

Consider applying "the art of working backwards": that is, reverse planning back from the designated date of your presentation to the initial steps of preparing it. Creating a timeline—and thinking backwards about it—is a useful way of judging the amount of time you have to devote to specific steps; your timeline will help you visualize the stages of preparation and keep on track.

Say, for example, that Mahima, our technical specialist mentioned at the beginning of this chapter, is to present information about notebook computers three weeks from today. Her timeline might look like Figure 2-1.

Figure 2-1 Mahima's Timeline

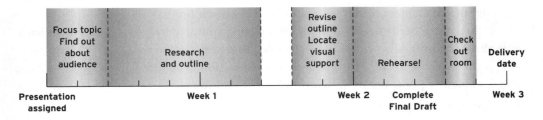

Notice that Mahima plans to complete the final draft of her presentation by the beginning of week three. Two or three days before her presentation date, she visits the venue to determine that all the equipment she needs—the projector and computer linkup, for example—are operational. Early in week three, she will spend two or three days rehearsing. Rehearsal time gives Mahima the opportunity to become so familiar with her material that she can maintain eye contact with her audience and harmonize her visual aids with her speech. Sufficient lead time also gives her the opportunity to revise and refine her presentation further, if necessary.

From the middle of week one to the end of week two she prepares her detailed outline and her visual support, and early in week one she determines her audience's needs, focuses her objective to respond to them, and begins her research. Note that Mahima devotes her first two days of the preparation process to thinking through her purpose and analyzing her audience. She will then spend about four days on research and on outlining her remarks. During this time she will continually ask herself questions that shape her understanding about her objectives and her audience and that direct her research. Although you might be tempted to start your research before you have thought through your purpose thoroughly, don't be hasty. Investing time in analyzing and developing your purpose will make the preparation process more efficient.

As you see, by allowing herself generous time to work on her presentation, Mahima will avoid feeling pressured and will be able to deal with any unpleasant surprises, such as faulty equipment, that can thwart her efforts. Admittedly, you may not always be given three weeks, or even two weeks, to prepare a presentation. In some situations only a short amount of time is required. If you give periodic progress reports on a project, for example, you are already familiar with your material and your audience's needs and expectations. In such instances the amount of research you may need to do is minimal. But whatever the amount of time you have to prepare your presentation, it is important to manage your time effectively.

Know Your Audience

It is impossible to overestimate the importance of analyzing your audience—it is the most vital step in planning your presentation. The objective, content, strategy, research, and level of language all follow from your understanding of your listeners.

Defining Your Audience

There are some basic questions you can ask about your audience to pinpoint their characteristics:

1. Who will be listening to my message? What internal departments or divisions, or outside organizations, do they represent? Are they members of the general public?

2. What is the size of the gathering?

3. What do they need to know?

4. Why does this audience need this information?

5. How knowledgeable is my audience about my topic?

6. What decisions might my audience make based on the information I am presenting?

7. Are all members of my audience eager to receive my message? Or are there individuals who are resistant to it?

8. Are all my listeners fluent speakers of English?

9. Will my listeners report the information I am presenting to their colleagues, to managers, or to executives? Would my information influence decisions these other people might make?

In many business situations, speakers already know who their audiences will be: they work with and report to these individuals as part of their jobs. We can call this audience the "internal" audience—a speaker's colleagues. Often you know about the attitudes and level of knowledge of an internal audience. If you don't, it is easy to learn about them: you can speak to them or to people familiar with them before your presentation.

Sometimes, as in the case of Andrew, the mutual fund sales representative who is to speak to his bank's customers, the audience is more of an unknown quantity. We can call this audience, people outside of an organization, the "external" audience. They may be an organization's clients, customers, suppliers, or the general public. Often a business or technical speaker is familiar with members of an external audience—for example, an employee may have been dealing with a particular group of clients over a period of time on a project. But sometimes an external audience is composed of people the speaker has never met. In this situation finding out about their attitudes, expectations, and knowledge involves guesswork as well as research.

To help you understand your audience, you should create an audience profile as an aid, as many business speakers do; Figure 2-2 is one type. Note that it covers not only the composition and level of knowledge of your listeners, but also the problems you might encounter when speaking to them and the decisions your audience might make based on your speech. Your audience profile will help you determine the level of language and technical explanation of your speech, how to overcome barriers to communicating with a specific audience, and the outcomes you desire.

Let's apply some of the questions in the audience profile form to the scenarios introduced at the beginning of this chapter. The purpose of Mahima's presentation is to recommend a notebook computer for her company's sales and marketing staff. We can speculate that her audience is composed of representatives from this division, as well as someone from the financial department, since this volume purchase of notebook computers involves a sizable investment. Mahima is aware that her audience has some knowledge of notebook computers. She decides to present a very brief overview of the capabilities of such computers in language her audience can understand, but not to define such terms as "memory," "hard disk," or "CD-ROM," for example, because her listeners are sophisticated computer users and have a general knowledge of the computer's components.

Mahima understands that a main concern is the computer's usefulness in the field, so she will discuss how effectively the computer can handle the necessary business and communication software. She will also deal with price and with the product's features in relation to its cost. Mahima decides to present information about two different notebook computers and compare them, showing she has investigated the problem rather than arbitrarily chosen one brand and model. Also, a comparative approach gives her audience themselves the opportunity to compare and analyze features and make an

Figure 2-2 Audience Profile Sheet

Date of presentation:

Topic:

Purpose:

Length:

Composition of audience:

Internal   *External*

Divisions or departments: Clients ❑   Suppliers ❑

                                                          Bankers ❑   Other ❑

Level in organization:

Comments: Comments:

People audience report to:

Decision-making responsibilities?

Comments:

Audience's level of knowledge about my topic:

· Advanced ❑   Intermediate ❑   Basic ❑   None ❑

Comments:

Potential problems in communicating to my audience (e.g., attitude, resistance to message, knowledge of English):

Decision(s) audience may make, based on my presentation:

informed decision. In other words, Mahima will do her best to speak to the needs and knowledge of her audience.

Lyndon is presenting the results of his marketing study. He has worked with his clients, owners of a small business, over some time and knows that they are not familiar with the jargon of market research. Because his clients do not have sophisticated business knowledge, he cannot assume that they know much, if anything, about his methods and techniques. Consequently, he decides to avoid specialized language, more so than Mahima, and to present his findings in terms his clients can easily understand, relying on uncomplicated explanations and definitions. Furthermore, he realizes that there is a language barrier between him and his audience. Although his clients know English, they are not native speakers. Consequently, Lyndon decides to use simple vocabulary and to speak more slowly than he would with fluent English-speaking listeners.

Finally, let's examine Andrew's understanding of his audience, who want to learn about investing in mutual funds. To a great extent, Andrew's audience is unknown to him. He will present his information to a large gathering of between 50 and 100 people, and he does not know which of the bank's customers he has met will attend. He will do some research by studying his bank's customer surveys to learn about customers' knowledge of mutual funds and investing. He learns that many people in his audience may never have purchased mutual funds, or have done any investing; consequently, he will organize his presentation to include explanations of terms and processes. He will discuss financial concepts as simply as he can. He will not direct his information above the heads of his listeners. And, considering the diversity of the bank's customers, he also will use accessible language and control his speaking pace.

As the examples of Mahima, Lyndon, and Andrew show, knowing your audience is critical to getting your message across and helping audience members make their business decisions. Speech scripts you may access on the Internet or obtain from corporations all indicate the speaker's audience. If your listeners do not understand your ideas, you have failed not only in your mission to inform or persuade, but you may also lose customers and suffer some deterioration in relations between the audience and the company, and in your own position at work. If your audience is resistant to your ideas, you have to use effective arguments and convincing evidence to turn them to your point of view: these methods are discussed in Chapter 6, on persuasive business speaking.

Some Special Audience-Related Problems

Many speakers have remarked that adjusting a presentation to the audience's level of knowledge is a greater obstacle to speaking than nervousness. One special situation is presenting technical data to nontechnical people or to people in unrelated technical fields. For example, John MacNaughton, retired president and CEO of Spar Aerospace Ltd., assumed the audience for his speech, "From Stem to Canadarm—Reflections," would understand such terms as "an orthogonal axis robot."[1] Probably most of his listeners did understand, as he spoke to the Canadian Aeronautic and Space Institute.

Another difficulty is ensuring your audience understands your referential remarks. In his presentation at the Invest in Saskatchewan Forum, Bernard Michel, president and CEO of Saskatoon-based Cameco, a uranium mining company, commented, "It will not come as a surprise to you, to learn that I am here to tell you that Cameco is a unique investment opportunity. I was pleased to see in last Saturday's *Globe and Mail* that the famous Dunnery Best agreed."[2] Michel assumed that his audience not only read the *Globe and Mail* but could identify Dunnery Best, a financial advisor and columnist.

Still another situation is presenting information to mixed audiences, such as high-level managers, who want an executive summary, attending the same presentation as technical people, who want the fine details. It can be difficult to satisfy a hybrid audience where one group wants an overview and the other wants technical data.[3] While in situations such as these you will have to accommodate everyone in your audience, discussion of the fine detail can also be allocated to the question-answer session following your speech, when you can deal with technical concerns more thoroughly.

Such situations clearly challenge the business or technical speaker. While there is no easy answer when you are faced with circumstances such as these, trying to understand who is attending your presentation and meeting the needs of the majority of your listeners will help ensure that most of the audience will grasp your message. A successful presentation has two characteristics: your audience should be more informed when they leave the session than when they arrive, and you should walk out knowing more about the audience than when you entered the room. You can apply this knowledge to analyzing audiences for future presentations.

The Shadow Audience

The level of knowledge of your audience and their familiarity with English are two concerns of business and technical speakers. Competent speakers are also aware that there is a "shadow" audience for their speech.

The audiences I've discussed above can be classified as the "primary" audience: simply put, the people who are sitting in front of you. These people are often the decision makers, the individuals who will act on the information you communicate. But there is always a "secondary" audience—the people your immediate listeners may talk to about your presentation after they leave the room.

We can draw an analogy between oral business communication and written business communication here. Written reports have both primary and secondary readers. The individuals to whom the report is addressed are the primary readers. But these readers may copy or summarize the report to other members of their organization. These other members, who may hold a lateral, subordinate, or superior position in the organizational hierarchy, are the secondary readers. The secondary readers, depending on the situation, may influence the primary reader's decisions based on the written report, or make decisions themselves after reading it. A proposal is one example: for instance, you determine that your division needs new project management software. You write a proposal to your division head justifying this purchase. After studying your proposal she agrees with it, but she needs further authorization. She forwards your proposal to upper management to persuade them—the secondary readers—that this software is necessary.

In a speaking situation, the primary audience, the actual listeners, may report on your presentation to others within your organization, or outside it, who were not present. Sometimes this secondary audience, who receive your information second-hand, make decisions based on it. In some situations, such as "train the trainer" sessions, only a few members of an organization are involved; their purpose after your presentation is then to train their colleagues. Your ability to present a clear and focused speech will help your primary audience (if they are effective listeners) relay your information accurately to your secondary audience.

The secondary audience may also gain an impression of your abilities as a speaker—your presentation style—through your primary audience. How well you perform when delivering a presentation—your skill at communicating information in a focused manner, your speaking pace, the clarity of your examples and visual aids, for example—is also talked about. I'm sure you have learned through conversations with colleagues which employees in your organization are effective speakers—and which are not. In other words, your reputation as a speaker is extended to this secondary audience by your immediate listeners. Your awareness of your status as a communicator is another factor that will motivate you to do a good job.

Noise

No matter how thoroughly you have analyzed your audience, and how much effort you have put into accommodating them in your presentation, there are situations where this hard work just will not be enough. This is the area of everyday attitudes, the emotional and mental state of the audience. In communication theory, barriers to communication are called "noise."

Two kinds of "noise" have already been discussed: the audience's level of knowledge and language barriers in terms of fluency in English. Other kinds of noise include the wavering attention of listeners and environmental distractions. No matter how effective a presentation is, it is likely that you will "lose" some members of your audience. Perhaps some of your listeners are distracted by other matters relating to their workday, such as their workloads, deadlines, and office gossip, and find it difficult to concentrate on your presentation. Others might be sleepy—a characteristic of after-lunch meetings—and many presenters try to avoid scheduling their presentations in the afternoon. Some people might be consulting with their colleagues while you are speaking, causing a distraction for you as well as for more attentive audience members. Attention-deficit problems are also compounded by extraneous noise. Loud ventilation systems, outside construction, or the sound of visual-aid equipment can be other barriers to a productive atmosphere.

What can you do about such interference? All speakers have to contend with barriers to communication that are sometimes beyond their control. It is important, first, to be aware of them, and, second, to try to avoid or overcome them as much as possible. Check out the room and equipment ahead of time; if they are not satisfactory, do your best to change them. If your audience needs to take notes, for example, be sure that your room has tables and proper lighting. Plan ahead and keep notes on the environment; Figure 2-3 will help you organize your venue.

Furthermore, be sure you use proven techniques for effective presentations, such as previewing, summarizing, and consistent eye contact, topics covered in Chapters 3 and 4. Applying these methods will help keep your audience alert and guide them through your material. And be sure that you have focused your objective in relation to your audience's needs, as you have determined them.

Formulating Your Objective

Diligent audience analysis will lead you to formulating the objective of your presentation accurately and concisely. *Canadian Banker* magazine believes that the objective should fit on the back of a business card; if it doesn't, it's too complex.[4] Indeed, it is important to write it down, if not on the back of a business card, then on a piece of paper large enough so that you can keep revising it until you phrase your objective just right. Writing out your objective makes it concrete and gives you some distance from it, allowing you to analyze it with clarity. If you write it down, you can pin it down.

Let's go back to the scenarios of Mahima, Lyndon, and Andrew, and phrase objectives for their presentations. As we see in their situations, they already know the general purpose of their presentations. For Mahima, it is recommending a notebook computer for sales and marketing staff. For Lyndon, it is advising clients about the marketability of a new product. For Andrew, it is educating investors about mutual funds.

But while these purposes are useful, they are far too general. Mahima, Lyndon, and Andrew now need to develop their objectives.

Figure 2-3   Venue Planning Sheet

Room #:

Topic of presentation:

Purpose of presentation:

Size of audience:

Size of room:

Audience needs: Note-taking? (tables available?)

                                   Microphones?

                                   Computer terminals?

Equipment: Overhead projector?

                                   Computer-linked projector?

                                   Lectern?

                                   Whiteboard? (electronic or conventional?)

                                   Computer terminals?

                                   LCD screen?

                                   Pointer? (laser or telescopic?)

                                   Microphone?

Lighting: Suitable for presentation?

                                   Location of controls?

General environment: Noise level?

                                   Special activities? (e.g., construction; meetings in adjoining rooms)

Determining Your Key Points

General business wisdom advises that presentations should be limited to three or four main ideas. It is difficult for an audience to retain much more. The dilemma the speaker faces is to determine which three or four ideas these should be. Experts apply the "must know" rule.[5] This means that with each key point, you ask yourself if the information is essential for your audience. If it isn't, don't use it.

We can perceive that the "must know" rule was applied to the speech "Consolidating at Home While Investing Abroad," by R. W. Osborne, president of BCE Inc., a Canadian telecommunications company, as he introduced his topic to his listeners at a global telecommunications conference:

> Just to let you know where I am going today, there are four parts to my presentation. I'll start with a brief descriptive overview of BCE, followed by a discussion of significant changes and opportunities as they relate to our domestic operations, then the same type of big picture as they relate to our international investments. Lastly, I'll give a quick wrap-up and make some investment points.[6]

Let's also look to Mahima, Lyndon, and Andrew for examples. Mahima has considered the needs of her listeners. She has done research into software the sales and marketing staff use and determined how much memory is needed to operate it. She has also learned about the duties of these employees: how much time they spend in the field, their communication needs, and their presentation needs. Since cost is a factor, she considered the price of these computers, warranties, and service contracts. Her general purpose, followed by her key points, might appear as follows:

General purpose: To recommend a notebook computer suitable for sales and marketing staff.

Key points:

1. ability to handle software

2. communication features

3. cost, warranty, and service agreement

As for Lyndon, he feels he should tell his audience about his research methods: doing so will educate his listeners as well as impart validity to his findings. He will then describe the results of his study, telling his clients about the response of the population sample he surveyed and about competing products. Here are Lyndon's notes:

General purpose: To advise my audience whether to market their new product.

Key points:

1. method of research

2. feedback from survey

3. analysis of competing products

Andrew wants to pitch his presentation to noninvestors, sensing that they will constitute the majority of his audience. He wants to tell them the basics:

General purpose: To inform my audience about mutual funds.

Key points:

1. general explanation of mutual funds

2. management of mutual funds

3. kinds of mutual funds

4. how to choose a mutual fund

When you develop your objective, be sure to consider your audience's needs carefully and to select the topics that are most relevant to them.

Developing Your Key Points

After you have confirmed your key points, the next step is to add supporting detail. The problem here is, how much? Once again, effective speakers consider the factor of audience need.

Let's return to Mahima, Lyndon, and Andrew to see how they go about developing their presentations. One element each must think about is how to organize the information in a way that suits their audience most effectively. Mahima has chosen to compare and analyze two notebook computers for her company's marketing and sales staff. She reports on these models—let's call one the Joey and the other the Piglet—by criteria, rather than by product description. Her more detailed list of points follows from her key ideas:

General purpose: To recommend a notebook computer suitable for sales and marketing staff.

Key points:

1. ability to handle software

    - memory

        - Joey

        - Piglet

    - speed

        - Joey

        - Piglet

2. communication features
   - fax/modem
       - Joey
       - Piglet
   - e-mail
       - Joey
       - Piglet

3. cost, warranty, service agreement
       - Joey
       - Piglet

Organization by criteria is useful for a sharp comparative analysis of two products, services, or concepts. By this method Mahima does the work for her listeners, rather than forcing them to try to make the comparisons as she speaks. The alternative method, which would look like this, would probably frustrate her audience.

1. Joey
       - ability to handle software
           - memory
           - speed
       - communication features
           - fax/modem
           - e-mail
       - cost, warranty, service agreement

2. Piglet
       - ability to handle software
           - memory
           - speed
       - communication features
           - fax/modem
           - e-mail
       - cost, warranty, service agreement

This presentation strategy might make it easier for the speaker to prepare the information, but such an arrangement amounts to a summary of sales brochures.

Lyndon's key points for his marketing presentation follow a procedural arrangement, mirroring the approach he took while doing his research and analyzing his findings. More development of Lyndon's key points might look like this:

General purpose: To advise my audience whether to market their new product.

Key points:

1. method of research
    - description of survey instrument
    - results of secondary research

2. feedback from survey
    - correlation of data
    - comments from people interviewed
    - interpretation of survey results

3. analysis of competing products
    - product A
    - product B

4. recommendation

Andrew's objective is to educate his audience about mutual funds: he organizes his material from the general to the more specific. He believes that this strategy will help his audience, inexperienced investors, understand the concepts most easily.

General purpose: To inform my audience about mutual funds.

Key points:

1. general explanation of mutual funds
    - definition of mutual funds
    - purchase options

2. management of mutual funds
    - management philosophies
    - management fees

3. kinds of mutual funds
    - equity funds
    - balanced funds
    - money market funds

4. how to choose a mutual fund
    - analyzing your risk level

- following fund trends and earnings
- understanding the prospectus
- choosing an investment advisor

These three detailed approaches give you an understanding of how to develop key points. It is important to keep in mind that our three imaginary speakers have analyzed their audiences and remembered their time limits when developing their organizational strategy and sub-topics. Mahima, Lyndon, and Andrew each has a firm foundation for developing his or her presentation further.

Managing Time

So far in this chapter we have examined the importance of careful audience analysis and explored some strategies for developing the key points of a presentation. The amount of time you have for your presentation is another essential consideration. Information overload is as much a barrier to effective oral communication as environmental distractions, lack of speech focus, inadequate audience analysis, and complex language and phrasing.

Determining Your Time Limit

As discussed in Chapter 1, it is critical that business and technical speakers respect the time limits determined for their presentations. As important as your presentation is to you, for your audience it is merely one segment of their workday. Often business speakers are told how much time they have: Mahima may have been told to keep her presentation to a maximum of 20 minutes. Andrew knows he has an hour and a half for his presentation, but about 45 minutes of that time is devoted to a question-answer session with his audience. Lyndon's clients did not tell him how long they want him to talk, but he does not plan to go over half an hour; discussion with his clients about his findings will take considerable time.

How do you judge the length of your presentation if you are not advised? If you are one in a roster of speakers, you can easily find out how much time is set aside for the entire session. You can then judge your segment—it's good if you can contact the other speakers to discuss how you will divide the time—and determine the length of your presentation. If you have an individual presentation scheduled on its own, and have no information about time limits, you can find out if a certain length is part of the "culture" of your workplace, that is, if there is a length that people generally follow. Typically, however, business and technical speakers know how much time they are allowed.

Correlating Content to Time

Another aspect of the timing problem deals with judging how much information will fit the time you are allowed. Make sure your information does not exceed your time limit; if it does, then cut out material that you assume is not a "must know" fact or idea for your audience. Keep in mind that your audience must not be overloaded with information.

Experience is one teacher in correlating speech content to time constraints: people who frequently give presentations develop a feel for how much information will correspond to their time limit. Otherwise, keep in mind this rule: generally, if you were to write out your presentation as a script, one double-spaced typed page constitutes about 225 to 250 words. It would take you about two minutes to read this page at a pace that is accessible to your audience.

Don't make the mistake of thinking that you must say everything you have learned through your research and analysis in your presentation. Your audience can only absorb so much information during a session, no matter how good your presentation is. The practice of including everything will lead you to go over your time limit, or to speak very quickly at the end of your presentation—usually speakers with too much information do both, and lose their audience's attention. Keep in mind that you can supply your listeners with a handout that covers information you did not include in your speech. An audience is always glad to walk away with material they can study at their leisure.

Furthermore, always save time for a question-answer session. It is practical even to overprepare, to have at hand more information than you plan to present, as many experienced speakers do. Consequently, you will be ready for the question-answer segment, when listeners who need more detailed information or clarification can seek it.

Chapter Summary

I don't want to conclude this chapter by making you more apprehensive about giving a presentation than you might already be. By setting aside sufficient time to plan your talk, you are well on your way to success. A calm and logical approach will help you avoid the pitfalls of poor presentations: lack of focus, inadequate audience analysis, and poorly managed time. Awareness of your purpose, your audience, and your time limits is essential. From this foundation, you can develop your subject matter effectively and tailor it to your specific speaking situation. Certain components of the speaking environment might be beyond your control, such as distracted listeners and extraneous noise. But despite such variables, your constant concerns must be a clear objective and insight into your audience's knowledge and needs. With these elements, your presentation will achieve its aims.

We next turn to shaping your presentation further, exploring the techniques you can use to guide your audience through your content.

Applications

1. What are the business outcomes of poor planning for a presentation? What are the personal outcomes?

2. Why is it important to analyze your audience? What are the problems of inadequate audience analysis?

3. How does a secondary audience influence a presentation?

4. What is "noise?" How does it affect a business presentation?

5. Distinguish between a presentation objective, key points, and subsidiary points. What is the relationship between key points and subsidiary points?

6. Choose a product or service with which you are familiar. Imagine you have been asked to deliver a presentation recommending it to a company. Formulate an objective, the key points for discussion, and the subsidiary points. Be sure your information fits into a time limit of 15 minutes.

References

1. John D. MacNaughton, "From Stem to Canadarm—Reflections" (delivered to the Canadian Aeronautic and Space Institute, April 29, 1997). [www.spar.ca/corp/speech_c.htm], July 14, 1997.

2. Bernard M. Michel, untitled speech (delivered to the Invest in Saskatchewan Forum, Regina, Saskatchewan, April 22, 1997). [www.cameco.com/investor/speeches/ invest_in_saskatchewan_forum.html], August 19, 1997.

3. See H. J. Scheiber and Peter J. Hager, "Oral Communication in Business and Industry: Results of a Survey on Scientific, Technical, and Managerial Presentations," *Journal of Technical Writing and Communication* 24, no. 2 (1994), 176.

4. Judith Humphrey and Ted Nichols, "Speak Up Persuasively," *Canadian Banker* 100, no. 1 (January/February 1993), 38.

5. See Carole McKenzie, "Preparation not Perspiration," *Chemistry & Industry*, no. 9 (May 2, 1994), 350.

6. R. W. Osborne, "Consolidating at Home while Investing Abroad" (delivered to the Salomon Brothers Global Telecommunications Conference, New York, December 2, 1996). [http://bce.ca/bce/fs/e/newsroom/communications/speeches], August 12, 1997.

CHAPTER 3

Making It Accessible: Openings, Closings, and In-Between

It's now time for the challenge of drafting a presentation. You have your purpose pinned down, a mental snapshot of your audience, and your time limit. You know basically what you want to say, but now you need to package it. You cannot jump right into your material and expect your audience to follow you. You need to lead your audience, to direct them through your presentation. And you need to do this in a way that is clear, accessible, and considerate.

This chapter gives you guidelines and techniques for pulling your presentation together. We will look at methods of introducing and concluding your material and of presenting it so that your audience can follow your key points. We'll also consider some stylistic matters and how they relate to business speaking. At the end of this chapter, you will see a preparation outline that demonstrates how you can organize your material effectively.

The Opening

To many people, the introduction is the most important part of a presentation, because that is when the speaker sets up the speech for the audience, and when the audience senses the speaker's ability to discuss the topic effectively. I want to lay down some ground rules about introductions.

Keep It General

Introductions are not detailed: they are deliberately general previews of the material that will be developed in the body of the presentation. It is very important to avoid the hazard of delivering a top-heavy speech, that is, one with so much detail in the introduction that you confuse and bore your audience, and you have little left to say in the speech body. Each of the three sections of your speech—introduction, body, and conclusion—must be distinct from each other. When you prepare a draft of your speech, make your opening and closing the shortest sections. Because your audience will not have a copy of your script or outline, it is your responsibility to make your presentation easy to follow. Limiting the detail in your introduction is one way of meeting this responsibility.

State Your Purpose and Preview Your Key Ideas

Virtually all speech introductions express the purpose of the speech and tell the audience what they will learn. Often, but not always, speakers state their qualifications for speaking on their topic—the research they did, their experience, for example. Finally, effective business speakers use a transition to lead their listeners into their discussion. Figure 3-1 summarizes the basic strategy of an introduction.

Figure 3-1 Basic Elements of an Introduction

1. State your purpose
2. Indicate the basis of your credibility, that is, what makes you qualified to speak on your topic.
3. Preview your main points.
4. Use a transition to move your audience from the introduction to the body of your speech.

However, I don't want you to follow a formula for writing your introduction, because your purpose, your audience, and your time limit will often govern which elements to include. In almost all situations, as the following excerpts from speeches by Canada's business leaders demonstrate, it is necessary to tell the audience the purpose and the key points of your speech. When to use other components such as an attention-getter—a quotation, paraphrase, anecdote, or joke—is left to your own judgment. So is whether to indicate your credibility to your audience.

Examples from the Real World

I want you to look at two introductions to see how they can be created.

The Full Introduction

The introduction to a speech delivered by Deborah Allan, formerly vice-president of Public Relations at Spar Aerospace, the developer of the Canadarm, is a good subject for analysis. She is speaking to the Canadian Association of Career Educators and Employers:

> Thank you, and good morning everyone. My topic for this morning has been billed: "Employment Trends for the Future and Skills for the 21st Century." But that sounds a little heavy. I prefer to think of it as "What I want to be when I grow up and how I plan to get there."
>
> As you may be aware, my original presentation of this topic was developed for student audiences. I think the message is every bit as relevant for business people and educators, however, especially given the reality of the need for "permanent learning" or "learning a living," as I like to call it.
>
> To talk about employment trends and employment skills, we really have to consider two other areas as well. They are employee knowledge and the employee workplace. In other words, what we'll be discussing this morning is:
>
> - What employees are going to have to know to earn a living—that is the basic knowledge they need before they acquire defined skills.
>
> - What they're going to be doing for a living—the industries and occupations in which they may be employed.
>
> - Where they're going to be earning their living—their actual physical location; and
>
> - How they're going to be able to go on earning a living all of their working life—the skills they will acquire on an on-going basis throughout their working life.
>
> Let's take a brief look at each of these areas, starting with What employees are going to have to know to earn a living.[1]

As I said in Chapter 2, topic, audience, and time constraints all condition the nature of a business presentation. The version of this speech on the World Wide Web is approximately 4000 words. My calculations suggest that Deborah Allan's speech lasted about 30 minutes. The introduction is 260 words, or about seven per cent of the total speech; in real time, just over two minutes to deliver.

Allan's speech is delivered to an external audience composed of both business people and educators who teach business skills. The audience may not know her personally or have worked with her. We can see from this introduction that she attempts to put her audience at ease, to reassure them that her subject matter will be delivered in an accessible way. First, she rephrases her topic in friendly, understandable terms: the original topic is "a little heavy." She "prefers to think of it as 'What I want to be when I grow up and how I plan to get there.'" Allan's revision is both humorous and easy to remember.

Allan then offers some personal credibility for presenting her topic: the second paragraph of the script reveals that she has spoken on the topic before, to students. In other words, she reassures her audience that the speech is prepared, not spontaneous.

Then she focuses her topic in a very clear way, explicitly, in no uncertain terms: she previews for her audience the four areas she will cover. As an executive of Spar Aerospace invited to speak to this association, she was assigned a broad topic, "Employment Trends for the Future and Skills for the 21st Century." Her job was to make it manageable so that her audience could leave the session with some insights into the future of the Canadian workplace and the Canadian worker that they can apply at their own companies and schools.

Finally, Allan uses a transition to signal that she is going to speak on her first key point: "Let's take a brief look at each of these areas, starting with ...." She eases the audience into the body of her speech.

The techniques Allan uses in her presentation conform to the strategy given at the beginning of this chapter. This is a practical strategy to apply to your own presentations. You can visualize it as funnel, a shape that progresses from wide to narrow, when you have trouble creating your opening remarks; it will remind you to make your introductions general, and the speech body specific.

The Succinct Introduction

Now, Allan's opening is but one example of an introduction to a business presentation. Not all business speakers have a lead-up as long as Allan's to the key points that will be developed. Some speakers are terse; they come immediately to the point. Consider the following opening from a speech, "Canadian Universities: Competing to Win?" by Peter Godsoe, chairman and CEO of Scotiabank:

Thank you ladies and gentlemen.

What I am going to talk about today is excellence, and the need for excellence in today's world. Specifically, I would like to talk about excellence in education. My main point today is this: I believe that we need to create centres of excellence within our university system to develop our best and our brightest students—our business, political, and academic leaders of tomorrow—to ensure that we are able to compete with the best and the brightest from around the world in years ahead.[2]

Note that even though Godsoe does not state his qualifications for speaking on his topic, the listener recognizes that he is qualified by virtue of his business position. He does articulate his purpose ("the need for excellence in today's world") and main point ("that we need to create centres of excellence within our university system ... to ensure that we are able to compete with the best and brightest from around the world in years ahead"). Note also that the very terseness of Godsoe's introduction establishes a mood for his speech; that characteristic in itself is an attention-getter. In other words, business speakers do not always need a preamble to get the audience to sit up. Sometimes, if speakers feel that the topic in itself will rivet their audience, they begin directly. However, no matter what strategy is used in an introduction, the entire speech must live up to the expectations the opening creates.

Using Attention-Getters

Neither of the two introductions quoted above use distinctive attention-getters. Speakers sometimes use special techniques—jokes, questions, anecdotes, quotations—to get the audience's attention, if they think doing so is appropriate to their speaking situation.

Should you use attention-getters?   When deciding whether to begin a presentation with a joke or an anecdote, you must take into account why your audience is listening to you, what business decision they may make based on your information, and your time restrictions. For example, if you are giving a routine update on your team's current project at a departmental meeting, an internal audience of colleagues, is it necessary for you to open with humour, or even to demonstrate your credibility, your qualifications for speaking on the topic? Your audience knows you, so you do not need to mention your technical background, unless the circumstances warrant this.

How should the business people introduced in Chapter 2, Mahima, Lyndon, and Andrew, begin their presentations? Mahima, our technical specialist, may consider it worthwhile to establish her qualifications for recommending a specific notebook computer to her audience. Her listeners are composed of upper management: telling them the extent of her research and how she arrived at the two products she is evaluating will enhance her credibility and establish the validity of her analysis. Because she has only 20 minutes to deliver her presentation, she may decide to forgo an attention-getting device in order meet her time limit. An internal business audience wants its information quickly, in the most accessible way. As we've seen, attention-getters aren't always needed.

Lyndon, our consultant who is presenting the results of his marketing study to new Canadian entrepreneurs, might also forgo attention-getting remarks in his introduction: since his clients are paying for his expertise, he already has their interest. However, because his listeners are not marketing experts, he might introduce his talk with remarks that would put them at ease—perhaps tell them that he will describe his findings in terms they can understand. Lyndon will also preview his key points before actually describing the details.

Andrew, our mutual funds sales representative, might also begin his presentation with comments that will establish a comfortable atmosphere. As Andrew analyzed his listeners, they are nonexperts, people who are not investors; prudently, he would remark that mutual funds will not mystify them and that he will explain things in a way that they can understand. He might also offer a quotation from a prominent financial advisor about the wisdom of investing wisely. Next he can describe his qualifications for presenting information on investing in mutual funds—such as his credentials and his research in the field. Andrew then can preview his key points. His overall strategy for his opening remarks involves instilling faith in his audience that he is speaking with expertise and knowledge, since his presentation may influence his listeners' financial decisions.

Now, let's examine some special techniques for openings.

The paraphrase or quotation.   Sometimes speakers like to begin their introduction with a paraphrase or quotation. Carol Stephenson opened her speech "Three Good Reasons and Ways to Profit from the Corporate Talent of Women," delivered when she was CEO of the Stentor Resource Centre, in this way:

> A wise person once said: "To see is one thing. To understand what you see is another. To learn from what you understand is something else. But, to act on what you learn is all that really matters."
>
> Today, I'd like to share with you what I've seen, what I understand, and what I've learned about women in the marketplace and in the business world. And then I'd like to share how Stentor and other companies are acting on what they've learned.[3]

Stephenson's introduction is philosophical, and sets a serious mood for her speech. Note also that, like Deborah Allan and Peter Godsoe, Stephenson fulfills the basic requirements of an introduction: she previews the specific areas of her speech and establishes her qualifications through her experience, and, obviously, her gender.

Humour.   When assigned the task of an oral presentation, speakers often ask if they should begin their speech with humour. Consider the following remarks by Rick George, president and CEO of Suncor, a major Canadian energy producer headquartered in Calgary, to the Global Energy Forum in Houston, Texas:

> I didn't need any encouragement to join this year's Global Energy Forum. Not only is the theme of this session, "Serving the Customer of the Future," a timely and important one ... but, just as importantly, it is warm in Houston—a lot warmer than where my company, Suncor, operates in Canada. To give you an idea of how cold it is: The average home deep-freeze is about 15 degrees below zero. In January and February, it routinely drops to 35 below at our oil sands plant in Fort McMurray. As the locals say, that's cold enough to freeze the chrome off a bumper hitch.[4]

If you do decide to begin your presentation humorously, your humour should work. Often, humour is most effective when it suits the situation, when it deals with a topic with which your audience can identify or can understand. Here, George's humour plays on the cold Alberta weather for his warm Texas audience. Yet the purpose of his speech is serious: he will discuss not only the oil sands industry in Canada, but also how the oil industry must change to meet the needs of their crude oil customers in the 21st century. His humour helps develop his likability factor: that is, he earns the audience's support—and their attentiveness—for his central message.

Questions.   Finally, some speakers open their presentations with a question, or a series of questions, as another way to get their audience's attention. Here is an example from a speech by Courtney Pratt, the former president of Noranda, headquartered in Toronto:

> I want to start this talk by asking you a question: If you think of the mining business, what are the images and words that come to mind? How about the forest industry? How about the oil and gas business? How about Noranda?[5]

Through his questions Pratt covers the three former areas of Noranda's business: mining, forestry, and oil and gas (Noranda dropped all operations outside of mining in December 1998). His questions intrigue his audience because they want to know how he will answer them.

The Closing

We've covered ways to introduce your subject to your audience. We'll skip the speech body for now, and jump ahead to ways to conclude your speech, because in many ways conclusions are mirror images of introductions.

Summarize, But Do More

It is commonly said that the basic overall strategy for a speech is to tell your audience what you are going to say, say it, and tell them what you just said. In essence, conclusions repeat your introduction. They tell the audience your key points once more. But they can do more. Closings can stress the one or two main ideas or interpretations of your presentations, and they can give the audience "something to take away with them" in an abstract sense, that is, an idea, an attitude, or an understanding that will help toward making an informed business decision. Let's consider Deborah Allan's conclusion to her speech on Canadian employment trends:

> Let me close, then, with one last thought on the subject of learning and the critical role it plays in all of our lives, especially in this knowledge economy. First, of course, learning gives us basic facts and figures—the information we need to do our jobs ... to function on a day-to-day basis. Second, by being open to continuous learning, we're more able to adapt in this rapidly changing world, and are better prepared for change when it presents itself. But third, and I think most important,

is the fact that, in learning we gain knowledge and knowledge helps us to gain confidence ... the confidence we need to succeed, both as individuals and as a society. After all, René Descartes is not famous for the phrase, "I think I am, therefore maybe I could be."[6]

If you compare this conclusion with Allan's opening statement, you will find some similarities: the references to "learning a living"; to the idea of the basic knowledge people need to be employed; and to the concept of adaptation, of continually acquiring skills. But in her conclusion Allan brings her themes to a higher level: the implications for people themselves and for society. She cleverly caps her final remarks with a humorous turn on the famous phrase by Descartes, the 17th-century French philosopher: "I think, therefore I am." In other words, she leaves her audience with something to think about.

Here's the conclusion from Peter Godsoe's speech, "Canadian Universities: Competing to Win?":

On that note, let me summarize. I believe that our economic future depends on our ability to create, use, and manage knowledge as effectively—more effectively—than the rest of the world. I believe that human skills—that people—are the only true source of comparative advantage over time. And I believe that we have to move toward the forefront of university education by developing the sort of institutional excellence that exists in other countries. Or we risk, over time, losing our best and most capable people—our leaders of tomorrow.

To do this, we need to unbundle our funding and allow universities to compete for research grants; we need to tolerate variation in tuition fees to promote institutional excellence; and we need to permit private institutions to play a role in our university system. Let the market, not the government, determine which universities succeed and where our centres of excellence are.

Ladies and gentlemen, we have a great country and I, personally, believe in its future—a future that demands the best and most challenging of educational systems.

Thank you very much.[7]

Godsoe's conclusion is 194 words, or only 7.5 per cent of the entire speech (2600 words). In this space he reviews his main points and leaves his audience with his theme: that the marketplace, not government, should play a key role in the future of Canadian universities. He ends his speech with his most significant remark.

Avoid These Mistakes

Here are two other considerations to keep in mind when writing your conclusion: don't add any new information, and don't say "that's it." Sometimes speakers add a fact or two to the conclusion that should already have been presented in the speech body: new information at the end of a speech confuses listeners.

Furthermore, many speakers feel they need to signal to the audience that the presentation is concluded, when they have already done so. Uttering "that's it" undermines the forcefulness of your closing remarks. A phrase such as "in closing" tells your audience you are about to conclude. So does the summary of key ideas that follow. If you wish to add another remark, ask for questions.

The strategy given in Figure 3-2 for concluding your presentation suits numerous situations: routine reporting as well as persuasive business speaking, such as presenting a proposal. Keep in mind that just as your introduction gives your audience a sense of your ability to deliver your information, your conclusion gives them a lasting impression that you did, and did so effectively.

Figure 3-2   Basic Elements of a Conclusion

1. Signal your audience that you are going to conclude with a phrase such as "in summary," "in conclusion," "let me close."

2. Summarize your key points.

3. Emphasize the main idea you want your audience to remember.

4. Thank your audience.

The Speech Body

Now it's time to examine ways of making the body of your presentation easy for your audience to follow. Several common devices are used for this purpose: transitions, signposts, internal previews, and internal summaries. These devices demonstrate the logic of your organization and reasoning. They give your listeners a handle on your speech. Let's look at their applications.

Transitions

We already saw in the introduction of Deborah Allan's speech that she uses a transition to move her audience into the body of her remarks: "Let's take a brief look at each of these areas, starting with What employees are going to have to know to earn a living." The purpose of transitions is to signal to your listeners the direction of your presentation. Transitions prepare the audience for what's ahead, as well as reminding them of what they just heard.

Statements as Transitions

Transitions can be independent paragraphs or phrases, and can bridge two parts of a speech or two sentences. Here is a transition, taken from Carol Stephenson's speech, "The Need for Competitive Equity in the Canadian Telecommunications Industry":

> Given our capital and operating expenditures, which total $13.6 billion a year, and the taxes we pay, about $1.5 billion—and you thought you paid a lot of taxes—our total contribution to the Canadian Gross Domestic Product is a hair under $20 billion, or 2.5 per cent.
>
> **But our impact is more than just a money game. We also contribute to the well-being of Canadians in many ways.**
>
> NB Tel is a leader in broadband communication with its VideoActive network. This initiative, which began in August, provides two-way, broadband services to 5000 homes ....[8]

The highlighted paragraph is the bridge, or transition, between two topics in this speech. Note the clarity of the transition, the clear reference to the section she just completed discussing and to the one she is about to begin.

Here are examples of transitional expressions and phrases, taken out of context from "The Changing Nature of Work," a speech delivered by Charles Baillie, president and CEO of the TD Bank Financial Group, to the Canadian Club in Orillia, Ontario.[9] I've numbered the phrases to make each distinct.

1. **Now the question is,** what, if anything, can be done about this?

2. **Having said that,** we clearly need a "new bargain" to replace the old one that has essentially disappeared.

3. **And so,** speaking as head of TD Bank—a leading employer in this country—**let me explore** some elements of what the new bargain might be.

4. **Not only are we** creating jobs in our own industry. **We are** creating jobs throughout the economy.

5. **Finally,** I believe we have to continue to strive to get the fundamentals right.

6. **In short,** the structure of incentives and disincentives in the economy is still not what it should be.

7. **And here, I want to focus on** a key element of "the new bargain"—the relationship between employee and employer.

8. **Next,** we provide a variety of *pension options* to help employees plan for their retirement. **As a result,** they no longer have to stay at TD to keep their benefits. This increases their freedom and flexibility.

9. **And so, let me close on a broader point.**

Notice how these transitional phrases clarify the flow of the speech for the listener. They are true aids in making the speech accessible. But they have to be used judiciously: overusing the same transitional expression in a speech can annoy the listener. Imagine listening to a speech in which the speaker uses the word "next" repeatedly. Variety is a key for effective transitions.

Transitions also must be used correctly. For example, if you are using the term, "in contrast," or "on the other hand," it is important that the point following this phrase show a comparison, as in this excerpt from Peter Godsoe's speech:

> **On the positive side,** public expenditure on education in Canada is among the highest in the world. In terms of the percentage of young adults enrolled in higher education, we rank highest in the world. We also have a very high proportion of university-educated adults by international standards.
>
> **On the other hand,** Canada scores second lowest among G-7 countries in terms of well-educated people staying employed in their own country, according to the 1995 World Competitiveness Report. This is the so-called "brain-drain"—the worst case scenario that I just mentioned.[10]

The comparison, signalled by the phrases in boldface, contrasts high Canadian expenditure on education with low rates of educated Canadians remaining in Canada.

The list in Figure 3-3 is useful for finding synonymous transitions in order to achieve variety when speaking.

Questions as Transitions

Sometimes speakers use questions as transitions. We see this, for example, in a speech by Peter Spelliscy, senior vice-president of Suncor:

> How do your employees feel about their jobs? How would you characterize the culture of your organization? And what are some of the common beliefs and values of your employees?
>
> A recent Canadian Towers Perrin survey gives us some general answers to these questions ...[11]

Figure 3-3   Transitions

Introduction	Conclusion	Sequence	Comparison
let me begin	in summary	next	in contrast
let's start by	in conclusion	then	on the other hand
	finally	first, second, third ...	likewise
	to summarize	now	however
		and so	yet
		here	not only ... but also
		let me turn now	

Addition	Example	Cause and Effect
in addition	for example	thus
furthermore	for instance	therefore
further	to illustrate	in consequence
also		consequently
too		

Questions can be thought-provoking transitions, and can involve your audience. Use questions sparingly, though, or they can lose their effect.

Internal Previews

Similar to transitions, internal previews also act as bridges, though they are a little longer than typical transitional statements. They tell the audience the topics in a subsection of the speech. Here is an example from Godsoe's speech on Canadian universities:

> I would like to touch on two issues. First, I would like to take a look at funding policies, because money for education is a major issue. And second, the role of business, which in part is related to the funding question, but is really much broader than that.
>
> So let us look at funding.[12]

Note that he announces the two subtopics his speech will cover next, and then uses a transition to guide the audience to the first one.

Here's another example, from Carol Stephenson's speech, "The Female Style of Leadership." She previews a subsection of her presentation:

But I want to begin by talking about the new approach to leadership that women bring to the corporate world. **I'll describe this style, and explain why it has become increasingly important.**[13]

Stephenson's audience knows exactly where she is taking them, and they know what to listen for.

Internal Summaries

Similarly, internal summaries work like transitions, but they too are a bit fuller. Here is an internal summary, from Courtney Pratt's speech, "Noranda: On the Leading Edge":

We invest heavily in exploring for metals and oil and gas. In 1995 alone, we invested $97 million in grass roots mineral exploration and $88 million in oil and natural gas exploration and development. Unlike a number of other companies, we continue to focus a lot of our exploration effort and funding in Canada ....

With this background of size, strength and growth, let me now talk to you about the "character" of our company.

Note that Pratt refers back to three previous areas of his speeches before continuing to the next subtopic. He reminds the audience of what he covered, and tells them where he is going.

An extract from Deborah Allan's presentation to the Canadian Association of Career Educators and Employers is another example:

Okay. So far, we've looked at the knowledge employees will need to have, the skills they'll need to acquire, and the occupations in which they'll be applying both. But where do you think they'll be working?

When to use internal previews and summaries depends on the number of subtopics you cover in your speech. Notice from the examples above that internal previews signal that two or more subtopics will follow; internal summaries refer back to the same number.

Signposting

Signposting, or numbering ideas or statements, is another simple and practical device for guiding your audience through your presentation. Signposting is often used in internal previews, as we saw in the excerpt from Peter Godsoe's speech on Canadian education. We also see this technique in Baillie's speech, "The Changing Nature of Work":

At the outset, some basics and some principles.

First, the blame game must stop. Now that we know governments are ineffective at creating employment directly, some are pointing the finger at the private sector and saying it's our fault that more and better jobs aren't being created—that it is our responsibility to turn things around.

Well, it's not. Our primary responsibility is to our customers, our shareholders, and our existing employees. But our *purpose* is not to create jobs. Our *performance* is what creates them.

Secondly, that does not mean the private sector has no responsibility whatever. We do. I strongly believe it is in the self-interest of all of us to treat the human resources of our country with all the care and respect they deserve. Not to be altruistic. But to be *successful.*

Thirdly, I believe we have to be clear on what doesn't work.

Like the other techniques demonstrated, simple signposting also orders and clarifies your presentation for your audience and helps to make it memorable.

Language and Style

I expect you sensed from the excerpts quoted so far in this chapter that Canada's business leaders try to speak in a personal and conversational style. Business speaking, like any other kind of oral communication, is an exercise in human relations. An effective speaker understands that to communicate a message successfully, to ensure that the audience receives it, the presentation must be personalized, or made conversational. Each listener should feel that he or she is spoken to as an individual.

The Mechanics

The following isn't intended as a grammar lesson, but grammar is relevant to the art of business speaking. I've detailed two elements to consider when writing your speech outline or speech script.

Personal Pronouns

Using personal pronouns in your presentation makes your listeners feel like individuals. Look at the introduction to Deborah Allan's speech on employment trends and skills. She uses such words as "you," "I," "we"—"as you may be aware," she says, and "what we'll be discussing this morning ...." Whether your audience is 2, 20, or 200 people, personal pronouns are essential in achieving a rapport with your listeners. Personal pronouns show that you recognize their presence, that you are not speaking to a vacant room.

Active Voice

Another element of effective business speaking involves using the active voice. Active voice means using the subject-verb-object pattern. Note the following excerpt from a speech by Fares Salloum, senior vice-president, International Operations, GTE Service Corporation:

One of the most daunting challenges **regulators face is** the Internet. Because, as I said, **it transcends** national boundaries. **It is eroding the** traditional barriers **that restrict or complicate international trade.**[14]

Phrased in the passive voice, this excerpt would be written like this:

One of the most daunting challenges **faced by regulators** is the Internet. Because, as I said, national boundaries **are transcended by** it. International trade that **is restricted or complicated by** traditional barriers **is being eroded by** it.

If you read the two passages aloud, you will quickly see how clumsy and confusing the passive-voice version sounds. As often as possible, use the active voice to create a lively speaking style.

Words

The topics discussed below fall under the headings of semantics, or the meaning of words, and of diction, or the use of words. Consider these elements also when creating your presentation.

Denotation and Connotation

Denotation refers to the dictionary meaning of words; connotation refers to the emotional or psychological associations we have with words. Consider the word "cheap." The dictionary meaning of "cheap" is "inexpensive." If a salesperson used the word "cheap" when describing a product, the listener would attribute the quality of shoddy workmanship to it. However, if the salesperson used the word "inexpensive" to describe the product, the listener would likely think of good quality for a good price. When creating your presentation, be sensitive both to the dictionary meaning of words and to their possible associations: doing so may mean the difference between a presentation that is well received by your audience, and one that isn't.

Level of Language

Obviously, the level of language of your speech also affects its impact on your listeners. Analyzing your audience will determine the complexity of your words. For example, in his speech, "Steel and the New Imperatives," John Mayberry, president and CEO of Dofasco, uses the word "metamorphosis": "I don't want to linger unduly on the past, but it deserves a few minutes' mention—if only to set up the metamorphosis that's occurred since."[15] Metamorphosis essentially means "change," but the word also has the connotation of "transformation." Mayberry is speaking to the Confederation Club, an educated group; he can safely assume that his audience understands the full meaning and implications of the word "metamorphosis." If he were speaking to a different audience, however, he might use the word "change," or a phrase, to communicate his meaning.

Idioms

Idioms are expressions unique to a specific language. They are another device speakers use to make their presentations conversational and interesting to their audiences. Mike O'Brien, executive vice-president of the Sunoco Group, uses idioms in his speech, "The Next Big Challenge: Moving from Downsizing to Growth." He says, "Now let's go back in time to 1992, when Suncor did not have all its ducks in line," and "When I got to Sunoco in November, earnings were going down the tubes ...."[16] Peter Spelliscy, senior vice-president of Suncor, uses idioms in his speech, "Moving From Survival to Expansion—Why Changing the Culture is Essential": "We're known for turning our oil sands business from a marginally profitable white elephant ...."[17]

Idioms add colour and interest to business speaking, but they have to be used judiciously. To a multicultural audience, one composed of listeners who may not understand English idioms, such phrases as "white elephant" and "going down the tubes" may be perplexing.

References to Popular Culture

References to popular culture also add colour and humour to a speech, but the audience must be familiar with their context. In his speech, "Voyage to Tomorrow," delivered at the Marine Club Annual Dinner, John Mayberry of Dofasco said, "With a title like that, maybe we could get Jean Luc Picard to be captain."[18] Discussing the influence of technology in the manufacturing sector, Deborah Allan uses the image of "Homer Simpson at the nuclear station controls" to stress for her audience "the implications of the need for technical skills training."[19] Most people in North America are familiar with these icons of popular television, but speakers should be sensitive to their audience's knowledge of North American culture when using references to film, television, and books.

Metaphors

Another element that adds interest to business speaking is the use of metaphors, or figurative language. In his speech on the Alberta oil sands, Rick George of Suncor says, "Sunoco has been playing in the sand since 1967...."[20] Discussing Dofasco's restructuring, John Mayberry said, "For those of us steering the ship, we now have a more responsive vessel at our command. And a happier crew."[21] Such invention can add colour and interest to a business speech, if the occasion is appropriate. Again, less is often more: use imagery sparingly for the best effect.

Unbiased Language

In her speech on employment trends and skills for the 21st century, Deborah Allan says,

> Many other workplace factors are also changing. In the olden days there was a simple answer to a simple question. What do you want to be when you grow up,

Johnny? What about you, Jane? Well, today Johnny and Jane may both want to be a police **officer** or a flight **attendant** or a fire**fighter** or a health care **worker** or an astronaut (my personal favourite).[22]

The emphasis in this excerpt is from Allan's script, not mine. Her emphasis points out the use of gender-neutral language in public speaking. When writing a draft of your speech, proofread it carefully to check for any inappropriate gender-specific terms, such as the pronouns "he" or "his" when your reference is intended to include both genders. Consider the following sentence:

The business speaker should be aware of his audience.

It can be revised in one of the following ways:

The business speaker should be aware of his or her audience.

or

Business speakers should be aware of their audiences.

To avoid a sentence that repeats the phrase "his or "her" more than once (such repetition can sound awkward), use the plural form.

Dignity and sensitivity should govern any business speaking activity. Mention racial or ethnic background or age in your presentation only if it is necessary to your meaning. Be respectful to your subject: refer to Canadian First Nations peoples by their correct names. Refer to the aged as "the aged," "senior citizens," "the elderly," or "seniors," for example.

Repetition

Often business speakers will repeat a word or phrase to reinforce a key idea or to add variety to their speech. For example, consider this excerpt from Gayle Stewart, vice-president, Corporate Communications, BC Telecom, on the information highway:

Change is never easy, particularly change of the magnitude I'm talking about. It's not easy for us at BC TEL. It's not easy for the new competitors. It's not easy for you, our customers. And it's certainly not easy for government, which is trying to regulate an industry that is literally re-inventing itself.[23]

The repetition of the phrase "it's not easy" adds force to the speech and maintains the attention of Stewart's listeners. Note also this passage from Peter Spelliscy's speech on Suncor's corporate culture:

I believe we need to go beyond a survival mentality to one that creates energy, excitement, and growth—a world where employees feel they have a future. A world where people want to come in to work in the morning. A world where we can have fun.[24]

This technique can add impact to a presentation. But just as you should use metaphors and idioms carefully, so should you be prudent when using repetition. Your topic and audience should govern when and how frequently within a speech to use special techniques.

Sentences

Successful business speakers try to vary sentence length to make their presentations sound conversational and interesting. They also use topic sentences effectively to cue their audience to the flow of their ideas.

Topic Sentences

A topic sentence contains the main idea of a paragraph. It is usually the first sentence of a paragraph, though sometimes it appears in the middle or at the end of a paragraph. Effective speakers use topic sentences to help their audience follow their presentations. Note the following example from Fares Salloum's speech on telecommunications and the Pacific Rim:

> I believe, ultimately, no one will be able to contain or curtail the impacts of the Internet. Even today, it has moved beyond the reach of regulators. The strength of the Internet comes from the sheer numbers of individuals who use it. Internet users wield tremendous power. They've created an environment where rules are extremely difficult to enforce. And national borders or distinctions are transparent.[25]

The first sentence in this paragraph is the topic sentence. It contains the general idea of the paragraph, in essence: that the Internet's influence cannot be controlled. The remainder of the paragraph develops the theme by describing the impact on users. When constructing your presentation, check that each section and subsection of your speech includes a topic sentence, so that your listeners can follow you.

Sentence Variety

Because you are speaking, not writing, it is important that your sentences be relatively short. We see this in many of the excerpts in this chapter, such as the passage from Gayle Stewart's speech on the information highway. Short sentences are easy for your audience to follow. But a presentation filled entirely with short sentences would sound choppy to the listener. Consequently speakers vary short and long sentences, to maintain the interest of their audience, and to try to mirror a conversational style. We see this variety, for example, in Mike O'Brien's speech on Sunoco's corporate culture:

> People were frustrated and unhappy. They had been trying to do things to make the company more efficient, but they weren't getting any traction. There had been a lot of reactive downsizing in response to pressure to cut costs, without much communication, understanding, or participation in the process.
>
> The whole organization was in a state of fear. People didn't know what was going to happen next. There were some good programs in place, but there had been so much change that many people didn't know what they were accountable for any more.[26]

Read this section out loud to get a sense of the pacing and rhythm. The variety in sentence length helps to make it sound like the cadence of conversational speech.

Pulling It Together

Looking back at this chapter, you may find the ideas and techniques rather disparate, separate, without cohesion. I'd now like to show you a typical speech preparation outline that pulls many of the techniques I've discussed together, so that you can see how the pieces fit. Figure 3-4 is an outline created by Radhika McDoom for a presentation to information management students on carpal tunnel syndrome. In Chapter 4 we will consider different note formats for presentations, but, for now, note some of the details in this outline: the separation of main ideas from supporting ideas by indentation; the inclusion of transitions; and the inclusion of sources, should your audience ask you for this information. From examining this outline, you can see how a presentation is organized and made accessible to an audience.

Figure 3-4   Speech Preparation Outline

Topic: Computer Related Repetitive Strain Injury

Audience: Computer users at X Corporation

Main Idea: To inform my audience about repetitive strain injury, its side effects, and what we can do about them.

INTRODUCTION

Among the people who suffer from repetitive strain injury, or RSI, are major-league pitchers, tennis players, musicians, assembly-line workers, and computer users.

RSI encompasses such disorders as carpal tunnel syndrome, tendinitis, and tennis elbow, to name a few.

So what is this potentially crippling condition and how is it related to computer use?

Preview Of Key Points: First I will define RSI and its symptoms, then show its causes, and then conclude with some advice on how to prevent it.

Transition: Now, I'll define repetitive strain injury and describe some of the symptoms.

SPEECH BODY

I.   What is RSI and what are the symptoms?

    A.   RSI is a description of a condition, not a diagnosis, that is rapidly becoming a hazard of the computer age.

        1.   It is injury to the hands and arms caused by the regular repetition of a particular movement.

        2.   The repeated regular movement causes damage to tendons, nerves, muscles, and other soft body tissues.

        3.   According to Dr. Barry Carlin, technical director at Future International Technologies, a California-based company specializing in injury prevention programs, a contributing factor to RSI is a prolonged period of looking down and holding your neck still.

            a.   Looking down shortens some muscles in the neck.

            b.   The result is a condition that puts pressure on the arteries, veins, and nerves going into the arms.

        4.   Stress is placed on the tendons and nerves in the hands, wrists, and even the shoulders and neck, by the following activities:

            a.   long periods of high-speed typing

            b.   clutching and dragging the mouse

            c.   using trackballs

Transition: Let's look at some of the symptoms of RSI and the damage it causes.

    B.   A repetitive strain injury develops slowly and can affect many parts of the body.

        1.   One of the symptoms is a tightness, discomfort, stiffness, or pain in the hands, wrists, fingers, forearms, or elbows.

        2.   Another indication is a tingling, coldness, or numbness in the hands.

        3.   Tension, sharp pain, ache, or cramping in the shoulder blades would indicate some degree of RSI.

        4.   Headaches that are caused by neck or eye problems could also be RSI related.

Transition: Now that we have an idea of what RSI is and how to monitor and recognize the symptoms, let us look at the causes.

II.   Why does RSI occur?

    A.   The restriction of circulation to muscles, tendons, and nerves during repetitive use can lead to RSI.

        1.   Normally, muscles and tendons get blood through capillaries that pass among the muscle fibres.

            a.   When you tense a muscle, you restrict the blood flow.

            b.   When you're typing too much, your muscles never relax enough to let the blood pass through.

    2.   Without fresh blood, the muscles use up stored energy.

        a.   The muscles then switch to anaerobic metabolism (that is, without using oxygen).

        b.   Anaerobic metabolism generates pain-causing by-products like lactic acid.

B.   Another factor that restricts blood flow is any existing injury.

    1.   Injured tissue becomes inflamed during repetitive motions. This pressure limits circulation.

    2.   Once one muscle hurts, all the surrounding muscles tense up. More tension results in less blood flow.

Transition: So far, we know the nature, symptoms, and causes of the problem. Let us now look at the most important and critical area, that is, ways to prevent repetitive strain injury.

III.   How do I prevent RSI?

A.   Workstation equipment must be set up to maximize comfort and support for the user.

    1.   The keyboard and monitor should be placed directly in front of the user's normal sitting position.

    2.   The monitor should be at eye level.

        a.   Be sure it is about 45 to 75 cm from your eyes.

        b.   This distance will prevent blurred vision.

    3.   Your chair should be adjustable and suitable to your body type.

    4.   Use a document holder to hold hard copy so that you don't look down.

    5.   Set your lighting, screen contrast, and ventilation at a comfortable level.

B.   But ergonomic equipment is not enough. Gary Karp, an ergonomics specialist with the San Francisco firm, Onsight Technology Education Services, says, "ergonomic equipment solves only 40% of the problem." Good posture also helps reduce tension.

    1.   Try leaning back in your chair and change your posture from time to time.

    2.   Place your feet flat on the floor.

    3.   Keep your wrists straight.

    4.   Don't slouch or lean forward.

    5.   Pull your chin in to look down; don't flop your head forward.

Transition: You should not only use comfortable equipment and practise good posture. You should also learn to relax.

C.   Relaxing also reduces muscle tension.

    1.   Let your shoulders relax.

    2.   Hold the mouse lightly instead of gripping or squeezing it.

    3.   Take brief, three-second breaks, every three minutes.

    4.   Take active breaks, to stretch and relax, every two hours.

Transition: In conclusion...

CONCLUSION

Summary of key points: We all have aches and pains that disappear in a day or two. But if you experience any of the symptoms of repetitive strain injury—pain, tingling, or numbness in your arms and hands, or clumsiness or loss of strength, on a regular basis—please see your doctor. Early treatment is critical to preventing further damage.

Concluding remark: I would like to leave you with this thought. The most important thing you should ask yourself is, are you comfortable throughout a day's work? If it feels good, then you are probably less at risk of injury.

SOURCES: "Prevention is the Key to Avoiding RSI," *Computerworld Canada* (March 14, 1997), pp. 18-20; [www.me.berkley.edu/ergo]; [www.cs.princeton.edu?~dwallach/tifaq]; [www.amara.com/aboutme/rsi.html]; [www.bilbo.com.wsj/html], April 5, 1997.

Chapter Summary

We've covered a lot of material here about drafting your presentation. As this chapter explained, all business presentations have three parts: the introduction, where you state your purpose and ease your audience into your material; the speech body, which develops your ideas and facts; and the conclusion, which summarizes and reinforces the key concepts you want your audience to remember. As I've said repeatedly, techniques, such as attention-getters, metaphors, and repetition, should not be used wholesale. Your purpose and audience are the key factors for using special devices.

Chapter 4 takes you one step further toward delivering your presentation. In that chapter I'll discuss how to deal with nervousness, the main obstacle many business people face when speaking to a group. I'll also deal with platform manner, vocal delivery, and note management. Your presentation may look good on paper, but maintaining a rapport with your audience is the key to successful delivery.

Applications

1. In what speaking situations might you use a full introduction? In what speaking situations might you use a succinct introduction?

2. What are the main elements of the conclusion of a presentation? What is the importance of these elements?

3. What techniques are used to guide listeners through a presentation? Why is variety important in applying these techniques?

4. Discuss the denotation and connotation of the following words:

    a. techie

    b. correction (as in "a correction in the financial markets")

    c. downturn

    d. downsize

    e. team player

    Why is it important to be sensitive to the connotation of words when preparing a presentation?

5. What are the dangers of using metaphors, idioms, and references to popular culture when speaking to culturally diverse audiences?

6. Change the passive voice to the active voice in the following sentences:

    a. An award was received by Rashid for exceeding his sales quota in the third quarter.

    b. Akiva Technology will spend $2 000 000 this year on training its employees, it was noted in the company's annual report.

    c. The employees will benefit by the introduction of a new insurance plan.

    d. The Yukon and the Northwest Territories are the sales regions serviced by Ellen Gold's team.

    e. Efficiency will be improved by the new software, and productivity will increase.

References

1. Deborah M. Allan, "Employment Trends for the Future and Skills for the 21st Century" (delivered to the Canadian Association of Career Educators and Employers, June 4, 1996). [www.spar.ca/corp/empltrnd.htm], July 14, 1997.

2. Peter C. Godsoe, "Canadian Universities: Competing to Win?" (delivered to the Canadian Club, Toronto, Ontario, March 4, 1996). [www.scotiabank.ca/speech1.htm], June 18, 1997.

3. Carol M. Stephenson, "Three Good Reasons and Ways to Profit from the Corporate Talent of Women" (delivered to the Arthur Andersen's Leaders of Influence Seminar Series, Toronto, Ontario, June 25, 1997). [www/stentor.ca/scripts/dbml.exe?template=/stentor/body.dbm&page_exsp10.html], June 20, 1997.

4. Richard L. George, "The Alberta Oil Sands—An Unconventional Alternative" (delivered to the Global Energy Forum: Strategies for the 21st Century, Houston, Texas, February 12, 1997). [www.suncor.com/05speeches/sp0197.html], August 18, 1997.

5. Courtney Pratt, "Noranda: On the Leading Edge" (delivered to Le Cercle canadien, Toronto, Ontario, December 12, 1995). [www.noranda.ca/news/prattspeech.html], June 20, 1997.

6. Allan, "Employment Trends for the Future and Skills for the 21st Century."

7. Godsoe, "Canadian Universities: Competing to Win?"

8. Carol M. Stephenson, "The Need for Competitive Equity in the Canadian Telecommunications Industry" (delivered to the Empire Club, Toronto, Ontario, December 5, 1996). [www.stentor.ca/scripts/dbml.exe?/template=/stentor/body.dbm.&page_id=exsp5.html], August 29, 1997.

9. A. Charles Baillie, "The Changing Nature of Work" (delivered to the Canadian Club, Orillia, Ontario, May 2, 1997). [www.tdbank.ca/tdbank/Speeches/sp-may97.htm], August 28, 1997

10. Godsoe, "Canadian Universities: Competing to Win?"

11. Peter Spelliscy, "Moving from Survival to Expansion—Why Changing the Culture is Essential" (delivered to the Human Resources Association of Calgary 1996 Conference and Expo, Calgary, Alberta, April 4, 1996). [www.suncor.com/05speeches/sun07spa.html], June 23, 1997.

12. Godsoe, "Canadian Universities: Competing to Win?"

13. Carol M. Stephenson, "The Female Style of Leadership" (delivered to the Chatelaine Women of Influence Luncheon, Vancouver, B.C., May 8, 1997). [www.stentor.ca/scripts/dbml. exe?template=/sentor/body.dbm&page_id=exsp14.html], August 29, 1997.

14. Fares F. Salloum, "Getting Connected in the 'Pacific Century'" (delivered to the University of British Columbia Bridging the Pacific Conference '97, Vancouver, B.C., January 24, 1997). [www.bctel.com/library/pacific.html], September 4, 1997.

15. John Mayberry, "Steel & the New Imperatives" (delivered to the Confederation Club Luncheon Meeting, Kitchener, Ontario, April 18, 1996). [www.dofasco.ca/news/news_speeches. html#Voyage], August 11, 1997

16. Mike O'Brien, "The Next Big Challenge: Moving from Downsizing to Growth" (delivered to the Strategic Leadership Forum, Toronto, Ontario, November 28, 1996). [www.suncor.com/ 05speeches/sun07spc.html], June 23, 1997.

17. Spelliscy, "Moving from Survival to Expansion."

18. John Mayberry, "Voyage to Tomorrow" (delivered to the Marine Club Annual Dinner, Toronto, Ontario, January 17, 1997). [www.dofasco.ca/news/news_speeches.html#Voyage], August 11, 1997.

19. Allan, "Employment Trends for the Future and Skills for the 21st Century."

20. George, "The Alberta Oil Sands—An Unconventional Alternative."

21. Mayberry, "Steel and the New Imperatives."

22. Allan, "Employment Trends for the Future and Skills for the 21st Century."

23. Gayle L. Stewart, "Yes, Virginia, There Is an Information Highway" (delivered to the Canadian Club, Kelowna, B.C., December 13, 1995). [www.bctel.com/library/845665305.html], September 4, 1997.

24. Spelliscy, "Moving from Survival to Expansion."

25. Salloum, "Getting Connected in the 'Pacific Century.'"

26. O'Brien, "The Next Big Challenge: Moving from Downsizing to Growth."

Establishing Rapport: Platform Manner, Vocal Delivery, and Note Management

In every business speaking situation, speakers must present their information in a way that fosters the audience's receptiveness and understanding. In Chapter 3, we saw specific techniques that accomplish these purposes. This chapter also describes methods that promote a speaker's rapport with his or her audience; in other words, methods that create a human connection.

Establishing rapport with your audience is crucial for the success of your presentation because, as a speaker, you cannot separate yourself from your message. In a sense, the manner of your delivery is the message itself. How you use your body and your voice can reinforce—or diminish—the communication of your ideas. Connecting with your audience involves more than what we discussed before: expressing your purpose clearly, previewing your main points, and using bridging methods such as transitions, internal previews, and internal summaries. It is more than using personal pronouns, the active voice, and unbiased language. Establishing rapport also means using eye contact to speak to your audience as individuals, whether your listeners number ten, twenty, or many more. It means controlling your pace and intonation. It also entails mastering mannerisms that may interfere with the clear communication of your message. This chapter considers the three main elements of creating and maintaining rapport: platform manner, vocal delivery, and note management.

Developing Effective Platform Manner

Delivering a presentation, making a point at a meeting, and speaking one-to-one are all exercises in human interaction. In some ways, speakers have more control when communicating than writers. For example, speakers regulate the pace of their presentations, whereas the audience controls the pace when reviewing written reports. Speakers hold their listeners' attention through eye contact and vocal delivery, perhaps by using their voices to stress key ideas, or by pausing at key points in a speech. Writers do not have physical and vocal resources to keep their readers' attention. Furthermore, in oral communication speakers have much more immediate opportunity to clarify and enhance the content of their speeches through question and answer periods. Writers lack opportunities for such immediate feedback.

Yet the control speakers have in communicating orally can be undermined by certain risks. Potential dangers include the unpredictability of the speaking environment, such as those elements covered in Chapter 2: equipment failure, for example, or a noisy, distracting ventilation system. The audience also may not live up to the speaker's expectations: they may be sleepy, bored, or resistant to the message. Another potential problem is insecurity, a crisis of confidence. Indeed, you might prefer communicating on paper to communicating orally because, customarily, you do not have to appear before your audience. You are not compelled to present yourself personally, warts and all.

How to Control Public Speaking Anxiety

In a speech delivered to the Human Resources Association of Calgary, Peter Spelliscy, senior vice-president of Suncor, recalled "one Suncor employee who had to make a presentation to the management committee. The senior people gave him such a tough grilling on the details of his project that he passed out from fright—right next to the overhead projector."[1] Spelliscy told this story as an example of the "lean and mean" Suncor corporate culture that was transformed into one "liberally sprinkled with humanity." He commented, "People attend meetings with a different attitude (no one has fainted lately)."

For most people, fear is an inescapable part of delivering presentations. Several terms are used to refer to this phenomenon: public speaking anxiety, communication apprehension, stage fright. Inevitably, however, to succeed on the job you must communicate orally, and you can certainly overcome any fear of formal business speaking that you might have. As you read the following sections, reflect on any anxieties you experience when speaking to a group.

Recognize Your Anxiety

One of the first steps to managing speaking anxiety is to understand the reasons why you feel anxious. It is important to realize that you are not alone in feeling apprehensive when delivering an oral presentation: even business people who give speeches frequently feel nervous. The reasons people feel this way include these fears:

1. **Inadequacy.** I am incapable of speaking effectively. The audience expects me to do a good job, and I don't know if I can meet their expectations.

2. **Vulnerability.** My weaknesses will be exposed to the audience.

3. **Potential problems.** The speech will be either too long or too short, the equipment will not work, I will misplace my notes and visual aids, I won't be able to answer questions.

4. **Audience hostility.** The audience will not like my presentation or me.

Physical symptoms of stage fright are an increased heart rate, sweaty palms, fast and shallow breathing, dry mouth, upset stomach, a shaky voice. Sleepless nights before a presentation are another symptom.[2] If you are familiar with some of these signs, don't be overconcerned about them. Mark Swartz, a career consultant, speaker, and author, remarks that "nervousness is natural, and, in some ways, beneficial. It stimulates you to be on top of things and present in an animated, energized fashion."[3]

Get on Top of Your Fears

To manage your fears, you must consider what factors you can control. Dealing with the ones you can manage will certainly give you more confidence when you meet your audience.

Face the task.   As Chapter 2 warned, don't procrastinate when you are assigned a presentation; face the task and start preparing. Chapters 2 and 3 gave some basic advice about audience analysis, focusing your topic, and using language. It is important to prepare in a positive way that is focused on the job itself, rather than on your own nervousness or lack of confidence. It has been shown that highly anxious people use their time unproductively when preparing a speech.[4] They tend to review sections of their presentation they have already completed and spend time hunting for the "right word," instead of moving ahead. They worry about their ability to deliver a presentation, instead of analyzing their audience. They leave preparing visuals to the last minute and do not check that the equipment they need will be available and in working order. Awareness of these habits in yourself will help you prepare constructively, and, correspondingly, subdue your nervousness.

Prepare, prepare, prepare!   The flip side of these negatives, of course, is in-depth planning. Understand the speaking situation and the business needs of your audience. Determine how your information will benefit them. Write the drafts of your outlines straight through, pausing only briefly for corrections. Create your visuals as early as possible in the preparation process, and reserve and check any equipment you need several days before you deliver your presentation. It is often useful to prepare your visuals as handouts for your audience, just in case the projector breaks down—such disasters do happen! You could then proceed with your presentation, and earn the admiration of your listeners at the same time.

Predicting questions and having the answers to them is another way to reinforce confidence. Also, full preparation means having back-up materials, such as a list of your sources, on hand if anyone asks about your research.

Rehearse.   Thorough preparation is one way to ease stage fright. Sufficient rehearsal is another. Allocate rehearsal time in your preparation schedule. Practising will help you pinpoint potential problems, such as a speech that is too long or too short. Practising is invaluable for becoming familiar with your material, so that you can maintain eye contact with your audience, instead of reading from your notes. Rehearsal also gives you the opportunity to see how your speech "sounds," that is, whether you need to change your content or language for your audience. Furthermore, if you can spend some time rehearsing to a small audience of acquaintances or fellow employees, you can get feedback on your speech, as well as encouragement.

Some speakers also stand in front of a mirror while rehearsing a presentation. Taping your rehearsal with an audio cassette, or videotaping, is also helpful; you can analyze your performance at your leisure, and determine what changes need to be made. All of these processes contribute to a more confident feeling when you deliver a presentation.

Check out your venue.   If your venue is unfamiliar to you, try to investigate it before your presentation: doing so will improve your confidence by taking away one of the unknowns. Indeed, even if you are familiar with the setting, it's also a good idea to inspect it; there may be changes made by a previous speaker that you need to correct for your own speech. If you can rehearse where you will present, that too will provide a feeling of security as well as give you the opportunity to resolve any technical questions—such as determining the proper placement of a projector or screen so that all your listeners can comfortably view your visuals. Many speakers like to sit in different parts of the room, so that they can determine the audience's sightlines and make sure they are not blocked. Figure 4-1 shows effective room arrangements that take into account the proper placement of projection equipment.

Think positively.   Another factor that helps speakers develop confidence is positive thinking. Don't focus on the possibility of making mistakes; instead, focus on what you can offer your audience. Keep in mind that, as long as you are well prepared, you probably know more about your topic than your listeners do. They are eager to hear you speak because you are imparting the benefit of your research and analysis to them. Most people, including your listeners, are nervous when delivering a formal presentation; your listeners will respect you for trying your best.

View your presentation as an opportunity: you have another occasion to practise a key communication skill necessary for advancement in the business world. You have to do it, so regard your presentation as another chance to show your best professional self.

Figure 4-1   Effective Room Arrangements for a Presentation

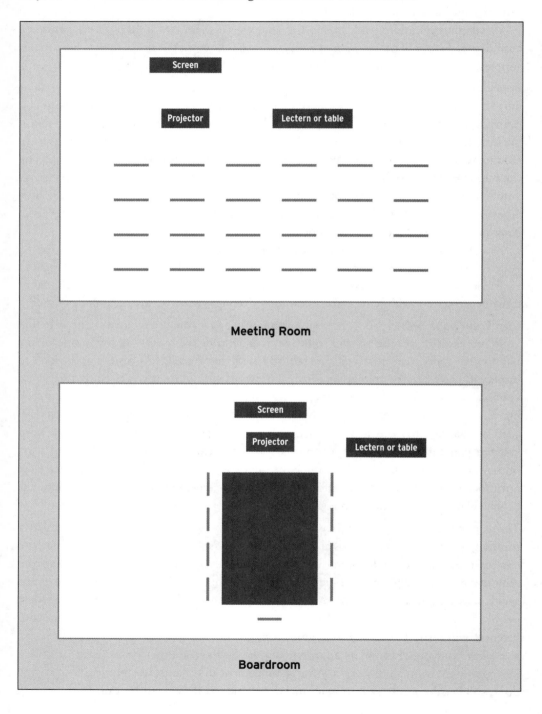

Visualize your presentation.   Some speakers try to visualize themselves speaking in order to boost their confidence. Picture yourself delivering your presentation in your designated setting, dressed as you will for the task. Imagine an audience in front of you, and picture yourself handling and discussing your visuals as you speak. Visualizing can help you focus on the activity of speaking and calm nerves by establishing familiarity with the experience.

Dress appropriately.   Dressing appropriately is another element that improves self-confidence. Appropriate dress means wearing clothes that don't distract from your message. Many female business speakers like to dress in solid colours because, they believe, the audience can focus on them better. Appropriate dress also means wearing clothes you feel comfortable in, while looking professional. A wardrobe has an impact on a presentation, for men and for women.

How to Energize Your Speech

Speakers want to be professional, yet natural, because they know an audience listens more attentively to someone who appears relaxed rather than someone who appears stiff and robotic. Overcoming nervousness through thorough preparation and a positive mind-set are two ways to help you achieve a more relaxed platform manner. There are other methods that will also help you present in a dynamic and meaningful way.

Channel Your Stage Fright

The *Royal Bank Letter*, a corporate newsletter available to the public, tells us that "fear concentrates the mind, lending a clear, sharp focus to the message we want to convey."[5] *Canadian Banker* magazine advises speakers to "think about the importance of what you are saying. This concentration will give you the energy to talk."[6] Channeling your stage fright will enliven your speech, and help you project interest and enthusiasm, rather than indifference.

Focus on the Needs of Your Audience

As we've already seen, it's important to develop the right attitude from the preparation stage; doing so will help you project concern as you deliver your speech. As you speak, keep thinking of your audience as a group of people you want to benefit, perhaps by improving their productivity or profits. Maintaining this mind-set will help you communicate with credibility and sincerity—it will show your conviction as a speaker. If you don't care, neither will your listeners.

Exercise!

I'm not suggesting you work up a sweat, but that you perform some simple exercises to help you relax. Pam Ennis, a fitness consultant and speaker who advises on healthy living, recommends some methods to loosen tight shoulders and to get your blood flowing. For example, try raising your shoulders to your ears several times, or squeezing your shoulder blades together. Hold the contraction for a few seconds, then release. Repeat the process as many times as you wish. The principle is that by forcing your muscles to contract forcefully, they tend to loosen up and relax once you release them.[7] Do these exercises at any time, not only before a presentation. You will feel a difference.

Maintain Eye Contact

Neophyte speakers say that the most difficult part of formal speaking is making eye contact with their audiences. Yet you can achieve a natural and impressive speaking style by looking at your listeners. The eyes command attention; it is difficult for an audience to be distracted if you keep looking at them.

The benefit of visual feedback.   Eye contact gives you valuable feedback on how you are communicating your message. You can sense whether you are communicating clearly, or not, by looking at your audience. Although the kind of presentation described in this chapter involves one-way communication (until the question-answer session), during the course of your speech you can determine whether to pause and explain a topic in more depth, or to shorten a section by noting if listeners are becoming restive or questioning their neighbours.

The benefit of more natural speech.   Another benefit of maintaining eye contact is that you will begin to speak more naturally, rather than in a stilted fashion. Eye contact is natural in casual discourse. You will find that sustaining eye contact with an audience of any size will help make your delivery sound more like an everyday conversation.

Tips.   There are certain tricks that will help you maintain genuine eye contact.

1. At the very least, memorize the introductory section of your speech, so that you establish eye contact with your listeners from the very beginning. They will sense your desire to connect with them and to communicate your message.

2. However, *don't memorize your entire speech!* Speakers who do so often fail to make real eye contact with their listeners. Instead, their eyes are often raised toward the ceiling, or focused on the back wall of the room or into the "middle distance," perhaps because they are trying keeping their place in the text they have committed to memory. It is, of course, acceptable to glance at your notes in order to prompt yourself. But be sure that your notes are not a crutch; to project genuine eye contact you need to look at your listeners.

3. Look directly into the eyes of individuals in your audience. Focus on one person for a few seconds, then move on to someone else. If your eyes focus on a listener's, his or her eyes will focus on yours. Also, try to encompass your entire audience with eye contact. Be sure your eyes travel the room and stop briefly here and there to

make eye contact. This technique helps to personalize your presentation and demonstrates to each individual your conviction in your topic and purpose, and, once again, your desire to communicate with him or her.

Movement and Mannerisms

Just as eye contact can enhance your message, so can your posture, gestures, and facial expression. Let's look at some specific pointers.

Be yourself.   One of the most important elements for establishing rapport with your audience is to be yourself. Don't try to mirror a personality viewed on television, perhaps someone broadcasting the news or selling a product on an infomercial. Trying to be someone you are not can damage the success of your speech. Audiences immediately sense artificiality, and lose interest. Be your best "professional" self for your presentation. (Remember the definition you created in an exercise following Chapter 1.) Your audience will respond to your genuineness and to your interest in your topic and purpose.

Look pleasant.   When faced with a presentation, try to remember the following advice for controlling your facial expression. If the situation is routine or positive—an informational speech or a training session, for example—be sure to smile, particularly in the beginning of your presentation. Smiling will relax you, and will also evoke a positive response from your audience. They will believe you are pleased to speak to them, and your facial expression will help set a positive tone for the event.

In difficult speaking situations—when you are communicating bad news—your facial expression could work for or against you. Be sensitive to the your audience's reaction and to the atmosphere; a smile can send the wrong message about your attitude.

Use natural gestures.   Being yourself means using natural gestures. As you rehearse, you may find that you gesture as you speak. Be sensitive to too much movement, which can distract the audience from your message. Try to control movement. If you find you make gestures at significant points in your speech—at key ideas and at the conclusion, for example—you can reinforce your content. But your actions should be natural, not contrived, to be convincing.

Control nervous gestures.   Also, be aware of nervous gestures—hand rubbing, tapping your hand on the lectern, playing with your jewellery, hair, or clothes. These movements also weaken the power of your message. Comfortable clothes will help you control nervous mannerisms and instill self-confidence. Gestures that we associate with casual conversation also weaken a formal presentation: crossing your arms across your chest, which presents a barrier between you and your listeners; keeping your hands in your pockets for extended periods of time; or putting your hands behind your back. Some authorities advise keeping your hands away from your face and neck, because touching these parts of your body suggests indecision or uncertainty.[8]

Don't hold things.   Try not to hold a pen in your hand—some speakers fall into tapping it on the lectern or clicking it. If you are holding a pointer as you speak, don't wave it at the audience! Place it on a table or hold it pointing down until you need it again. Similarly, turn off your laser pointer when it is not needed.

Should I hold my notes while I speak? is a question speakers ask. Anything in your hands can present a distraction. If you do hold your notes, consider using 5" × 7" cards, not letter-size paper, and hold them in one hand only.

Maintain good posture.   Pam Ennis says, "When you are standing tall and you are standing confident, people will listen. It's more than just getting up there and having the credentials. When you walk into a room, you have to fill it with your presence, then you'll capture people." She also sees a link between posture and confidence: "No matter how nervous you are, stand tall, and confidence will follow."[9]

Control movement.   The purpose of a presentation often dictates the need for movement. So does the environment in which a presentation is delivered. In training sessions, as Chapter 5 explains, the speaker and audience typically interact during the instructional segment and during the hands-on session. To check on the progress of the participants, the instructor must walk around the room and speak to people individually. In formal presentations, however, a speaker usually stands in front of the audience for the entire speech, and tends to limit walking to moving between the lectern and projector. It is important to be the centre of focus for your audience. If you stroll across the front of the room while you are speaking, you will probably distract your listeners from the message. A speaker who is self-possessed and maintains consistent eye contact with his or her listeners is a compelling focal point for an audience.

Many effective speakers like to restrict their movements to necessary walks between the lectern and the projector or other essential equipment. Sometimes, to reinforce a point, you may take a step toward your audience. Think of containing your movement within a triangle, as Figure 4-2 shows. In other words, use movement to underscore ideas in your presentation.

Use the lectern judiciously.   Should you use a lectern if one is available? This too is a concern for speakers. Many nervous speakers like to use a lectern because they believe it conceals them; the audience mainly sees their heads and shoulders. The lectern also provides a place to rest your hands if you tend to put them in your pockets or gesture too much. But a lectern can also be a barrier between you and the audience. The more an audience sees of you, the more personal the presentation becomes.

If a lectern is available for your presentation, consider using it only as a place to put your notes, so that you can consult them conveniently during your speech. Movement between the lectern and the open space in front of the audience will add a bit of variety to body movement, but not too much.

Figure 4-2   Triangle of Controlled Platform Movement

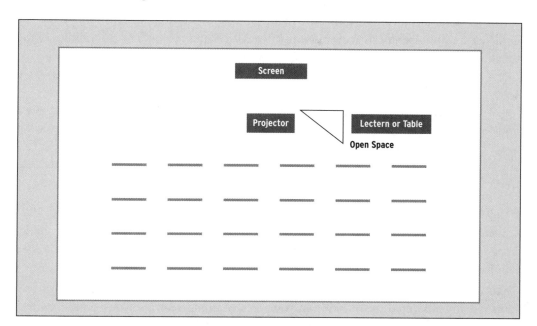

How to Present with Partners

Another dimension of effective platform manner is managing joint presentations, which are common in business speaking. If you and your partners don't plan joint presentations ahead of time, they will be confused and disorganized. There are several tips you can follow.

1. When preparing for a collaborative presentation, divide the research by area of expertise. After each participant completes his or her draft, it can be exchanged with a partner for editing and evaluation. Allocate the drafting of the overall introduction and concluding remarks to one person for efficiency, but be sure to have these sections reviewed by a colleague as well.

2. At the joint presentation, have the first speaker introduce each participant briefly. Then, the first speaker will deliver the opening remarks and his or her segment. Next the floor is turned over to the next speaker. The final speaker can present the concluding remarks in addition to his or her part.

3. During the question-answer session, let the best-qualified individual answer each question. Doing this will ensure that the most knowledgeable response is given.

How to Deal with Question-Answer Sessions

These sessions are an important part of business presentations because they give the audience an opportunity to acquire more information and to question the validity of the speaker's analysis and recommendations. Look at corporate Web sites that replay actual Q&A sessions, such as Suncor (**www.suncor.com/05speeches/sp0497.html**), to get a sense of how executives handle them.

Again, preparation is key for a successful question period. Always try to second-guess your audience's questions. Review your presentation outline carefully to predict what areas might solicit questions, such as generalizations with limited evidence, and controversial remarks. And bring along your list of references (you can include it in a handout) to direct listeners to specific sources and any data you used to analyze your findings.

Managing the Q&A Session

Controlling the question-answer session is important. Try to apply the following guidelines so that you give as many listeners as possible the opportunity to speak and to feel comfortable about asking questions.

Treat all questioners with respect.   Even if you think a question is stupid, or if you have already answered the question in your presentation, treat it seriously and respond, although you may need to repeat information. Spotlighting the speaker by indicating the question has already been asked is discourteous.

Maintain eye contact with both the questioner and the group.   Although you are answering one person's question, everyone in the audience is interested in it and in your answer. Roam the audience with your eyes to include all your listeners and to maintain their attention.

Repeat or summarize the question.   Not everyone in the audience might hear the question, so paraphrase it before you answer. If the question is preceded by a long comment, give the gist of the remarks.

Keep your answers to the point.   Avoid digressions. If a questioner seeks more information, he or she will have ample opportunity at another time. Let as many people as possible have the floor.

Politely suppress hijackers.   You may experience occasions when questioners seize the question-answer segment to promote their own positions. These people are annoying to your audience, who either want to ask a question or hear your responses. If you cannot deal with hijackers when they pause for breath, interrupt them and say you will be happy to discuss their concerns after the session.

Types of Questions

The following strategies will help you prepare for different kinds of questions people normally ask.

Questions that challenge your assertions or evidence.   Don't let challenging questions put you off. Treat the question as friendly, not hostile. You can begin your answer by restating the question and then refuting it politely using the evidence in your speech as well as findings you didn't include. Also point out the weaknesses in the questioner's comments. If the questioner's point is valid, be sure to acknowledge it, and indicate you will keep it in mind for future research. If your evidence is questioned, show that your source material is unbiased and your research methods sound. If there is anything uncertain about your research, be honest.

Questions that seek clarification.   Your questioner is confused or missed something you said. Repeat your remarks and amplify if necessary.

Questions that aren't questions, but comments.   Here you can paraphrase what the speaker said, and either try to extract a question from the remarks or ask the speaker to formulate a question.

Questions you can't answer.   Don't hedge. Admit you are unable to respond, and make arrangements to contact the questioner with the answer at a future time.

Improving Vocal Delivery

Good platform manner is essential for an effective presentation. Yet, although you may project ease and confidence through your platform manner, these qualities can be undermined by poor vocal delivery. Our voices, obviously, are an inescapable part of ourselves, and perhaps the part most difficult to change. Cecily Berry, a British voice coach, remarks, "A great many people worry deeply about how they speak and how they sound," and that effective speaking "has to do with discovering the vitality of your own speech and having confidence in it ...."[10] Effective business speaking demands a controlled pace, natural variety without fillers, and correct pronunciation.

Controlling Pace

Pace is one of the easiest elements of vocal delivery for a speaker to control. In times of stress or excitement, we tend to speak quickly. Our speaking pace also tends to be fast in normal conversation. But when we are delivering a presentation, it is important to control pace. The content may be authoritative, the analysis convincing. Our eye contact may be consistent and encompass our entire audience. But if we speak quickly, all the work on preparing and delivering a presentation can be wasted, because the audience won't be able to grasp and remember what is said. In business situations, the audience is there because they believe your information and analysis may benefit their business activities. If you are able to communicate in an accessible way, your listeners will leave with the facts they need, and with a positive impression of you.

How do you control pace? Try to practice the following methods when rehearsing and delivering a presentation.

Train Your Ear

It is important to train your ear. Listen to news broadcasters, for example, and announcers. Determine how quickly or slowly they speak. Choose a personality whose pace is effective, and try to pace yourself similarly.

Listen to the people with whom you work and associate. How quickly do they speak? Can you easily grasp what they are saying?

Listen to yourself, in everyday casual conversation or when speaking in a formal situation, such as making a point at a meeting or delivering a speech. Do you speak quickly, or slowly? Be conscious of your pace, and practise speaking more slowly if your pace is quick. Ask friends and fellow-workers if you speak quickly. Their honest response can help you become a better business speaker.

Read Poetry Aloud

Any poetry will do, modern or past. The strong iambic pentameter of Shakespeare's verse, for example, can help discipline your voice to speak at a moderate pace. You may wish to choose from any one of Shakespeare's plays. Figure 4-3, Lear's speech from the beginning of Shakespeare's great tragedy, shows the stressed syllables marked. Read the verse slowly, following the natural rhythm of the lines, to see how you can control your pace.

Figure 4-3   Practicing Pace: Reading Out Loud

Choose any poetry you enjoy, or read the following scene from Shakespeare's *King Lear*, in which Lear announces the division of his kingdom among his daughters.

Meantime we shall express our darker purpose.

Give me the map there. Know that we have divided

In three our kingdom; and 'tis our fast intent

To shake all cares and business from our age,

Conferring them on younger strengths while we

Unburdened crawl toward death.

King Lear, I, i, 35-40

Use Strategic Pausing

A controlled pace means not only speaking at a rate that makes your content accessible to your listeners, but also pausing every six or eight words, and at key points in the presentation. Pausing after every few words helps slow your pace, and pausing at key points gives emphasis to important parts of your speech, and gives your listeners an opportunity to relax and retain your ideas. For example, stopping briefly between each major section of your presentation will help listeners remember the point you just explained, and will help them prepare mentally for your next point. Pausing briefly before your conclusion is also a good idea, because it can cue your audience to your summary and final remarks. Practice strategic pausing when you rehearse your presentations.

Preventing Needless Fillers

Another speaking fault that can easily be managed is using needless fillers. These are the "ums" and "uhs" that invade the empty space as we form our thoughts. In everyday conversation "ums" and "uhs" are not usually irritating to listeners. They indicate that we are formulating ideas as we speak. We also often utter "um" or "uh" as a way to indicate to speakers, in interpersonal communication, that we are listening to what they say.

In a formal presentation, however, such fillers may suggest to the audience that you are not completely prepared. They imply that you are composing your presentation as you speak. This impression may be erroneous, but it is a negative impression nonetheless. "Ums" and "uhs" also suggest nervousness that cannot be channeled into effective speaking.

Suppress the "Ums" and "Uhs"

One way to conquer the "ums" and "uhs" is simply not to utter them! Be conscious of how you express yourself, and when you feel an "uh" coming on, just press your lips together and say absolutely nothing until the urge to "uh" passes. You may wish to take the opportunity to look at the audience as a way of reinforcing the point you just made, or to glance at your notes in order to prepare for the next section of your presentation. Suppression of the "ums" will supply another pause to your speech, a brief moment for the audience to relax and to reflect on what you have just said. You will come across as a controlled speaker, in charge of your presentation, through your brief silence.

Suppress Other Needless Fillers

Other fillers include expressions such as "okay," "really," "right," "and stuff," "whatever," "and whatnot," "et cetera, et cetera." Do these words and phrases actually add anything meaningful to a speech? In Chapter 3, we saw Deborah Allan, formerly of Spar Aerospace, introduce an internal summary with the word "okay." She used it as a transition into the final part of her speech. It adds a conversational tone. It serves a purpose.

But it is used only once. The other phrases listed above are, in essence, meaningless, and should be avoided completely.

Injecting Variety

Many speakers are concerned that they are expressing themselves in a monotone. Reading to your audience or delivering a fully memorized speech, instead of speaking extemporaneously, will inhibit vocal variety. Note the following tips.

Maintain Eye Contact

Consistent eye contact combined with the right attitude—believing in your message and purpose—will add interest and conviction to your voice, a natural delivery of your speech instead of a stilted one.

Avoid Uptalking

A problem that is linked to a monotone is that of uptalking. In uptalking, the voice rises at the end of statements. As Figure 4-4 shows, the voice inflects upward, making the speaker sound as if he or she is asking a question, instead of making a statement. Speakers who express themselves in this manner project the impression of being unsure and weak, as if they lack confidence in their facts and ideas.

Figure 4-4 Avoiding Uptalking

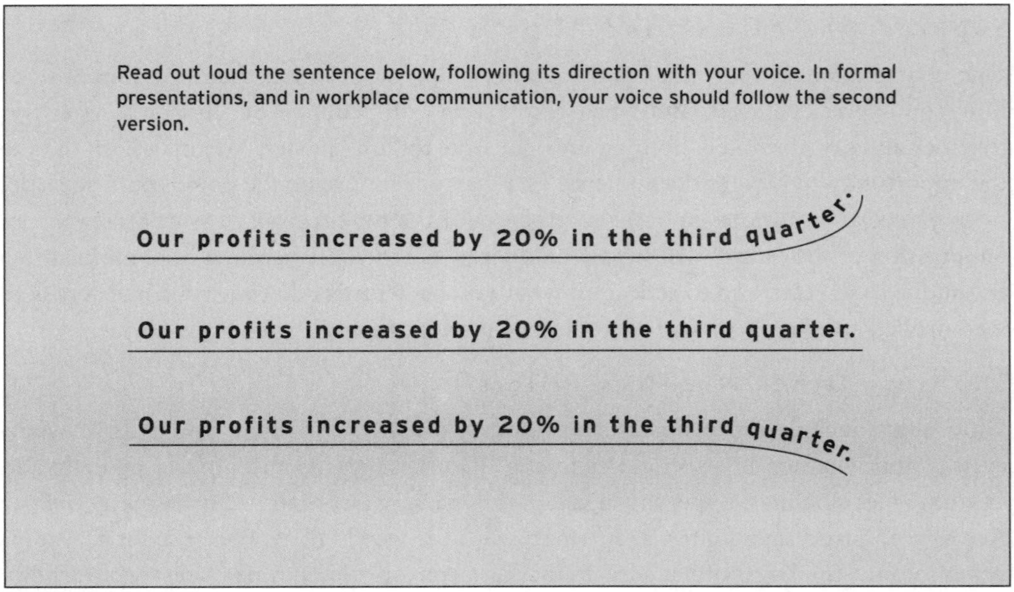

Read out loud the sentence below, following its direction with your voice. In formal presentations, and in workplace communication, your voice should follow the second version.

Our profits increased by 20% in the third quarter.

Our profits increased by 20% in the third quarter.

Our profits increased by 20% in the third quarter.

Control Pitch and Tone

The pitch and tone of your voice—whether you sound shrill, or sleepy, or nervous—can also block the success of a presentation. Although a tape recording of your voice will not give a true replication of how you sound, it is worth making a recording to determine if you sound shrill, whine, or speak through your nose, giving your voice a stuffy quality, as if you have a cold. Voice coaches recommend breathing from the diaphragm, from the bottom of the chest, rather than higher up in the chest area (that is, your stomach should extend as you breathe in), to achieve a resonant vocal quality and a relaxed voice.

Maintaining Volume

When inspecting the venue for your presentation, take note of its size. Will your voice carry throughout the room? Remember that there is no guarantee that a small audience will sit at the front in a large room. You may have to speak to a scattered audience. Project your voice, but don't shout. Again, breathing from the diaphragm will result in your natural voice, rather than a loud or shrill voice, reaching the entire audience.

Sometimes it is effective to modulate your volume, that is, to speak a little quietly to emphasize a point instead of at the volume you have sustained most of the time. A softly spoken phrase, when appropriate, can get your audience to sit up and pay attention more than words expressed in a loud voice.

Enunciating

It's important to pronounce your words correctly. Accurate pronunciation projects your concern for getting things right, for the details.

Don't Slur Words

Listen to yourself to determine if you slur your speech, that is, if you combine words instead of expressing each one distinctly. A mispronounced phrase of the National Anthem of the United States is often used as an example of slurred speech: "for Richard Stans" is a blemished version of "for which it stands."

Transliterate Difficult Names

Names can sometimes be challenging. Not infrequently in presentations it is necessary to acknowledge important people in the audience or people who have helped you in some way. People often feel slighted if their names are mispronounced. It is a sign of respect to get it right. You can help yourself by transliterating an unfamiliar name in your notes. Put the transliteration in brackets, as the following example shows:

And I want to thank Cecilia Cesare [Chay-CHILL-yah CHAY-zar-ray] for her help ...

Practice Technical Terms and Foreign Words

Some technical terms or scientific words, such as "orthogonal axis robot," might also need some practice. Pronouncing technical language aloud several times will help ensure correct speech.

Also do your best to pronounce any foreign terms correctly. Consulting a foreign-language dictionary, or colleagues who speak that language, will certainly help. Your audience will acknowledge your efforts.

Don't be Overconcerned About Accented English

Speakers with accents often worry about their spoken English. As long as you try to enunciate each word as clearly as you can, and speak at a pace that is accessible to your audience, you will be understood. Perfect pronunciation does not make a successful presentation: as already explained, a demonstrated interest in the topic, the desire to speak to an audience as individuals through effective eye contact, and a composed platform manner are more important elements. Indeed, a speaker who pronounces each word correctly, but does not employ the most important methods that create an effective speech, will lose the audience's attention.

Managing Notes Sensibly

Effective platform manner and vocal delivery are key elements in creating successful presentations. But they cannot be achieved without good note preparation. Let's now look at the issue of note management, the third element in establishing rapport with your audience.

The kind of notes we use for presentations can make or break a speech. Poorly devised notes become a crutch, and take your attention away from your audience. Well-prepared notes become an aid, assisting you in maintaining rapport with your listeners. We'll look at scripts and outlines, the most common forms speakers employ.

Scripts

A script is essentially the text of your speech, more or less as you will deliver it. If you do use a script, be sure that it helps you to read easily. As we know, speakers tend to experience some nervousness when delivering a speech. If you print out your script in small type, you can easily lose your focus and you will probably fumble to get yourself back on track. A large font, generous use of white space, and numbered pages will make your speech easy to read, and consequently project the assured image you want.

Figure 4-5 is a page from a script of a speech delivered by a TD Bank Financial Group officer. Note that the font is 14 point, larger than that used for conventional business correspondence. The text is double-spaced.

Mark Places for Emphasis

Remember also to use graphic devices—underlining, boldface, capital letters—to high-light words and phrases you want to emphasize. In Figure 4-5 the key word "strategy" is printed in capital letters, and the word "too" is underlined. These graphic techniques remind the speaker to stress these terms.

Figure 4-5   Example of Speech Script

Good morning, Ladies and Gentlemen. As you all know, the theme of today's conference is "Thriving in the Nineties" and I have been asked to discuss TD Bank's strategic plan for the remainder of this decade.

The word STRATEGY. It has a nice ring to it. It always makes me think of an all-seeing all-knowing group of thinkers deep in the core of an institution, or in some management consulting company, pontificating on the future of the markets and consumer's preferences – and directing strategy to benefit present and future generations. The trouble with this approach to strategy is that it tends to be biased toward a rear view mirror picture of the world, static, rigid, even brittle, while the world around us is increasingly dynamic and uncertain. <u>Too</u> rigid a view of the future can leave a corporation inflexible and unwilling or unable to seize new opportunities or react to sudden shifts in the environment or in customer preferences.

Source: G. F. Kym Anthony, "Thriving in the Nineties: TD Bank's Strategic Vision (the Tao of Your Bank, Your Way)" (delivered to the Gordon Capital Corporation, Toronto, Ontario, February 21, 1995). Print copy courtesy of TD Financial Group.

Mark Visuals and Pauses

If you employ visuals in your speech, as many presentations do, note in your script when you will show them, so that you can coordinate the visuals with your text.

You may forget to pause at appropriate places because of nervousness or your interest in your information. Many effective speakers find it useful to remind themselves when to pause. Simply write the word "pause" in your script in large letters and in a contrasting colour at the appropriate places.

Outlines

As I explained earlier in this chapter, most business speaking situations require that speakers maintain eye contact. Consequently, you need notes that will simplify the job of maintaining rapport with your audience. Outlines are very handy—they organize your material between main points and supporting points, and, if created properly, serve as a visual representation of the relationship of your ideas and facts. Figure 4-6 shows the two basic outline notation systems, alphanumeric and decimal format. As we saw in Chapter 2, Mahima creates successive outlines of her presentation. They are very useful in the preparation stage because they help you separate your presentation into its three main parts—introduction, body, and conclusion. Furthermore, since an outline requires separating primary, secondary, and tertiary topics, they encourage you to analyze your information carefully and to arrange it logically.

The kinds of outlines speakers usually create are either sentence or key-word outlines. Although each outline is different, each follows the same organizational principles. The outline in Figure 4-6 distinguishes between main ideas and supporting ideas, and demonstrates how indentation provides a visual reminder of the hierarchy of your information. Your word-processing software probably includes an outline function; using it will facilitate outline preparation.

Key-Word Outlines

You might want to begin drafting your presentation with a key-word outline, because this kind of outline, as Figure 4-7 shows, is a quick way to jot down your main ideas and to arrange them in the order that best suits your purpose and audience. You can see from Figure 4-7 that Radhika's sentence outline can be easily transformed into key-word format. Key-word outlines consist of just one, two, or a few words that express your point. Outline notation can be added to Mahima, Lyndon, and Andrew's notes in Chapter 2 to turn them into key word outlines.

Note also that "stage directions" are included in the outline, to remind Radhika when to pause and when to show visual aids.

Figure 4-6   Alphanumeric and Decimal Format Outline Systems

Some Rules:

1. One idea for each letter or number

2. Try to limit each entry to one sentence or point

3. When you subdivide, you should have two or more subsections; if you don't, then
   a) you are not subdividing sufficiently, or b) you are repeating the same idea

Alphanumeric System

I. First main idea
   A. First supporting idea for I.
      1. Supporting evidence for A.
      2. More supporting evidence for A.
   B. Second supporting idea for I.
      1. Supporting evidence for B.
         a. Supporting evidence for 1.
         b. More supporting evidence for 1.
      2. More supporting evidence for B.

II. Second main idea
   A. Supporting idea for II.
   B. More supporting information for II.
      1. Supporting evidence for B.
      2. More supporting evidence for B.

Decimal Format Outline System:

1. First main idea
   1.1 First supporting idea for 1
   1.2 Second supporting idea for 1

2. Second main idea
   2.1 Supporting evidence for 2
   2.2 More supporting evidence for 2
      2.2.1 Supporting evidence for 2.2
      2.2.2 More supporting evidence for 2.2

I strongly recommend using a key-word outline when delivering a presentation because it will prevent you from reading a text; key-word outlines are a prompting device. Obviously, you must be very well prepared to use them. Using a minimum number of words forces you to speak extemporaneously: that is, to make extensive eye contact and sound more conversational and natural than you would if relying on a detailed outline.

Sentence Outlines

An example of a sentence outline was given in Figure 3-4, Radhika McDoom's outline of her presentation on repetitive strain injury. Sentence outlines are an extension of key-word outlines. It's useful to write one after you have done much, if not all, of your research; doing so will ensure that you have covered your topic sufficiently. Writing out all your ideas and evidence will also reinforce your material in your mind. Keep in mind, however, that while sentence outlines are excellent preparation tools, they are poor speaking aids: their thoroughness tempts speakers to read rather than maintain eye contact with their listeners.

Handling Your Notes

Being comfortable with your notes helps ensure the success of your presentation. Here are some useful practices.

Use a Large Font and a Lot of White Space

Like a script, outlines require a large font so that you can quickly glance at your notes to track your presentation. With outlines, it's prudent to place each main point on a separate sheet of paper, as shown in Figure 4-8.

Mark Your Visuals

Clearly mark when you are going to show the visual on each page, as shown in Figures 4-7 and 4-8. Using a different colour than that of your notes, such as red, will remind you immediately when it's time to show your graphic aid.

Mark Your Transitions and Pauses

We've already seen the importance of including your transitions, internal previews, internal summaries, and connectives, such as signposts, in your speeches. We've also seen that it's useful to remind yourself when to pause. Either completely, or in short form, indicate these methods that will guide your listeners through your presentation.

Figure 4-7   Example of Key-Word Outline

Topic: Computer Related Repetitive Strain Injury
Audience: Computer users at X Corporation
Main Idea: To inform my audience about repetitive strain injury, its side effects, and
              what we can do about them.

INTRODUCTION: *Visual*

   - SUFFERERS

   - DISORDERS

   - DEFINITION AND COMPUTERS

PREVIEW OF KEY POINTS: DESCRIPTION, CAUSES, PREVENTION

TRANSITION   *Pause*

SPEECH BODY

I.   DESCRIPTION / SYMPTOMS   *Show bullet chart*

      A.   CONDITION
            1.   repetitious movement
            2.   tendon, nerve, muscle, tissue damage
            3.   Dr. Barry Carlin (technical director, Future International Technologies,
                 California)–contributing factors

      B.   ACTIVITIES CAUSING STRESS
            1.   high-speed typing
            2.   mouse   *Show bullet chart*
            3.   trackballs

      C.   SYMPTOMS   *Pause*
            1.   tightness–limbs
            2.   tingling, coldness, numbness–hands   *Diagram*
            3.   tension, pain–shoulder blades
            4.   headaches   *Pause*

TRANSITION

II.   OCCURRENCE–REASONS
      A.   REPETITIVE USE
      B.   EXISTING INJURIES   *Pause*

TRANSITION

III. PREVENTION
      A.   ERGONOMICS   *Diagrams*
      B.   GOOD POSTURE

TRANSITION

      C.   RELAXING   *Pause*

CONCLUSION: SYMPTOMS and PREVENTION

COMMENTS: COMFORT and WORK

Figure 4-8 Separating Notes

INTRODUCTION: PAGE 1

SUFFERERS   Visual

DISORDERS

DEFINITION AND COMPUTERS

PREVIEW OF KEY POINTS: DESCRIPTION, CAUSES, AND PREVENTION

TRANSITION   Pause

I. DESCRIPTION/SYMPTOMS: PAGE 2

A.   CONDITION   Show bullet chart

    1.   repetitious movement

    2.   tendon, nerve, muscle, and tissue damage

    3.   Dr. Barry Carlin (technical director, Future International
       Technologies, California)–contributing factors:

B.   ACTIVITIES CAUSING STRESS   Show bullet chart

    1.   high-speed typing

    2.   mouse

    3.   trackballs   Pause

Track Your Notes Carefully

Most important, be sure to keep your notes in order. Mark the page number on the top right hand corner, in red ink or another contrasting colour. Be orderly about your notes: put one page to one side after dealing with that point. Be sure your notes are in the correct order *before* you begin your presentation; it is embarrassing to reorder your notes as you speak. Place your notes in a secure place on the lectern, or on a table: you don't want to pick them up from the floor in front of your listeners.

Use a Cover Sheet for Notes

Finally, you can trick your audience into thinking you have a good deal of your presentation in your head, even if you do not, when showing certain transparencies—usually bullet charts or tables. When showing a bullet chart to your audience, do not display the entire chart at once. Instead, use a sheet of paper to cover up the points you are not yet discussing. This sheet of paper contains the remarks you want to make about that point on your bullet chart. As you reveal the points on the transparency by moving the paper down, you continue with commentary about each succeeding point. However, be sure you use the notes on your cover sheet only to prompt you: you want to make eye contact with your audience, not read from the projector.

Chapter Summary

Maintaining rapport with your audience is a key ingredient for successful presentations. As I've said, a speech is not a report—your mannerisms, eye contact, and vocal delivery are vital elements for communicating with your audience. Remember to relax, and channel your nervousness into preparing your presentation effectively, rather than focusing on your anxiety about speaking. When delivering your speech, be sure to keep your purpose in mind, and remember that your audience wants to hear what you have to say: you will energize your speech, and appear animated and interested. Try to make consistent eye contact, encompassing all your listeners, and moderate your pace. And, be sure to use notes that will help you maintain your connection with your audience, not hinder it. Your goal is to appear assured and composed, your best natural, yet professional self.

Now that you are armed with the basics of speech preparation and delivery presented in Chapters 2 through 4, we can turn to specific kinds of business speaking situations. In the next chapter, we'll look at reporting and training.

Applications

1. How can you maintain eye contact with an audience? Create a short extemporaneous speech on one of the following topics.

   a. the importance of good customer service

   b. how to invest in mutual funds

   c. how to choose a good stock investment

   d. how computer technology can help you prepare a presentation

   e. how the Internet can help you prepare a presentation

   Deliver your speech to a small audience of friends or family, and ask them to tell you how effective your eye contact was.

2. Deliver another short speech on one of the topics in Application 1 to your audience of friends or family. This time ask them to focus on your gestures. Ask them to note if your gestures reveal nervousness or are distracting.

3. Read poetry aloud several times a week to practise vocal delivery. Take careful note of your pace and pronunciation. Ask a friend or family member to evaluate your delivery and to recommend areas for improvement.

4. Create a sentence outline for a five-to-seven-minute speech on one of the topics in Application 1, or a topic of your own choosing. Use either the alphanumeric or decimal point format. Be sure to distinguish main points from supporting points by using the correct notation and indentation.

5. Create a key-word outline based on your sentence outline, and use your outline to deliver a presentation on the topic, applying the techniques for eye contact, movement, and vocal delivery discussed in this chapter. Practise this presentation until you feel you have mastered your material and can make consistent eye contact with your audience.

6. Practise the posture exercises and breathing techniques discussed in this chapter several times a week to improve your comfort level and vocal delivery for presentations.

References

1. Peter Spelliscy, "Moving from Survival to Expansion—Why Changing the Culture is Essential" (delivered to the Human Resources Association of Calgary 1996 Conference and Expo, Calgary, Alberta, April 4, 1996). [www.suncor.com\05speeches\sun07spa.html], August 23, 1997.

2. Elizabeth H. Winslow, "Overcome the Fear of Speaking in Public," *American Journal of Nursing* 91, no. 5 (May 1, 1991), 51.

3. Mark Swartz, e-mail to author, June 11, 1997.

4. See John A. Daly, Anita L. Vangelisti, and David J. Weber, "Speech Anxiety Affects How People Prepare Speeches: A Protocol Analysis of the Preparation Processes of Speakers." *Communication Monographs* 62, no. 4 (December 1995), 383–397.

5. Royal Bank of Canada, "Giving a Performance," *Royal Bank Letter* 76, no. 2 (March/April 1995). [www.royalbank.com/english/news/letter/giving.html], June 16, 1997.

6. Judith Humphrey and Ted Nichols, "Speak Up Persuasively," *Canadian Banker* 100, no. 1 (January/February 1993), 39.

7. Pam Ennis, interview with author, Toronto, Ontario, September 16, 1998.

8. Stephen D. Boyd, "What's a Body to Do?" *Public Management* 76, no. 4 (April 1996), 26.

9. Ennis, interview with author.

10. Cecily Berry, *Your Voice and How to Use it Successfully* (London, England: Harrap, 1975), pp. 7, 30.

CHAPTER 5

Presentations I: Reporting and Training

I hope you have gained confidence for facing your business audiences after reading the last three chapters. Focusing your purpose, understanding your listeners' needs, using effective techniques to guide your audience through your speech, and rehearsing (and rehearsing and rehearsing) will help you to speak credibly and meaningfully. With the basics behind us, I now want to look at elements of some typical business presentations you might deliver.

In this chapter, we'll consider what can be classified, for the sake of convenience, as informational business speaking. This category includes such activities as updating colleagues on the progress of a project, presenting summaries, and providing new information. In the next chapter, we'll discuss strategies of persuasive presentations, that is, business speaking that tries to change listeners' minds or urge them to pursue a particular course of action.

Although my discussion of business presentations is divided between informational speaking and persuasive speaking, the distinction is hazy. As either a speaker or a listener, you have probably felt that persuasion is an inescapable element of informational business speaking, an activity that guides audiences toward making business decisions. For example, if you have already delivered informational speeches, you may have highlighted certain facts, ones you believed your audiences should especially notice because they might influence your listeners' choice of options. Furthermore, your method of organization, vocabulary, tone of voice, and manner of delivery all shaped your audience's attitudes toward your subject matter. And, from the other side of the lectern, as a listener, you probably viewed informational speeches, to some degree, as persuasive. You likely evaluated the validity and relevance of the speaker's information, and judged his or her credibility. In short, either you were, or weren't, persuaded by the speaker, even if the purpose of the talk was informational.

This chapter looks at two kinds of informational business speaking—reporting and training. We'll focus on strategies that will help you perform these speaking tasks effectively, and we'll also look at their persuasive elements.

Oral Reporting

As routine business speaking tasks, oral reports help organizations run day to day. They may summarize written reports or original research, describe progress on a project, or explain procedures and policies. To deliver an effective oral report, you must make certain decisions. What information should you select? How concrete and specific should you be? How should you organize your facts?

Reporting on Written Documents

You may find that a number of your oral reports will be based on ones you have recently written. Let's imagine that, for the past six months, at his manager's request, Andrew has been tracking the questions and problems presented at the customer service desk at his bank. His task includes following how staff deal with customer concerns and what products customers purchase. Andrew's supervisor asks him to write a report based on his findings. Andrew produces a document about 20 pages long, including tables and charts.

After reading his report, Andrew's manager asks him to deliver an oral version to other managers and to customer service representatives at the next staff meeting. Let's imagine these meetings typically last one hour, and Andrew learns that he will have 10 minutes to speak.

The problem facing all business people when they need to adapt a written report into an oral report is deciding what information to omit, and what to present. Ask yourself the following questions, as Andrew would:

- What is the purpose of my oral report? Is it different from the purpose of my written report?
- Will my audience have read the report?
- What information will be most useful to my audience?
- Will everyone understand the facts and analyses I am communicating?
- What will they do with the information I give them?

The Purpose of an Oral Version of a Written Report

Written reports are filled with much more detail and analysis than speakers can expect to include in their presentations. What is the purpose, then, of a speech when the audience may have read, or can expect to read, the written version?

For one thing, an oral presentation gives you, the speaker, the opportunity to reinforce the most significant concepts and facts in the written report. The oral report also lets you interpret the facts more than the written one. In addition, you have the chance to update information and to answer questions from your listeners. In other words, an oral presentation of a written report, including a report that has a strong informational purpose, can be highly persuasive. It lets you influence your audience's reading and understanding of your material. An oral interpretation of a written business document can be a powerful device, because it provides you with more control over the decisions your audience makes from your information and analysis.

Selecting Your Information

If you have any doubts about the purpose of an oral version of a report you wrote, ask your supervisor why he or she wants you to speak, and find out whether your audience will receive copies of the written report before your talk. If so, you will have the opportunity to focus entirely on the most relevant points for your listeners. For example, you might wish to exclude background information, such as your discussion of your report's limitations (that is, the areas your report does not cover) and your research methods.

Let's say that Andrew's supervisor tells him that the main purpose of his oral report is to improve his audience's awareness of customer concerns so that the staff can improve service. If Andrew's listeners have already read his report, he might decide to omit a discussion of limitations and background material entirely. He might say to his audience, "You are already familiar with the reasons for my focus, and with my research methods, as discussed on page 3 ...." Using a simple reference like this one would signal to your audience that they can review such details. You will then be able to devote all of your speaking time to highlighting the most relevant information for your listeners. Andrew would devote his time to discussing his findings, particularly the service areas that can be strengthened.

Alternatively, if Andrew is told that his audience will not have the opportunity to read his report, he might then shape his presentation differently. He might decide to outline both his report's scope and his method of collecting his information, so that his audience has a context for his findings. Then he would discuss the results of his research.

You can see how important it is to know the purpose of your oral report when adapting your written one, and whether your audience will have read it, so that you can focus your objective and facts appropriately.

Presenting Detail

One of the challenges in any oral report is deciding how much and what kind of detail to include. The three main issues regarding detail are ethics, selection, and concreteness.

The Ethics of Details

In Chapter 1, I mentioned the importance of ethics to business speaking. The discussion of how oral reports amplify written reports also touched on this concern. Let's now consider the matter of ethics in relation to the information you communicate. Your power as a speaker comes with responsibility: ethical business practice requires you to do your research thoroughly, ensure the validity of your sources, credit your sources, and communicate your information accurately and objectively.

Doing responsible research.   The concept of responsible research means that you are thorough and up to date in investigating your topic. When speaking to his audience of novice investors, a task assigned to Andrew in Chapter 2, he has the responsibility to communicate the most recently available information about mutual funds to his audience. By learning about the most relevant and reliable sources for your topic and by speaking to the most knowledgeable people about your subject, you can use your time efficiently to obtain information for your presentation.

Obtaining valid evidence.   Another dimension of the ethics of details involves determining the validity of the results of your research. Is the information accurate? Is it factual? Is it opinion? A contribution from a writer to an Internet discussion group on notebook computers claiming one brand of computer is better than another is merely an opinion. It is up to you to gather information from several manufacturers, and to compare and analyze the specifications in relation to the needs of your audience. If you are expressing an opinion in a presentation, you must clarify for your audience that it is opinion, not fact.

Crediting your sources.   No one has ever given a presentation without help, either from colleagues, specialists outside the organization, or secondary sources such as books or magazine articles. It is to your credit to credit your sources. Doing so enhances the credibility of your presentation—an audience is suspicious of presenters when it appears, intentionally or unintentionally, that all information is original. Acknowledging help also enhances your integrity as a business speaker—it shows your honesty. Mention the names of people who assisted you and the authors or titles of books or articles where you obtained specific ideas or that you quote or paraphrase. Using known and respected sources gives you their authority. Neglecting to give credit will leave you open to accusations of plagiarism, that is, theft of someone else's ideas and material. Being honest can only improve your stature in the eyes of your audience and your organization. Later in this section on reporting you will learn how to acknowledge your sources.

Communicating your information accurately and objectively. Sometimes, while doing research for a presentation, speakers are careless when transcribing information. Sometimes they make mistakes while preparing overheads. Keep in mind that in the business world audiences make decisions based on the information you communicate. One respondent to a survey of scientific, technical, and managerial presentations said that a mistake made when preparing data "can cause a very good ... presentation to go right down the drain. It can ... cause numerous questions and lead to lengthy discussions."[1] In worst-case scenarios, such as inaccuracies in training employees on machinery, the safety of workers may be at stake. Double-check, even triple-check your facts when preparing a presentation.

You may also discover new information that supplants your current data. In some fields, technology is changing so quickly that it is difficult to keep yourself up to date on innovations. In such situations, you may be forced to redo a large part of an oral report, to revise your analysis, or to come to different conclusions. As frustrating and time-consuming as the process is, it is necessary to make these major revisions. Personal feelings must be put aside in such situations. You are accountable for presenting timely data, as your listeners expect.

Objectivity is another ethical concern when deciding what details to include. While doing your research you may discover information that disagrees with or weakens your argument. The temptation might be to omit this information, but doing so would misrepresent the issues to your audience. Such an approach to a presentation misleads your audience and can be damaging to you as well as harmful to your organization. Loss of business as well as legal actions are possible outcomes. As Chapter 6, on persuasive speaking, demonstrates, developing counter-arguments is one way to deal with opposing information.

Selecting Your Facts

To determine how specific your oral report should be, consider the three elements discussed in Chapter 2: purpose, audience, and time. If your purpose is to update your listeners on the project, select information that describes developments. If your audience need specific data to complete their work, you must include this information. And, obviously, you must fit your presentation into your time slot.

As we saw, Andrew, for his presentation on customer service, selected detail that would give his colleagues a profile of their customers' problems and needs, and would help them improve service. To look at a common, real-life example, we need only turn to the presentations delivered by CEOs at annual general meetings (AGMs). One of the main goals for CEOs on these occasions is obviously persuasive, to maintain stockholder confidence in the company. To do this, they highlight the achievements of the past fiscal year, and the problems, showing how management is dealing with them. For instance,

Paul Tellier, president and CEO of the Canadian National Railway Company, reviewed accomplishments of the previous year to the audience at the 1997 AGM:

> ... CN has met or exceeded every goal we set for 1996.
>
> We beat our operating ratio target. Since 1992, our operating ratio has improved more than any other railway in North America.
>
> We produced $610 million in operating income. It was the best year in the 77-year history of the company.
>
> We cut $30 million off the cost of material and services ....
>
> Having said this, let me tell customers in the audience that I am very much aware of the need for us to improve our service. Meeting commitments to you is a top priority. We will concentrate our efforts on meeting your needs.[2]

Note the way in which Tellier recounts CN's successes. By dealing with each point briefly, he avoids belabouring his material and covers many areas. This concise list of achievements, while being informative, is very persuasive: note, for example, the positive language ("met or exceeded," "beat our operating target," "improved," "cut"—often a favourable word in business). And, because Tellier also admits that service must be improved, and with it, profits, his presentation is also convincing to an audience who have invested money in the company. His forthrightness shows that he isn't glossing over problems. Tellier has selected the details to fulfill his business purpose for this particular business event. The lesson here for all business speakers, once again, is to focus your objective, and to select your facts and analyses honestly to meet it.

Interpreting Your Facts

Note also that it's important to show the significance of the facts. Here is another persuasive element in informational speaking, because as a business speaker you will often influence the way your audiences view the facts. For example, Tellier interprets facts when he remarks that the $610 million produced in operating income "was the best year in the 77-year history of the company." This comment tells the audience why the figure is important, and shapes their view of Tellier's leadership as CN's CEO.

For his part, Andrew might say in his report, "Of the 7000 customers who visited our branch in the last three months, 2500 purchased GICs, or about 36 per cent. As you recall, during this period the stock market experienced a downturn. One interpretation of this figure is that customers wanted a secure investment for their savings." Andrew's interpretation of the facts would likely persuade his listeners to consider promoting GICs to customers as a secure alternative to investing in equity mutual funds.

Again, select your facts to support your purpose. Do not only supply them, but also comment on them, so that they are meaningful to your audiences.

Being Concrete

Another consideration for oral reporting is the degree of concreteness. Your purpose and the needs of your audience will determine how explicit you should be. When delivering financial information, for example, many business speakers tend to round off figures. For instance, in his presentation to shareholders at the Dofasco 1997 AGM, John Mayberry describes the strong balance sheet. He says, for instance, that "Our cash flow from operations ... grew significantly to $409.5 million, an increase of more than 57 per cent over 1995."[3] When discussing mutual fund performance to his audience of novice investors, Andrew might note that a $10 000 investment in the (fictitious) Akiva Technology Fund grew to about $15 000 over three years, for a gain of 50 per cent.

Rounding dollars and cents when delivering financial information is usually done for two reasons. First, if the audience already has a copy of the numbers, or will receive them (you can distribute financial information in a handout immediately before or after your speech), they can see the precise amounts. Second, it is difficult for listeners to retain fine financial detail. Imagine if Andrew said, "A $10 000 investment in the Akiva Technology Fund grew to $15 396.00 over three years," and used precise figures throughout his speech. An oral delivery of such numbers may well daze your listeners instead of fostering their understanding. What is most meaningful to your audience is the pertinence of the details.

You can see how focusing on the meaning of your information contributes to the persuasive element in your speech, because you are shaping your listeners' responses to the facts. For example, as Dofasco's CEO, John Mayberry uses percentages to highlight Dofasco's financial strength, thus positively influencing shareholders' impressions of how the company's executives are managing it. Although Andrew would be using the Akiva Technology Fund as an example, and not recommending it as an investment, his remark might sway his novice audience to consider this fund seriously as an investment choice.

Using Supporting Evidence

Here I want to highlight ways to credit your sources. Showing off your research is critical to gaining your audience's trust in you as a credible speaker. We've already seen Deborah Allan, formerly of Spar Aerospace, credit Robert Fulghum, author of *All I Really Need to Know I Learned in Kindergarten*, for many of the ideas about learning in her presentation to the Canadian Association of Career Educators and Employers. Whether your sources are in-house studies, studies commissioned from consultants, Internet sources, or print sources, such as books and periodicals, it is necessary to acknowledge them. The testimony of experts lends your presentation their authority and makes your speech more reputable, and, consequently, more persuasive. Figure 5-1 offers some guidelines for citing source material.

Figure 5-1   Guidlines for Citing Source Material in Oral Presentations

Newspaper and magazine articles: mention author, journal, and date the article appeared.

Books: mention the author, title, and date of publication

Web sites: mention the company that owns the Web site and the date you obtained the information (Web-site information is updated on a regular basis).

Independent or commissioned study: mention the author (individual or group), title of the study, and date.

A question that speakers often consider is, how detailed should my attribution be? With a recent and popular book, it is usually sufficient to mention the author and title, as Deborah Allan does. If the book was published some time ago—three years, perhaps—or if the date of publication is relevant to your topic, then it is worth mentioning the date to your audience. More examples can be drawn from Allan's speech, which uses a variety of sources, including Statistics Canada and professional and research organizations. For instance, when noting a statistic, she says,

> Current statistics about the literacy rates of Canadian adults are startling, to say the least. According to Statistics Canada in its Canadian profile of Adult Literacy Skills used in Daily Living, 16% of Canadian adults have reading skills too limited to allow them to deal with the majority of the written materials they encounter every-day—newspapers, memos, bulletin board notices, drivers licence renewals. Another 22% can't cope with complex instructions.

Instead of saying "statistics say," as many speakers are tempted to do, she is scrupulous in citing the source by mentioning the research organization and the report title. More factual matter is also attributed:

> It is just as important for science and math students to study communications as it is for arts students to study math and science. Don't just take my word for it. According to a Conference Board of Canada survey, more than one-third of Canadian companies say they have difficulty introducing new technology and training employees in new skills. Why? Because of lack of basic literacy and numeracy skills.

Regarding the skilled occupations, such as engineering, computer programming, and health care, she remarks,

> What do all of these occupations require? That's right: a background in science and math. The Canadian Council of Professional Engineers predicts that by the year 2000 there will be a shortage of between 25 000 and 45 000 engineers in Canada alone.

Mentioning the "real-world applications for mathematics," she comments,

> As Simon Fraser University Professor Katherine Heinrich noted: "Mathematicians are the ones who, among other things, schedule airline flights, provide the language for error-free satellite and computer communication ... enable you to listen to music on compact discs, design the statistical components of cancer studies, and model the beating of the human heart."[4]

Note how the source material not only provides information and strengthens the authority of the speech, but also enlivens it—and heightens its persuasiveness—through its sources. You may have observed that, in contrast to the guidelines in Figure 5–1, Allan omits mentioning the dates of her references. The question arises: why should she, or any speaker, include dates? Let the speaking situation dictate the answer. Ask yourself: does my audience need dates? Does my audience expect them? Will dates add credibility to my presentation?

Furthermore, you must consider how many sources to include in your speech. A profusion of dates may well make your speech sound pedantic, and might overload your audience's ability to retain information. One can assume from Allan's speech that she used recent sources; an audience trusts a speaker to use the most recent, relevant, and reliable supporting evidence. One occasion for dating a source is its age; you don't want your audience to think that you are using current research when you are not.

If you are questioned on a date of a source after your presentation, be sure to have the answer. Keeping a thorough list of references for your speech is practical; you might even have extra copies for interested listeners.

Two Common Types of Informational Reports

Now that we've seen certain techniques used in oral reporting, I want to consider two frequent types of oral reports: overviews and progress reports.

Overviews

A large part of oral reporting involves presenting overviews, or summaries, of an issue, a policy, a development, or a product. Overviews are important because they help managers make decisions about prevailing concerns. Like much informational business speaking, overviews contain persuasive elements. By showing the history or evolution of the subject at hand, overviews provide a context for new developments and strategies, giving managers a framework for evaluating their direction. In addition to enlightening management, overviews also provide information to listeners at any level of a company, as well as to the external public. Your organizational approach will be determined by your topic, purpose, and audience.

Topical organization.   As we saw in Chapter 2, Andrew's approach to his presentation on mutual funds is topical. He begins by explaining what mutual funds are, then he discusses how they are managed, describes the different kinds of funds on the market, and completes his talk with a discussion of how to choose a mutual fund. Note that this topical organization clearly has a logic behind it. Because Andrew is speaking to an audience of novice investors, he begins his talk with a general description to give his listeners a context. He then moves into important basic information—management approaches and types of funds—before he discusses the critical step of selecting funds for personal investment. His topical arrangement—from fundamentals to guidelines for making the highly individual investment decision—is suitable for his audience. Like Andrew, you, too, may find that developing your talk by topic is an appropriate structure for some of your speaking situations.

Chronological organization.   Sometimes an entire speech comprises a history of a project or event, or a speaker may find it necessary to include an historical overview as a segment of a presentation. When organizing material chronologically, ask yourself what is the point of presenting this history? Is it to give your audience a context for understanding a current situation? Is it to show the development of a product?

For example, you may need to include a chronology as a section of a persuasive speech in order to give your audience a perspective on current events, with the aim of influencing how your listeners view them, and, correspondingly, of influencing their decisions. In her 1996 presentation, "Opportunities in Broadband Services," Carol Stephenson, then president and CEO of Stentor Resource Centre, told her audience, members of the International Engineering Consortium,

> My primary purpose here today is to outline the strategy the Canadian telephone companies are pursuing as we evolve toward a multimedia interactive future. But I recognize that many of you may be unfamiliar with the Canadian regulatory and business environment. So I thought I'd begin with a brief chronology of key milestones.[5]

Stephenson then reviewed developments between 1994 and 1996, leading up to Industry Canada's decision in 1996 to exclude both telephone and cable companies from bidding on wireless telecommunications services. As her speech shows, she views this ruling as restricting competition, and tries to gain her audience's agreement with her.

In presenting overviews, be selective about your examples. One or two representative examples are sufficient, because you are illustrating your main ideas rather than being comprehensive. Be sure to present your chronology fairly and accurately: you want to maintain your integrity as a speaker and to educate your audience fully, without bias.

Procedural organization.   Use a procedural organization to show the steps in a process, from beginning to completion. The process may be mechanical, managerial, or financial. For example, in his presentation, Andrew might lead his audience of novice investors through the procedure for investing in a mutual fund. The first step, he might tell them, is to analyze their own financial situation. Then, Andrew would explain the second step of evaluating their comfort level regarding financial risk. Following that, he might tell his listeners their next step is to investigate the types of funds in which they might consider investing their money. Finally, he might end his talk by telling them how to place their money into a particular mutual fund by using a stockbroker.

Progress Reports

A common type of oral and written business report is the progress report. In their written form, progress reports provide detailed documentation of a project's course from inception to completion as well as a record of accountability for its management. Progress reports are submitted at regular intervals, as determined by the project's complexity and requirements. For example, progress reports on the set-up and installation of a company's computer network may be submitted weekly, because of the complexity of such an undertaking.

Typically, progress reports briefly review the purpose of the project and list the advances made during the reporting period. Your choice of topics could include the following, based on their relevance to your project.

- the extent to which the goals for that reporting period were achieved

- budget considerations, such as cost overruns

- problems encountered during the reporting period and how they were managed

- scheduling considerations

- goals for the next reporting period

Primary readers for written progress reports are often department or project managers. Your document may be copied to other division heads or staff who need to be informed of developments. On the other hand, your oral progress reports may be delivered one-to-one or in a meeting. Your audience may include team members as well as other staff who need the information you are delivering. Supervisors usually participate in these meetings, and you may be on a roster with other employees who report on their group's role in the project.

Because your audience probably will have studied the written version, your purpose in your oral report will be to direct them to the most significant developments of the project for the period under discussion and to comment on their relevance and implications. Keep in mind that you have a limited amount of time, and will need to emphasize the information most important to your listeners.

Training

The second half of this chapter on informative speaking deals with a job function you have also probably performed, informally if not formally. The purpose of this section is not to discuss training theories and methods; you can easily find many books as well as professional journals on the subject at your library. You might also investigate the American Society for Training and Development Web site (**www.astd.org**), which includes many links to Canadian and U.S. organizations. I want to focus on two areas here: preparation for training, and the delivery, or communication, of training.

The Learning Organization

Many Canadian corporations are learning organizations; that is, they incorporate training as an integral part of the workplace. As an employee, you might already have been sent on a course to learn a new skill. You might also have trained a colleague yourself, either in a brief, one-hour session or over the course of several days.

Sylvia Chrominska, executive vice-president of Human Resources at Scotiabank, cites training as one factor that helps companies thrive and employees remain employable. Noting the importance of new technology, she says successful organizations recognize that "managing change is really about managing changing work. Training must be forward looking, and it should help employees acquire skills that are adaptable to the new work environment."[6] Deborah Allan comments, "learning ... needs to be on-going ... the minute we stop learning is the minute we become irrelevant. And irrelevant is just another way of saying obsolete. And that's another way of saying unemployed—or worse still—unemployable."[7] An organization that perceives the need for continually training its personnel, and that is able to predict the areas for training, will not only flourish but also preserve worker loyalty.

Professional trainers classify learning into three areas: knowledge learning, skills learning, and attitude learning.[8] Knowledge learning involves learning company rules and policies. Skills learning means learning how to perform a task, such as operating machinery or programming a computer. Attitude learning deals with values, such as a company's code of ethics. Obviously, these three areas interrelate: for example, acquiring a new skill also requires learning the rules for performing it.

Because the workplace is changing so rapidly, it is sometimes difficult to hire trainers with up-to-date knowledge. They may be both greatly in demand and costly. Consequently, knowledgeable employees who have not been trained as trainers are often asked to perform the training function. For example, an employee is sent on a course, perhaps to learn new presentation software, and upon returning to the workplace trains colleagues on its use. In other situations, an employee is asked to share knowledge already acquired on the job.

Preparing to Train

To share your knowledge effectively, so that your "students" apply your information reliably and contribute to the overall success of the organization, it is important to prepare in a constructive manner. Figures 5-2 and 5-3 are examples of training courses offered by the Canadian Council for Occupational Health and Safety. Examine them with me to understand the foundation for effective training.

1. Determine Your Purpose

As the course titles show, you must focus your purpose precisely. Course titles typically include the following components: topic, application, level, and duration of the course. This information helps employers and participants decide if the course is suitable.

2. Analyze Your Audience

As I discussed in Chapter 2, it is essential to determine your audience's level of knowledge. Find out as much as possible about the participants so that you can design your course effectively. Learn what they do at work, and what they need your information for most of all. Learn what functions they perform most frequently. For trainees to be persuaded that the training is valuable, the trainer must show how the instruction will benefit them.

Note how the health and safety courses in the illustrations are targeted toward specific audiences with different levels of proficiency in using the Internet. The basic course, shown in Figure 5-2, opens with a general introduction to the Internet; the first segment, on e-mail, covers concepts and buzz-words. There is much lecture and demonstration of different Internet tools, leading up to the research session using the tools taught earlier in the day. For its part, the advanced course described in Figure 5-3 is oriented toward more sophisticated learners, who are familiar with Internet applications. Here, the emphasis is on research and networking. The best approach for any training session is to build later on what you taught first.

3. Be Systematic

As the examples suggest, planning a training course is different from planning a presentation. Segregating your information, allocating your time to different "hands-on," or practice sessions, and preparing the training site are all vital elements for effective training.

Organizing material.   Plan your presentation of information very carefully. Adjust your mind to the beginner's vision. Be sure to reinforce the purpose of the training. Furthermore, keep in mind that your audience may include people who are resistant to the training that the changes in their organization have demanded. Thus, consider

Figure 5-2   Agenda for a Beginners' Training Course

Using the Internet to Access Health and Safety Resources: A Basic Hands-On Course

Designed to help you use resources on the Internet—effectively.

The focus will be on health and safety resources, including message-based discussion groups and WWW resources.

This practical course provides you with ample opportunity to try out Internet-based software, search tools, and resources.

Course Outline

Morning (9 AM – 12 Noon)

Introduction
- Introduction to the Internet
- Discussion of its history, size, growth, and types of resources

E-Mail and Mailing Lists
- Discussion highlighting concepts and buzz-terms
- Workshop using both E-mail and public mailing lists (e-mail-based discussion groups)

Usenet Newsgroups
- Brief lecture/demonstration showing newsgroups, their hierarchies, useful news reader software, and health and safety newsgroup resources

Telnet, FTP, and Gopher
- Brief discussion/hands-on exploration of these three technologies for connecting to, and transferring information from, other computers on the Internet. The focus will be on their application to health and safety.

Afternoon (1 PM – 4:30 PM)

World Wide Web
- Introduction to World Wide Web (WWW) technology
- Discussion/hands-on exploration of key health and safety WWW sites
- Discussion/hands-on exploration of WWW directories and search engines
- Hands-on workshop

Research Session
- Research health & safety topics using tools learned throughout the day

How To Get Connected
- Discussion about finding Internet service providers and hardware/software requirements for access

Wrap-up
- Question and answer period
- Course evaluation

Source: The Canadian Centre for Occupational Health and Safety, "Using the Internet to Access Health and Safety Resources: A Basic Hands-On Course." [www.ccohs.ca/products/courses/internetcourse.html], February 8, 1999.

Figure 5-3   Agenda for an Advanced Training Course

Using the Internet for H&S Research and Networking—An Advanced One-Day Course

Explore the potential for serious research and professional networking on the Internet.
* Locate various types of H&S information—e.g., regulatory info., research reports, chemical hazard documents, etc.
* Network with other H&S professionals
* Learn about the most useful search tools
* Learn the basics of building your own H&S Web site

This practical course provides you with ample opportunity to try out Internet-based software, search tools, and resources.

Course Outline

Morning (9 AM – 12 Noon)

Introduction
* Introduction of instructor and participants. Discussion of participants' levels of experience with the Internet.

Health and Safety Research
* Discussion/demonstration of techniques for locating various types of information, such as: regulations and interpretive documents, research reports, and chemical hazard documents. Hands-on workshop where participants use the tools and sites discussed.
* Hands-on Workshop

Networking with other Health and Safety Professionals
* Discussion/evaluation of major health and safety mailing lists and newsgroups, and techniques for maximizing their potential.
* Filtering messages from mailing lists
* Using mailing list and newsgroup archives
* Hands-on Workshop

Afternoon (1 PM – 4:30 PM)

Cornucopia
* Discussion of assorted "tips and tricks," such as:
    * using "meta" directories and search engines to locate health and safety information
    * choosing appropriate Internet software
    * locating colleagues through "white pages" search engines
* Hands-on Workshop

Establishing Your Own Health and Safety Web Site
* Discussion of issues associated with planning your organization's site, such as:
    * rationale
    * technical issues
    * maintenance and publicity

Discussion of Web page creation basics, authoring and maintenance tools

Wrap-up
* Question and answer period
* Course evaluation

Source: The Canadian Centre for Occupational Health and Safety, "Using the Internet for H&S Research and Networking—an Advanced One-Day Course." [www.ccohs.ca/products/courses/advintcourse.html], February 8, 1999.

incorporating into each step of the session the benefits of the new procedures so that reluctant listeners will be persuaded of your purpose.

Try to think yourself into your listeners' heads in order to organize components in a logical manner. The term "chunking" is often used to describe isolating information into manageable segments. The basic health and safety Internet course in Figure 5-2 logically reviews and demonstrates various Internet tools individually before introducing the specific health and safety application. The advanced course, for knowledgeable users, is organized around the themes of research and networking, rather than Internet methods.

Training also means choosing the most relevant material for your audience. Apply your knowledge of the participants, and stress in your training the most important concepts and tasks. Minor points can be omitted. Responsible trainers make themselves available after the training session: leaving your phone number or e-mail address for the trainees, with a friendly note that they contact you with any questions, goes a long way.

A dry run of your session with colleagues as your audience will help you target problem areas. Practising also gives you the opportunity to coordinate your visual support with your commentary and to polish your demonstrations.

Preparing handouts.   Preparing documentation for your audience is another step in planning a training session. Always give participants a copy of the agenda ahead of time so that they know what to expect. Consider creating a manual of your handouts: reproduce your visual aids, computer screens, and other relevant material, including reference lists of details you may find too numerous and too picky for you to cover. Follow the rules given in Chapter 7, on visual support, for effectively prepared documentation.

Time management.   Just as managing time is necessary for a successful presentation, it is also essential for effective training. As a trainer, you will often be required to judge how much overall time you will need, and how you will divide the time you have. Time allocation means including breaks for coffee, snacks, and lunch. It is important not to overload participants with too much information and activity, and to provide time for relaxation; such "downtime" will help your students absorb their new-found knowledge.

Another consideration of time management is realizing when to schedule certain activities. Typically, training sessions last for an entire business day. The post-lunch segment is sometimes called the "graveyard session," for good reason: this is the time when participants are unable to focus effectively on the work. Consequently, try to schedule a hands-on activity right after lunch to stimulate your trainees.

Hands-on sessions.   Hands-on activities are incorporated into most training sessions, particularly skills training: they give participants the opportunity to apply the theories and rules they learn, and instructors have the opportunity to determine how effectively they taught their topics and who needs extra help. Your challenge will be to calculate how much time to allow for practice, so that participants will have some opportunity to become comfortable with their new skills.

4. Prepare the Venue

As we saw in Chapters 2 and 4, an important component of preparing a speech is investigating the speaking environment. For training sessions too it is essential to select and organize the location appropriately. The training purpose dictates the equipment needed and the configuration of the room. Training involves a good deal of interaction with participants. The arrangement of tables and chairs can encourage or discourage participants from asking questions. It also promotes your ability to communicate with members. Figures 5–4 to 5–8 show different room arrangements and how they affect trainer-participant interaction.

Special equipment is also an important consideration. If participants need computers, for example, are workstations available for all? Doubling up is awkward because one student observes while the other practises, and the trainer must ensure that each participant gets equal time. Furthermore, trainers must check that all equipment is functional. If participants are to use computers, you must also determine that the lighting is suitable; direct sunlight on computer screens makes them impossible to see.

Another consideration related to preparing the venue is the physical comfort of participants. It may be your responsibility to check that food meets your specifications and will be available at the times you want.

Figure 5-4 Traditional Classroom Arrangement

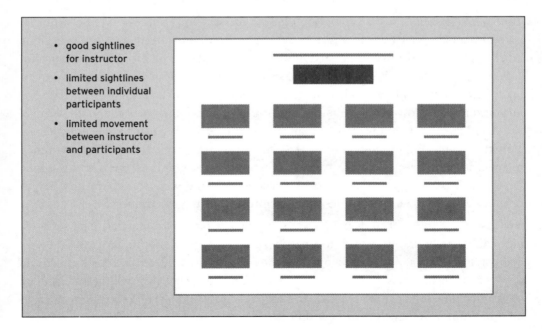

Figure 5-5 Amphitheatre Arrangement

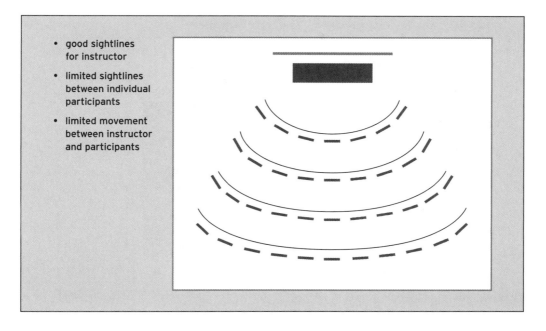

Figure 5-6 Horseshoe Arrangement

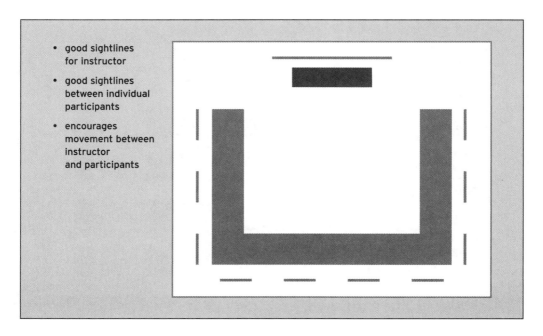

Figure 5-7   Boardroom Arrangement

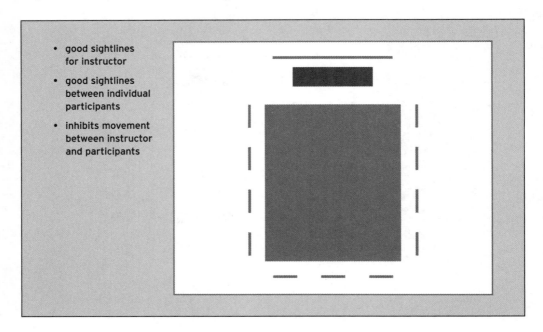

Figure 5-8   Parallel Workstation Arrangement

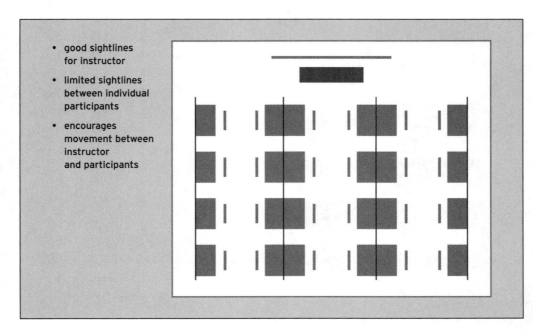

Clarifying Technical Terminology

As a trainer, you will frequently be faced with the need to explain concepts or techniques to colleagues or clients. We've already seen this requirement in the cases of Mahima, Lyndon, and Andrew in Chapter 2. As you recall, Mahima determined that her audience's level of knowledge of notebook computers was rather sophisticated, so she decided to explain only terms with which computer specialists, but not necessarily managers, are familiar. To present the results of his market research to his clients, Lyndon relied on uncomplicated explanations and definitions, and reported his findings in terms his listeners could understand. Similarly, facing an audience of inexperienced investors, Andrew needed to educate them on the terminology and concepts relating to mutual fund investment.

When you help your audience understand unfamiliar concepts, you are directing them toward your persuasive purpose. If elements of your training sessions bewilder your listeners, they will discredit your assertions. Your audience will be convinced of the training's benefits if they understand the specialized terminology. Indeed, an inability to explain unfamiliar terms and procedures clearly weakens a speaker's credibility—that key element in persuading audiences to listen seriously.

The term "technical communication" means communicating unfamiliar concepts in ways your audience can understand. This term is used not only in technical fields, such as computer programming and engineering. It also pertains to any field in which communicators need to explain terminology, jargon, or concepts that may be foreign to their audience. Thus, a programmer may need to explain the workings of a local area network to an office administrator, and an accountant may need to explain the concept of an impaired loan to a client. Employ the following methods as needed when communicating unfamiliar terms to your listeners.

Definition

One frequently used method of explaining technical terminology is definition. In the constantly changing world of technology, new terms often need defining. But sometimes you might need to define old terms to remind your audience of what they mean, or to communicate to your listeners a particular meaning of a common word or phrase, suitable for a particular topic or occasion. We define terms and phrases every day; consider how often at work a colleague asks you what something means.

Defining the new.   In a speech about the future of telecommunications, L. R. Wilson, chairman and CEO of BCE, told his audience, "I will be talking about the new frontier of cyberspace and the telecosm. And while cyberspace is already becoming a household word, what on earth is the telecosm?" As Wilson explains,

The telecosm is a term coined by the technology guru, George Gilder, to represent

the linkages in cyberspace—the telecommunications networks that began 120 years ago with the telephone system, but that now also connect tens of millions of computers around the globe. In short, the telecosm is the "road network" of cyberspace.[9]

Note that Wilson introduces the word by first noting its origin (George Gilder) and then describing what it represents in terms accessible to the audience. He also includes a useful synonym—the "'road network' of cyberspace"—as an alternative term.

Sometimes, however, you may only need to supply a brief definition. Glenn Falcao, vice-president and general manager, Public Data Networks, Nortel, defines "an emerging new phenomenon called 'extranets,' which are really intranet extensions to corporate customers and suppliers."[10] Of course, Falcao assumes that his audience already knows what an intranet is.

Furthermore, you can define technical concepts by what they do. Lynn Patterson, formerly Sales and Service president, BC Telecom, defines multimedia in this way:

Multimedia enables you to present video, voice, and data—simultaneously. What's more, multimedia is interactive. You can put information in and pull it out. It's a two-way information exchange.[11]

As we see in this example, sometimes it is also necessary to define a term in your definition, as Patterson does with the word "interactive."

Defining for common understanding.   Sometimes you will want to ensure that you and your audience share a common understanding of a term that may not be specialized, but familiar. You may do this, for example, when posing an argument or making a distinction. Peter Spelliscy of Suncor defined the term "workplace culture" for his audience, the Human Resources Association of Calgary:

But before I tell Suncor's story, I'd like to define what I mean by workplace culture. It's a bit smoky, hard to pin down. And it's a term that's used so much that it's getting a bit worn out.

By culture I mean the essence, the makeup, of a corporation. It's what employees believe. It's how they behave. It's what they value and what they don't value. It's how people feel about their jobs.[12]

Using acronyms.   Acronyms, or the first letters of words used in place of the full name, also need defining. Consider the following statement in a speech by John Mayberry of Dofasco to the Canadian Institute of International Affairs (CIIA) 1996 Foreign Policy Conference: "The synopsis for the first session tomorrow asks: 'With NAFTA and the EU well down the path to integration, where do APEC and the FTAA fit?'"[13] Such a combination of acronyms for an unknowledgeable audience can be overwhelming, with the result that some listeners tune out. Mayberry's CIIA audience, of course, is familiar with the North American Free Trade Agreement, the European Union, the Asian-Pacific Economic Cooperation summit and the Free-Trade Area of the Americas. You see the hazard of letting acronyms stand by themselves.

You can easily solve this problem when you use acronyms in your presentations. The first time you use an acronym, also give the full term: for example, "the EU, or, the European Union." It is wise to remind your audience occasionally, throughout your presentation, of the full name of the organization, product, or service if you suspect the acronym is new to them.

Description

Description is another device used to clarify technical terms. For instance, engineers, who may work with marketing experts on a project, often find it necessary to describe technical processes or objects to nonexperts. An interesting example of making a technical term understandable to nontechnicians appears in a speech by John MacNaughton, retired president and CEO of Spar Aerospace, about the development of the Canadarm. Describing the "space transportation system," he remarks,

> It would be the first part of post Apollo and entailed the reusable spacecraft, which ultimately became known as the space shuttle. It was composed of two elements—the booster rockets to launch it into low earth orbit and ... the "orbitor"—the airplane-looking vehicle on which the astronauts would ride into space and back to earth, where it would land like an aircraft. The orbitor was about the size of a DC-9 and featured a crew area which could hold six astronauts, and a big cargo bay, 60 feet long and 15 feet in diameter. Big enough to hold the biggest satellites that could be conceived of at the time.[14]

McNaughton paints a clear picture of this spacecraft for us, by relating it to familiar things (it is an "airplane-looking vehicle") and by comparing its size to a common type of airplane and noting its general dimensions.

Analogy

Analogy is another device that clarifies technical words. An analogy is an extended metaphor, or picture, relating the unfamiliar item to something familiar in the audience's experience. Lynn Patterson, formerly president, Sales and Service, BC Telecom, for example, uses analogy successfully in a speech to health care professionals. Discussing how the "information highway" will transform the ways in which government and educational and health care institutions will provide services, he says,

> . . . let me define exactly what I mean by the information highway. The information highway is not something you can see or touch. It's not something you can point to and say, "There it is."
>
> Just like the human body is a connected network of respiratory, muscular, and circulatory networks, the information highway is a connected network of communication networks.[15]

Considering the profession of his audience, his analogy is apt and helps foster his audience's identification with his topic. Gayle Stewart, Vice-President, Corporate Communications, BC Telecom, also charms her Kelowna, B.C., audience with an apt analogy for the information highway:

> Let me begin with a definition of what we're talking about. At its simplest, the information highway is a network of communications networks. It operates much like a road system. For example, here in Kelowna, Highway 97 is the main route into and out of the city. There are all sorts of roads that cross and intersect with Highway 97.
>
> They may carry different types of traffic, but they're all interconnected. The information highway is the same, although it's still very much under construction.
>
> As a user of the information highway, your biggest challenge today is getting an on-ramp to it. For some people, this will be a phone system. Others will use the cable network, but both on-ramps will eventually get you where you want to go.
>
> Ultimately, the information highway will be as well integrated as the road system here in Kelowna. It will connect you to each other. It will enable you to send and receive information anywhere, any time. It will provide interactive, two-way communications. Voice communications like a traditional telephone call, visual communications like dial-up movies on demand, and data communications like electronic home banking and home shopping.[16]

Stewart's description of the information highway explains the problems and potential of this technological thoroughfare. Within the extended analogy she includes brief examples, in the last sentence, of the different kinds of communication as a way to maintain her audience's understanding of the concepts. This careful, extended description serves an important purpose in her speech. Her presentation argues against the recent restrictive CRTC rulings against BC Telecom. By developing her audience's understanding of the information highway, she can win their support for her cause more easily.

Delivering Training

Now that we've reviewed training preparation, let's look at special considerations for delivery. Establishing your qualifications, creating a positive atmosphere, using an effective delivery style, and handling demanding participants are important training issues.

Establish Your Credibility

A large part of successful training involves earning the trust of the participants. Early in the session you may want to provide evidence of your abilities: you may wish to state your credentials—your previous training experience as well as hands-on experience in performing the tasks you are teaching. You should also explain to your listeners how the training will benefit them.

In training, credibility also means letting your students know that you do *not* know everything about the topic. It is important to project confidence, but if you don't know something, say so. Students have more confidence in instructors who are honest about their own ignorance.

Effective platform manner also contributes to your credibility. The elements that create a credible and likable presenter are the same as those that make a credible trainer: consistent eye contact, open body language, and a pleasant facial expression.

Create the Right Atmosphere

Your students are there to learn; it is up to you to sustain a positive and relaxed atmosphere. Treat your students with respect instead of talking down to them. Understand their confusion and bewilderment, when it appears, and respond in an understanding and helpful manner. It is important to motivate your students. Offer praise when a participant demonstrates understanding of a concept or function, and encourage those who are puzzled.

An ice-breaker at the beginning, when you and your students introduce yourselves and they discuss their current knowledge and their reasons for taking the course (see Figure 5-3: Introduction segment) helps you to get to know each other and creates a level of comfort. Ice-breakers are also useful for helping trainers determine how they should adapt their lessons, and for targeting participants who might need extra attention.

Use Effective Presentation Techniques

Much that can be said about your delivery style for training has already been covered in Chapters 2, 3, and 4, as well as in this chapter's section on technical communication. But let's review some important points for the sake of reinforcement, and introduce some new ones.

Guiding the learner.   Just as it is important to use guiding techniques to direct your audience through a presentation, so it is also necessary to do so when training. Preview your main points (see Figure 5-3, for example, where the course description cites the skills to be acquired), repeat and reinforce key ideas, and focus on the information your learners need to know. Develop key concepts with sufficient detail, but not enough to overload your listeners. And stress practical applications of the training—your students want to know, most of all, how they can use the information on the job.

Using language.   It's important to develop your ability to repeat the same idea in different ways. Not all participants will grasp a concept the first time you express it. Some trainees may also have limited knowledge of English. Thus, it is useful to find different ways of phrasing an idea in order to reach all your listeners. Use simple language so that your entire audience will understand you, and avoid using jargon. You will also find the techniques used for clarifying technical terms helpful, such as analogy.

Be a Facilitator

One difference between the delivery styles of training and of presenting, however, is called "facilitation." In training, facilitation means that the instructor evolves from presenter to guide. In the beginning of a training session your role is more that of a teacher, because the trainees lack knowledge. As the trainees develop their skills during the session's progress, you become more of a resource, or consultant, to the participants. As the participants practice in hands-on sessions, your role will be less dominant as you answer questions and encourage people. Good facilitators are effective listeners and have good interpersonal skills. You should show genuine interest in your students' questions, be patient, and listen objectively, without making judgments. The attributes of effective listening and interpersonal skills are discussed in Chapter 9.

Deal with Difficult People Effectively

The time will come when you will face difficult people. Examples include individuals chatting while you are speaking, challenging your abilities and instructions, and asking questions or making comments unrelated to the course. Maintaining your credibility, and the respect of the participants, means keeping control of the group.

To keep control of the group, you must maintain your own self-control. Never show anger or degrade anyone who is disruptive. Deal with problem people civilly: you will retain your integrity, and the group will support you, rather than the transgressor.

There are techniques for managing difficult participants. When there are private conversations, stop your discussion. Your silence will draw attention to the individuals, and they will probably stop chatting. If they persist, you can politely ask them to continue their conversation during the break. If your message hasn't penetrated, you can ask what they have learned so far, and what they want to take back to their office from the training session.

Digressers can be dealt with by gently pointing out that their question is unrelated to the topic currently under discussion, and that you will be happy to deal with it during a break. Challengers are more difficult to handle because of their arrogance. Sometimes the group, in their frustration, reins in such an individual; but you should take charge first. You can tell the participant that you will speak with him or her at a suitable time about the concern. If the behaviour continues, try to involve the person in an activity. If such tactics do not work, confront the person, but be civil. Point out how the behaviour is affecting the session. Tell the person that you and everyone else is there for a purpose. If this doesn't work, stop the training session and ask the participant to leave. On the rare occasion, you may need to call someone to help.

Remember that disrupters waste an organization's investment in training and weaken others' ability to learn. If you manoeuvre well, you put disrupters in a position where they realize that everyone else knows that they are wasting the company's time and money. It is your responsibility to keep the training session on track.

A Final Word on Training

Training is a gratifying activity, because you will acquire satisfaction from seeing your students learn, and from their appreciation of your services. Training is more demanding than delivering a progress report or an overview because there is much more interaction with individuals. Yet with the challenges of training comes the reward of seeing the practical applications of your course for the trainees and their companies.

Chapter Summary

Most business presentations, including ones with a strong informative focus, are also, inescapably, persuasive. Whether you are presenting progress reports or overviews of policies or developments, or training employees in new techniques, you are undoubtedly directing your audiences toward a business decision or shaping their attitudes. With informational business speaking, as with any business speaking task, the issues of integrity and credibility come into play: your audience will not be convinced of your facts, or of the benefits you explain to them, if they don't believe that your research is reliable.

The next chapter continues with business presentations by examining ones that have a strong persuasive focus. That chapter builds on the material presented here: to persuade your listeners to change an attitude or to act as you would like, it is necessary first to inform and educate them. Consequently, I'll be referring back to certain principles here as we consider persuasive strategies of business presentations.

Applications

1. What issues must you deal with when adapting a written report into an oral report?

2. What are the "ethics of details?" Why are they important?

3. Find an article in a business magazine or newspaper, such as *Canadian Business* or the *National Post* or *Globe and Mail* financial sections. Prepare an overview of it as an oral report.

4. Prepare an oral progress report on a current activity at work or at school. Consider the reasons for your arrangement of your material.

5. Define the following for nonexperts, using any of the techniques described in this chapter:

    a. hard disk

    b. savings bond

    c.   annual report

    d.   compound interest

    e.   gigabyte

    f.   palmtop computer

6. What are the persuasive dimensions of training?

7. Distinguish between the roles of "teacher" and "facilitator" for trainers.

8. Create an outline for a training session for a software product with which you are familiar. Consider carefully your purpose, audience, and topics.

References

1. See H. J. Scheiber and Peter J. Hager, "Oral Communication in Business and Industry: Results of a Survey on Scientific, Technical, and Managerial Presentations," *Journal of Technical Writing and Communication* 24, no. 2 (1994), 176.

2. Paul M. Tellier, "CN Looks Ahead" (delivered to the CN Annual General Meeting, Edmonton, Alberta, May 5, 1997). [www.cn.ca/cn/english/news/speeches/edmonton.html], August 21, 1997.

3. John Mayberry, Remarks delivered at the Dofasco Annual General Meeting (May 2, 1997). [www.dofasco.ca/news/news_speeches.html#Voyage], August 11, 1997.

4. Deborah M. Allan, "Employment Trends for the Future and Skills for the 21st Century" (delivered to the Canadian Association of Career Educators and Employers, June 4, 1996). [www.spar.ca/corp/empltrnd.htm], July 14, 1997.

5. Carol M. Stephenson, "Opportunities in Broadband Services" (delivered to the Broadband Multimedia World Forum, International Engineering Consortium, Colorado Springs, Colorado, November 11, 1996). [www.stentor.ca/scripts/dbml.exe?template=/stentor/body.dbm&page_id=exsp2.html], August 29, 1997.

6. Sylvia D. Chrominska, "Falling Down: Avoiding the Pitfalls of Restructuring" (delivered to the Ethics and Restructuring Committee, Sir Wilfrid Laurier University, Waterloo, Ontario, October 25, 1996). Print copy courtesy of Scotiabank.

7. Allan, "Employment Trends for the Future and Skills for the 21st Century."

8. See Tom W. Goad, *The First-Time Trainer: A Step-by-Step Guide for Managers, Supervisors, and New Training Professionals* (New York: American Management Association, 1997), pp. 45–46; and Tony Pont, *Developing Effective Training Skills: A Practical Guide to Designing and Delivering Group Training*, 2nd ed. (London: McGraw-Hill, 1996), 43–45.

9. L.R. Wilson, "The New Frontier of Cyberspace and the Telecosm" (delivered to the Canadian Club, Montreal, Quebec, November 10, 1997). [www.bce.ca/fs/e/newsroom/communications/speeches/97.11.10.html], December 9, 1997.

10. Glenn Falcao, "Ideas have Consequences" (delivered to the 1997 Masters Executive Conference, Point Clear, Alabama, July 31, 1997). [www.nortel.com/home/about/articles/falcaospeech.html], August 20, 1997.

11. E. Lynn Patterson, "Advances in Information and Communication Technology: The Prescription for Tomorrow's Healthcare Industry" (delivered to the Child Health 2000 Science & Technology Plenary Session, Vancouver, B.C., June 3, 1995). [www.bctel.com/library/845664984.html], September 4, 1997.

12. Peter Spelliscy, "Moving from Survival to Expansion—Why Changing the Culture Is Essential" (delivered to the Human Resources Association of Calgary, 1996 Conference and Expo, Calgary, Alberta, April 4, 1996). [www.suncor.com/05speeches/sun07spa.html], June 23, 1997.

13. John Mayberry, "Global Success Begins at Home" (delivered to the Canadian Institute of International Affairs 1996 Foreign Policy Conference, Hamilton, Ontario, October 26, 1996). [www.dofasco.ca/news/news_speeches.html#Voyage], August 11, 1997.

14. John D. MacNaughton, "From Stem to Canadarm—Reflections" (delivered by Canadian Aeronautic and Space Institute, April 29, 1997). [www.spar.ca/corp/speech_c.htm], July 14, 1997.

15. Patterson, "Advances in Information and Communication Technology."

16. Gayle L. Stewart, "Yes, Virginia, there IS an Information Highway" (delivered to the Canadian Club, Kelowna, B.C., December 13, 1995). [www.bctel.com/library/845665305.html], September 4, 1997.

CHAPTER 6

Presentations II: The Strategies of Persuasion

In the last chapter you saw that informational business speaking contains elements of persuasion. As I said, the two can't really be separated—even if your primary purpose is informative, you are also persuading your audience to accept your presentation of the facts and to acknowledge your credibility as a speaker. In this chapter, we'll look more deeply at persuasive speaking and its special attributes.

Whether you are an employee, entrepreneur, consumer, or investor, you know that persuasion is indispensable to business. For example, managers need to motivate workers to improve productivity. Entrepreneurs need to persuade lenders to finance the ventures they propose. Company officers must defend business decisions to employees, shareholders, special interest groups, and other audiences.

Not only must business people be persuasive, but so must technicians, according to Shahid Hussain. As the former managing director of product development, Enhanced Local Services division, Stentor Resource Centre, Hussain sees persuasive speaking as an integral skill for Canadian telecommunications engineers. In a speech to the Engineering Institute of Canada, he said that "narrow specialization is no longer enough." These professionals must be "skilled communicators to ensure that government regulators understand our position in the marketplace. And, to ensure we can explain the benefits of our products and services to our customers."[1]

When you deliver a persuasive presentation, you want to convince your audience of the benefits of your ideas, to shape your listeners' attitudes, and (often) to urge them to pursue a designated course of action. In this discussion I'll refer back to Chapter 5, because not only are elements of persuasion a part of informational speaking, but elements of informational speaking are essential to successful persuasion.

Preparing to Persuade

When planning your persuasive business presentations, follow the same first steps as you would for any speech: formulate your objective and analyze your audience. With both a firm purpose and audience profile, you will be able to organize your material to achieve the results you would like.

Your Audience for Persuasive Speaking

Being aware of the needs, knowledge, and attitudes of your audience, as we have already seen in this book, is the key element of successful business speaking. Audiences in persuasive speaking situations are often demanding ones, for the following reasons:

- *Audiences for persuasive presentations want to know how your suggestions will benefit them.* Will they save money? Will their companies become more efficient? Will their businesses become more productive? Safer? Will the morale of their employees erode or improve? Will their customers be more satisfied and loyal?

- *Audiences for persuasive presentations are skeptical.* They will need proof that following your suggestions is the right thing to do.

- *Audiences for persuasive presentations are resistant.* They will likely oppose doing what you suggest. They may believe that their prevailing way of conducting business is satisfactory, or that what they want is what they need.

Persuasive business presentations ask for a commitment from audiences: either a change in their attitude, a change in their organizational strategy, or a change in their procedures. And, certainly, these three are almost always intertwined.

Your audiences will want to know why they should comply with your requests. They may not see that the current situation is unsatisfactory, and may doubt that it can be better. They may not see that a policy or regulation should be changed, because their business is operating well enough under current rules. As a business-systems consultant, Cal Smiley must explain to his clients why they should alter their business processes in a particular way. He must show why his method is more effective than the one his customers envision. He frequently finds that "business people tell you what they want, but they do not know what they need."

To understand your audiences, and to persuade them, you must do extensive research into their businesses. You should also understand the industry in which the business operates. Sometimes, says Smiley, you "have to get to know their business better than they do."[2] Your research may require speaking to and observing employees at work and studying company reports. It also means reading articles in newspapers and professional journals and examining Web sites, for information about consumer, industry, and government concerns, as well as about research and development in related fields. Such investigations will give you a refined sense of the atmosphere of a business, of the issues that affect your business audiences, and of their attitudes. Backed with this knowledge, you will be able to choose the right strategies for speaking to your audiences, and to make informed, knowledgeable recommendations.

Approaches to Persuasive Speaking

How you approach your persuasive business presentations will be closely linked to your audience profile. Because of the nature of your audience, you will need to choose your overall structure and your language carefully.

Let's turn again to Lyndon and his clients. Let's imagine that after completing his research, Lyndon realizes that the launch of their product would be a disaster: similar products already exist, and there seems little demand for a new version. But Lyndon realizes that his clients have their hearts set on manufacturing and selling their device. Indeed, Lyndon is concerned that they might disregard his recommendations and go ahead with production.

You can see how important it is for Lyndon to persuade his clients to abandon their efforts. He hopes that his clients will agree with his recommendations. The problem Lyndon faces, however, is how to present such unwelcome news to his listeners. If Lyndon begins his presentation with his advice, he might meet with outright rejection because his clients want to sell their product. Furthermore, they may not listen to the evidence and arguments supporting Lyndon's recommendations. How, then, should he present his information to them? The problem Lyndon faces—convincing a resistant audience of a course of action—is one that presenters often meet in persuasive speaking situations.

Choosing the Direct or the Indirect Strategy

Persuasive speakers can choose either a direct or an indirect method when trying to convert their listeners to their viewpoints. The following guidelines are not hard and fast rules. Always use your analysis of your audience to help you to determine the best strategy for the specific situation.

The direct strategy for persuasion. The direct strategy means that you tell your audience your persuasive goal at the beginning of your presentation. This strategy can be used in the following situations:

1. You believe your audience will consider your argument, and not reject it outright.

2. You believe your audience will agree with your argument.

3. You are communicating bad news that you believe should be given immediately.

4. You want to use your persuasive goal as an attention-getting device.

For example, Mahima's task, discussed in Chapter 2, is to recommend a notebook computer for her firm's sales and marketing staff. Her audience, marketing managers who will make the decision, is obviously a receptive one, because they expect that her presentation will help them toward the right choice. Consequently, Mahima chooses to announce her recommendation in her introduction, and then support it with her facts and reasons. The direct strategy will also help her listeners evaluate her arguments because they will have a context in which to judge her reasoning.

Also consider using the direct strategy when delivering bad news to your audience, if you think it is appropriate to do so. Once again, you must analyze your audience carefully. Judge their expectations for the specific speaking situation. In some circumstances, your audience might feel deceived if you delay a negative message. For example, when telling shareholders about poor corporate performance at a company's annual general meeting, CEOs often use the direct approach. The main purpose of a CEO's address is to keep the faith of their shareholders—to persuade them that they should maintain their investment in the company. Delaying unwelcome news may anger shareholders more than the message itself, because, as part owners of the company, they would feel that this news is of paramount importance to them. For example, Bernard Michel, president and CEO of Cameco Corporation, a uranium mining company, begins his message with unwelcome news: "Following an outstanding year in 1996, it is true that 1997 can be seen as a year of setbacks for Cameco, if your view is short-term."[3]

Note, however, that although Michel is straightforward, he puts the news in perspective by comparing the 1997 fiscal year to the previous one, and by asking his audience to take a long-range view. When you begin your persuasive message with bad news, put it in context, if possible. Your audience will then listen carefully to the positive points while you are explaining the negative ones.

The direct strategy is also used in persuasive speaking as an attention-getter, as a way to make audiences sit up and consider the speaker's arguments. Courtney Pratt, Noranda's former president, uses the direct approach in a speech about the mining company's corporate culture and operations. In his introduction, he cites the popular impression of the company as "dirty, polluting, unsafe, uncaring, low technology," and says, "Today, I want to change that picture in your mind."[4] With this direct statement, Pratt challenges his audience to listen to his evidence.

The indirect strategy for persuasion.   Using indirection means that you delay your request for action or for a change in viewpoint until after you have developed your arguments, highlighted the benefits of your ideas, and provided firm supporting evidence. Consider using the indirect approach when you believe that your audience will resist your arguments if they hear your persuasive goal first. I'll repeat—you must analyze your audience and your speaking situation carefully.

Lyndon's knowledge of his clients' attitudes leads him to choose the indirect strategy when he presents the results of his market research. He has met with his clients over a period of time and has become familiar with their personalities and attitudes. He knows that their project is dear to their hearts. Yet his responsibility is to steer them onto the right path. Consequently, because his audience might be stubborn, Lyndon decides to use the indirect strategy. He employs the organization we saw in Chapter 2. In his presentation, Lyndon first describes how he went about doing his research, and then he discusses his findings. Next, he analyzes the competing products and their popularity in the market, and puts his clients' product in this context. It is only in his conclusion that Lyndon recommends that his clients abandon their efforts, summarizing the benefits of this action and supporting it with his evidence.

Lyndon's method is subtle because he wants his clients to feel as if they are making the decision on their own, without his guidance. He tries to have the facts speak for themselves as much as possible. If his clients feel that they are coming to their own conclusions, without direction, they might accept his recommendation more readily than otherwise. Indeed, Lyndon might not even need to state outright that they abandon their project. As a persuasive speaker, you need to understand the personality, attitudes, and concerns of your audiences, and work with these elements, rather than against them.

The Language and Tone of Persuasion

Just as the right strategy is critical to the success of persuasive presentations, so is language and tone. Again, your analysis of your audience will help you decide how to phrase your ideas and requests.

Don't be pushy.   One key principle to remember is to avoid language that will make your audience feel pressured. Business audiences don't like feeling forced toward actions and decisions. Most persuasive business presentations ask an audience to take some sort of risk, one that will affect their company's, or their personal, financial situation. While the commitment you seek from your audience may, for example, require them to adapt to a new method of manufacturing, to hire consultants to do computer programming, or to support or oppose certain regulations, in most cases the risk is monetary. Audiences for business presentations are careful about their financial well-being, and will resent coercion when they are being persuaded to gamble with their money.

Thus, when seeking the support of your audiences, treat them gently. For example, in a speech asking his listeners to build business partnerships with Aboriginal peoples, Charles Coffey, the Royal Bank's executive vice-president of Business Banking, introduces his topic by saying that he wants to "explore" with them "the business case for expanding and strengthening corporate Aboriginal relations." He does not seek a commitment; instead, he invites his listeners to participate in a mutual exchange of ideas.

This advice against forceful language does not mean you shouldn't urge your audience toward an action. In the end of his speech about partnerships with Canada's Aboriginal peoples, Coffey uses direct language:

> ... those of you who've begun to see the business benefits of constructive relationships with Aboriginal people—I would urge you to speak out.
>
> Talk to your peers. Share your experiences. Convince others they have a role to play and much to gain from building relationships with the First Peoples of Canada.[5]

Note, however, that Coffey still gives his audience the option of inaction. He "urges" his listeners to speak out and directs them how to do so, but he is not commanding them. When preparing your speech notes, be sensitive to the language you will use when telling your audience what you would like them to do.

Use a light tone, when appropriate. Another feature of persuasive language is humour. Of course, the situation and audience must warrant your efforts in this direction. A brief, light remark can go a long way to engage your audience. In his speech to the Ontario Chamber of Commerce seeking their support of the proposed merger between the Royal Bank and the Bank of Montreal, Robert Sutherland, vice-chairman of the Royal Bank, appeals to his audience by saying, "There are people who don't want these mergers to be approved .... We need to ensure any decision is based on the business issues. And I assure you we can use all the help we can get!"[6] This last sentence, part of Sutherland's conclusion, is a humorous way of expressing the ultimate motive of his speech, and may charm his listeners toward support.

Speak plainly. You must, of course, use concrete and clear language in all of your presentations. One benefit of speaking plainly in persuasive speeches is that you show that you are clear about and confident of your goals. Another benefit is that your audience does not feel misled or befuddled. Use simple, straightforward, and concrete words whenever possible. Note how Don Calder, the president and CEO of BC Telecom, describes the "drivers" of change in the telecommunications industry to members of the Vancouver Board of Trade: "First and foremost, it's you. Your need to reach your customers, employees, and suppliers wherever they are in the world. Your need to lower your costs. Your need for creative solutions."[7]

Calder's language makes his meaning immediate and obvious. No word is longer than three syllables, and they are all understandable. We've seen plain speaking in the quotations throughout this book; apply the principles to your own persuasive presentations in order to convince your audiences of your beliefs.

When speaking plainly, you may also need to speak bluntly, if doing so will make an impression on your audience. For example, Matthew Barrett, the former CEO of the

Bank of Montreal, confronts his listeners with their own doubts about the proposed merger with the Royal Bank: "Some particularly harsh critics say in deadly earnest, 'You want to merge so you can stiff your customers and make your profits even more humungous than they already are.'"[8] This straightforward language clearly demonstrates Barrett's awareness of strong anti-merger emotions. You can certainly risk speaking colloquially, as long as it serves your persuasive purpose.

Building Persuasion

Your strategy and tone will help to engage the attention of your audience. Your appeals, evidence, and arguments will help to persuade them to support your goals. In order to develop your persuasive speeches effectively, you should view your presentation from your audience's perspective. I'm sure that when you've been on the receiving end of persuasive speeches, you've asked yourself questions about their relevance and validity. I've categorized these questions into three groups to help you answer the common concerns of your audiences.

Questions of Personal Value

Your answers to this set of questions will help you engage your audiences on a personal level. The responses you give will spotlight your credibility as a speaker and will foster your listeners' belief in your cause.

Why Should I Listen to You?

Your audiences will want to know what makes you qualified to speak on your topic. If you are trying to influence your listeners in some way, they want to hear about your own experience and knowledge. In short, they want to know if they can trust you.

Your position in your workplace and your training, for example, reveal your qualifications to speak on work-related topics. Andrew might tell his audience of novice investors about his credentials as a mutual funds advisor; this information would show his listeners that his talk is based on extensive knowledge of the industry.

If you are seeking funding for a venture, for example, you should describe your previous experience as an entrepreneur and describe the successes of your other endeavours. To establish his credibility as someone who will do a thorough and effective market study for their product, Lyndon might wish to review his previous work as a marketing consultant.

Another source of personal credibility is the research you have completed on your subject. As we saw with informational presentations, prudent speakers reveal the sources of their supporting evidence, thereby enhancing their credibility.

Why is Your Speech Relevant to Me?

Your audiences will want to know not only about your qualifications for speaking on your topic, but also why they should bother to listen to you. As a persuasive speaker, you must demonstrate the importance of your subject to them personally.

Establish your listeners' identification with the issues. It is difficult to persuade your audiences if they feel distant from your subject. Effective persuasive speakers develop a relationship with them. These speakers show how they and their listeners have certain concerns or activities in common, and how the issues being discussed are significant to them. For example, to show the relevance of the proposed merger between the Royal Bank and the Bank of Montreal to his audience, the Ontario Chamber of Commerce, Robert Sutherland comments,

> This province and the entrepreneurs you represent are very important to our bank. Last year, more than 200 000 small and medium-sized businesses in Ontario chose to deal with the Royal Bank, and to borrow $4 billion from us to finance their operations.
>
> Royal Bank is also important to Ontario. In 1997, we purchased more than $400 million in goods and services from local companies, paid more than $460 million in provincial and local taxes, and paid 10 000 Ontario employees more than $375 million in salaries and benefits.
>
> So in many ways, we have a mutual interest in each other's future. That's why I want to speak with you today about our proposal to merge with the Bank of Montreal, and explain why we want to build a new Canadian bank for the 21st century.[9]

Note that Sutherland uses concrete details when showing the connection between the Royal Bank and Ontario's business people. Be sure to do the same: concreteness makes the reasons for identifying with your causes compelling.

Highlight the needs of your listeners. Sometimes your listeners may not know that they require what you are proposing. In this situation, you will have to demonstrate that a need exists. Certainly, you will meet many audiences who know what their needs are. But to ensure that even they understand how their needs can be met, you will have to describe the obvious.

For example, in her presentation recommending a notebook computer for her firm's sales and marketing staff, Mahima will review how they currently keep track of their accounts, deliver presentations, and communicate with head office. She will show the shortcomings of these methods, such as the problems of entering client information manually, thus highlighting the need to computerize these functions.

Note how Carol Stephenson, of the now disbanded Stentor Resource Centre, describes the need of Human Resources Development Canada (HRDC) for effective electronic communication:

... The federal government completely overhauled the old U.I. (Unemployment Insurance) program in 1996. And since then, there have been many changes and innovations in program delivery.

Keeping HRDC's 25 000 employees across the country current with new policy regulations is a huge challenge. The department used to send trainers out to the regions and employees would participate in face-to-face sessions outside the office.

But, with accelerating change, this process was proving too costly and inefficient.[10]

Stephenson elaborates on the need; she doesn't simply mention that there is one without developing the point. Many business audiences are skeptical: they need proof that they really have a need. As a business speaker, you must make their need apparent.

How Will I Benefit?

Your business audiences will want to know what they will gain from following your recommendations. Your requests will fall on deaf ears if you do not demonstrate how their businesses will profit. Stating the benefits clearly is crucial for achieving your persuasive goals.

For example, Carol Stephenson explains how electronic communication benefitted Human Resources Development Canada. She remarks,

In close consultation with Bell Canada and Stentor, HRDC developed a Business Broadcast solution. The Business Broadcast service transmits high quality video and audio signals from one central broadcast studio to many sites simultaneously.

Cancom, a partner in the delivery of this service ... developed an innovative keypad system with built-in microphones. It allows participants to ask their instructor questions just as they would in a classroom ....

This technology provides many of the advantages of face-to-face classroom instruction, such as effective teacher-student interaction.

But there are other distinct advantages. For example, the system uses only one instructor for each broadcast. This reduces costs and also ensures consistent training. It's also easier to incorporate late-breaking program changes.[11]

Note carefully how Stephenson differentiates between the *features* of the solution and the *benefits* of the solution. The features show how the technology works; the benefits show the advantages of the features. For example, a feature is that "the system uses only one instructor for each broadcast." The benefits are a reduction in costs and "consistent training." While your audiences will be interested in the features of your solution, they will only be persuaded of its usefulness if you demonstrate its benefits to them.

For her part, Mahima may point out that the notebook computer she is recommending runs at a speed of 233 MHz and has disk space of 3.2 gigabytes. These facts mean little to her audience. The benefits of these features will mean a lot: Mahima would stress that with a speed of 233 MHz, the computer will run programs very quickly, and that the disk is large enough to hold wordprocessing, spreadsheet, and presentation software simultaneously. These products would permit the sales staff to carry all necessary information into the field for customer meetings, and thus benefit by working more efficiently.

Questions of Evidence

Business audiences, as I've said, are skeptical. They will want proof that you are telling them the truth and that complying with your proposals is beneficial. Your answers to this set of questions will help you to resolve these doubts.

How Do I Know Your Solution Works?

You must supply your audiences with firm evidence supporting your assertions in order to persuade them. Such evidence includes relevant examples, the testimony of experts, facts, and statistics. In Chapter 5, we saw how to incorporate supporting evidence into your presentations. Showing how the solution you are proposing has worked successfully in other, similar situations is one way of convincing your listeners of the effectiveness of yours. As we have just seen, in a speech promoting the applications of technology to solving certain business problems, Carol Stephenson depicts how videoconferencing benefitted Human Resources Development Canada. Her example would help to change the thinking of audiences who doubt that computer technology can improve their own businesses.

What Are Your Numbers?

We've already seen the importance of providing concrete information in business speaking. Your audiences will want the figures supporting your assertions. Vague statements such as "our business employs many people" and "a large percentage of our profits is reinvested" will not convince your audiences. Instead, you must answer their questions of "how many" and "how much." For example, to persuade his audience that the Royal Bank is serving Aboriginal communities, Charles Coffey tells them it "was the first bank to open a full-service branch in a First Nation community. We now have four such branches and one branch in each of the three regions of Nunavut."[12] The numbers help to prove that the Royal Bank is taking specific action. When preparing your persuasive speeches, take careful note of vague, general terms, and replace them with concrete detail whenever possible. Your business audiences will want to know your numbers.

What Do the Experts Say?

We saw in the discussion of informational speaking how to incorporate expert testimony into your presentations. Your references to authorities will enhance your own credibility as a speaker and will help to convince your audiences of the reliability of your claims. In Chapter 5, we saw several examples from a speech delivered by Deborah Allan, formerly of Spar Aerospace. Speaking of the need for liberal arts students to study math and science, she says, "Don't just take my word for it," and offers evidence from a Conference Board of Canada survey. Allan knows that her audience wants proof from reliable sources; so will yours.

Questions of Argument

Finally, when developing your persuasive presentations, you must answer the questions your audience will ask about the integrity of your argument.

What Are the Challenges to Your Argument?

You will demonstrate the validity of your case by refuting opposing arguments. For example, let's say that a marketing manager asks Mahima why the Joey notebook computer, which runs at a speed of 233 MHz, is preferable to the Piglet computer, which runs at a faster speed of 300 MHz. Mahima's answer might be that the users' software can easily run on a less powerful computer. She might explain that the slower speed will serve their purposes for two or three years, and the company will save money on this purchase.

For his part, in his speech discussing the proposed merger between the Bank of Montreal and the Royal Bank, Matthew Barrett answers the criticism that the amalgamation would "stiff" customers and create "even more humongous profits." He states that the reproach doesn't "make any sense at all …. In a world that is more competitive every day, why would we want to do something as, well, as boneheaded as alienating our customers …?" Barrett also notes that "75 per cent of our business is done by meeting the needs of individuals and small businesses," and that

> Last year we took in $57 billion from individual Canadians in deposits and lent $58 billion to those Canadians so they could buy homes or start their own businesses ….
>
> … the merger will give us the increased investment capacity to provide a service offering to our customers equal to anything foreigners can throw at us, and do it *both* through our branch network and the new electronic channels.[13]

When refuting opposing arguments, don't sidestep the issues. Be open and direct, and offer concrete evidence to support your case. Doing so will help you to convince your audiences of your points.

What Are the Weaknesses in Your Arguments?

No argument is perfect. Check for defects in yours, and be sure to admit them. Perhaps the plan you are recommending hasn't worked in some situations; perhaps it means a significant financial risk. Discussing the flaws in your case shows that you have considered the issue from many perspectives and demonstrates your freedom from bias.

For example, in her speech urging her listeners to promote the practical applications of information technology to business, Carol Stephenson says, "our critics are worth listening to ... because some of what they say is true. And it points to serious weaknesses in our industry." She cites the common complaints that technology does not provide the promised financial returns as an investment and that "'cutting-edge computer systems fail to live up to expectations or fail altogether.'"[14]

Stephenson does not refute these criticisms because, as she admits, they are true. You, too, will deliver persuasive presentations in which you will need to acknowledge your own argument's shortcomings for what they are. Don't hesitate to bring them up. Not only will you show your audiences that you are fully aware of the issues surrounding your case, but you will also prove that you are not trying to conceal information that is damaging to it. But be sure to balance the weaknesses in your case with its strengths. Whenever possible, reinforce benefits after citing problems.

But Aren't Things Fine the Way They Are?

Another question your audiences may ask themselves regards the status quo. My business is running fine as it is, your listeners may think, so why should I undergo the upheaval of change? You will need to show that the present condition isn't good enough. You will need to paint a positive picture of the future to convince them, showing both the problems with the current situation and the benefits of change.

For example, Mahima may respond to listeners who question the usefulness of notebook computers by demonstrating the current problems with using only the desktops located at the central office. She might say that desktops prevent staff from delivering computer-generated presentations in the field, from communicating easily with headquarters, and from updating customer files quickly. With notebook computers, she would note, staff can communicate via e-mail at customers' sites, enter information into a database immediately, and deliver dynamic presentations.

But you will also need to convince your audiences that the status quo is acceptable. For example, Peter Godsoe defended Scotiabank's decision to remain independent when the Bank of Montreal and the Royal Bank announced their proposed merger in January of 1998. Speaking to shareholders at the 1998 Annual General Meeting, the CEO explained Scotiabank's position, noting "we see no reason that the proposed merger would cause us to change our course or shift our very successful strategy." Godsoe supports his case by citing Scotiabank's financial health—the "26 per cent return over the past five years—a winning strategy for our owners" by global operations "in 53 countries—still more, by the way, than the Royal and Bank of Montreal combined!"[15] When your audiences seek change, but you disagree with them, be sure to support your argument with evidence.

Three Types of Persuasive Business Speaking

Your audiences will ask themselves questions about the value, evidence, and weaknesses of your argument as they listen your persuasive presentations. If you predict and respond to their concerns as you prepare your speech, you will have a better chance of convincing your listeners of your viewpoints. The following discussion shows approaches to developing speeches that motivate, propose, and justify.

Motivational Speaking

How do business speakers inspire audiences to support their causes? Whether a motivational presentation is delivered externally, perhaps to special interest groups, or internally, to employees, its central purpose is to convince audiences to endorse an "agenda," that is, specific objectives and goals. They may be ones that concern an individual company, such as achieving higher productivity. Or they may be more general endeavours, such as participating in community service activities, which the speaker believes are important for all businesses. As these examples suggest, motivational presentations will seek a personal commitment from audiences, and may appeal not only to their reason, but also to their emotions.

Understand the Climate

To be a persuasive motivational speaker, you must be particularly sensitive to the attitudes of your listeners. When planning your speech, consider the circumstances surrounding the occasion for your presentation. Motivational speeches are delivered in good times and bad, to audiences who feel committed to their company or to a particular cause, or to audiences who feel apathetic, skeptical, or angry. For example, a manager or executive may give a motivational speech when a company is prospering and employees feel secure in their jobs; the speaker may want to urge employees on to even greater productivity. On the other hand, such speeches are also delivered when prospects are gloomy: orders have fallen, share prices have dropped, and the media have spotlighted the organization in its time of distress. It's time to convince the audience that they must stay loyal to the company.

Adapt Your Strategy to Your Audience

It's relatively easy to motivate audiences who already feel positive about their employer or about the undertaking you want them to consider. It's obviously more difficult to motivate listeners who feel neutral or negative. Be sure to get in tune with your listeners and to predict their concerns.

Involve your audience immediately.   Identify both the issue and your audience's connection with it early in your speech, whether their attitude is positive or negative. At the jointly sponsored Royal Bank–Council for the Advancement of Native Development

Officers Symposium, the Royal Bank's executive vice-president, Charles Coffey, clearly presents the purpose of the meeting: "Your participation today marks the beginning of what I hope will be a three-way effort among Aboriginal peoples, governments, and corporate Canada to address economic development and opportunity for the First Peoples of Canada."[16] Speaking at an employee dinner in British Columbia, Scotiabank's CEO, Peter Godsoe, expresses his theme: "the positive role that banks—particularly Scotiabank—play in the economy—and in Canada." He then tells his audience, "of all the professionals—and we Scotiabankers are highly skilled professionals—bankers and banking—continue to come under attack—by the media—by members of the federal government—by our competitors."[17]

Both speakers demonstrate the significance of the issue to their listeners and foster their identification with it. They heighten the bond by using personal pronouns—"your participation," "we Scotiabankers"—thus including their audiences on a personal level. In your motivational presentations you will ask your listeners to take action; if you involve them from the outset, you will have a better chance of persuading them.

As I've said, motivational speeches are also delivered when an audience gathers to hear bad news and is asked to maintain its commitment to the company despite pessimistic forecasts. In such situations, be direct and candid about the reason for the gathering, even if it is a negative one. Express your understanding of how the audience feels about the situation: showing that you recognize your listeners' concerns will earn their respect when emotions may be running high.

Illustrate the issues.   In motivational speaking, it's important to explain the background of the need for action, so that your audiences see the logic of your requests. For example, in a speech urging the Liberal Caucus Task Force on Financial Services to assess the need for bank mergers carefully, Scotiabank's Peter Godsoe discusses the issue of competition, saying that the proposed mergers would

> ... **significantly reduce choice for Canadian consumers and business. On the Royal/BMO and CIBC/TD proposals specifically, we suggest that these ... two mega-banks would have 70% of core banking markets. The Royal/BMO alone would be at almost 40% of personal banking deposits here in Canada.**
>
> **On small business, the two mega-banks would control more than three-quarters of the small and medium-sized business market, and well over 80% in some provinces.**[18]

To be credible, you must be concrete and specific. Statistics and clear explanations will help you to convince your audiences that they should take action.

Admit risks.   Motivational speakers ask audiences to take risks; they cannot guarantee a positive outcome. It is difficult to motivate an audience under a cloud of uncertainty. You are more likely to persuade your listeners to comply with your requests if you don't make any promises. For example, should Andrew, our mutual funds expert, try to persuade his audiences to invest in mutual funds, he must be frank about the risks involved: he must tell them that past performance does not necessarily predict how the funds will perform in the future. He can only advise his audience to do their research thoroughly, and to analyze their own comfort level when investing their savings.

Honesty always means admitting any shortcomings in your case. Doing so will earn the trust of your audiences, and then their commitment. Speaking of the Royal Bank's own efforts in helping Aboriginal communities to become economically self-sufficient, Charles Coffey comments, "Have we achieved our goals? Not yet. Do we have a distance to go? Certainly. And are we on the right path? We believe that we are."[19] When trying to motivate your listeners to follow your example, be realistic about the opportunities for success.

Refute criticisms logically.   To convince your audience of the validity of your viewpoint, you must deal with opposing arguments to your case and show their weaknesses. Let's imagine that, in his presentation on investing, Andrew says that common stocks are a good investment option. A member of the audience challenges him on this point during the question-answer session, citing major market corrections over the years. To respond, Andrew would explain that stocks should be seen as a long-term investment, and would point to the history of the stock market. He would show that, while the share prices of stocks do drop, over a period of time wise stock investments increase in value. Andrew would use concrete evidence, citing specific examples to show how much an investor has gained over the past 10 or 15 years.

Answer the question "What's in it for me?"   Your motivational business presentations, like any business presentations, have the greatest chance of persuading your listeners when you demonstrate the direct benefits to them. The Royal Bank's Charles Coffey tells his audience of business people the advantages of doing business with Aboriginal Canadians by explaining that they are a source of new customers and skilled, reliable employees. Whenever possible, show how the course of action you want your audience to follow will benefit them by using logical arguments and telling examples.

End on a note of constructive action.   A motivational speech emphasizes action. Be sure to conclude by telling your audience what you want them to do. Charles Coffey urges his audience to "work in partnership with [Aboriginal Canadians]—toward goals that we can both share—to get the results we both need."[20] If he wished to motivate his audience to invest in mutual funds, Andrew might urge his listeners to look carefully into them as an alternative to Canadian savings bonds, which are more secure but potentially less rewarding as investments. In other words, remember to end a motivational talk by sending off your audience in a practical and beneficial direction. If you don't answer the question, "What do you want us to do?" your audience may not see the point of your speech.

Oral Proposals

In essence, an oral proposal is another kind of motivational speech. Its purpose is to persuade a business to purchase a product or service that will improve that organization's productivity or profits. Proposals may also recommend a change in procedure in some way that will improve an organization. They are delivered after an organization has studied the written document and believes the plan might be worthwhile.

The Written Proposal

Proposals may be solicited or unsolicited. In the first instance, a company or a government agency, for example, sees a need that must be addressed and issues a "request for proposal," or RFP. The RFP is, essentially, an advertisement detailing the specific areas of concern and asking vendors to submit a proposal demonstrating how they will help the company. An unsolicited proposal is initiated by an individual, such as an employee or a consulting company, who sees a need within an organization for a product or service that will improve operations. In both circumstances, the proposal must be credible and convincing.

The content of written proposals.   In your written proposals you will include the following:

1. *Your purpose.* What specific product or service are you recommending that will make the company more productive, efficient, or profitable?

2. *Your understanding of your reader's situation.* What are the company's specific needs? What are their problems? Why do they need the product or service you are proposing?

3. *The benefits of your plan.* What will your reader gain by implementing your proposal? What are the short-term gains? What are the long-term gains?

4. *A description of your plan.* How will it work? How will you implement it? Has it been successfully implemented elsewhere? Will staff need to be trained? Will equipment be purchased?

5. *A timetable for completing your plan.* How long will it take from beginning to end? What are the different time considerations for different stages for implementing the proposal?

6. *Personnel requirements.* Will you need to hire extra staff to implement the proposal? Will the company need to hire outside staff for training?

7. *A budget.* What will implementation of the proposal cost? Are any guarantees or service contracts figured into the budget?

Depending on the problem to be solved, a written proposal can be short, perhaps three to five pages. On the other hand, a proposal can range from 20 pages to 200, or even longer, depending on the complexity of the company's problem and the nature of the writer's solution. An effective written proposal is highly detailed, considers all sides of the reader's problem, presents a realistic timeframe and budget for completing the project, and, most importantly, stresses the benefits of the plan. A written proposal grabs the reader's attention in the opening by stating the proposal's purpose and goals and by previewing the key benefits for the reader. The conclusion briefly summarizes the main facts and restates the benefits, thus leaving the reader with the most important elements to consider.

Planning the Oral Proposal

Creating a written proposal is a major undertaking. The final document demonstrates that you have thought the problem through and that your project is both workable and beneficial. An oral proposal is a distillation of the written document. If you are asked to deliver a presentation based on your written proposal, you must decide what information you will include, because you will only be given a limited time for your presentation.

Reasons for oral proposals.   Why should readers want you to prepare an oral proposal, when they have already scrutinized the written product? For one thing, your readers may become your clients: they have seen how you write; now they want to hear you speak. A competent business person is able to communicate both on paper and orally—how skillful are you in each area?

Your audience is investing their money and time in your venture, project, or company if they select your proposal. Your live presentation tells them about your confidence. In this situation you are performing under pressure, and demonstrating your ability to handle it. Furthermore, answering questions after your speech will disclose how thoroughly you prepared and your ability to maintain your professionalism as you argue any challenges to your plan. Your performance gives your potential investors important clues about your competence should they decide to hire you.

Determining content for your audience.   The most difficult part of preparing the oral version of your written proposal is selecting information. You will not have the time to say everything, nor does your audience expect (or want) you to.

To ensure your proposal has the best chance of adoption, you will need to analyze your audience in order to decide what information to repeat and enhance. Use the following guidelines for choosing material from your written proposal:

1. What needs are most pressing for your audience? Review the needs that concern them the greatest. Are they related to employees? Technology? Strategy?

2. How much is your audience concerned about the costs of implementing your plan? Cal Smiley says, "Make sure that you understand and can articulate the financial impact of proposals. The client needs to know what it will cost and what they will save."[21]

3. What details of implementation would they want to know? Is there any technical process you should highlight and explain? Will your plan disrupt the day-to-day running of the company?

4. What evidence will they want that your plan will work? Select examples of similar companies where your plan has been effective. Stress the results of your surveys, not how they were conducted.

5. What are the key benefits for your listeners? Select the benefits that will help to win acceptance of your project.

Furthermore, be sure to prepare answers to the questions you suspect your audience will ask about evidence and the soundness of your plan, using the strategies outlined earlier in this chapter. Your preparation will demonstrate your foresight and competence, two qualities business people value in those they seek to solve their problems.

Benefits, not features.   For your proposal to succeed, you must describe the benefits of your venture. As I've already noted, remember to phrase them as benefits, not as features. To repeat: a feature of a product or service is a function that it performs; a benefit is the way that function will help your listeners.

Speeches That Justify Decisions and Actions

For a business to operate smoothly, managers must justify decisions and actions to employees, clients, shareholders, special interest groups, and the public at large. They must seek the understanding, and, often, the agreement of these shareholders, the people who depend on an organization for their livelihood or have another interest in it. Otherwise, a company may be prevented from achieving its business goals. How decisions are explained frequently determines whether the shareholders will approve them. As with presentations that motivate and presentations that propose, those that justify decisions and actions depend on careful audience analysis and the ability to present information clearly and logically.

Present an Overview of the Problem

When businesses formulate strategies and policies, they do so in response to problems that need to be solved, be they technical, financial, or human. To convince audiences that your solution is valid, you must first review the problem itself.

Determine your audience's level of knowledge.   Like most business speakers, you will face audiences whose knowledge of a particular issue varies from member to member. To gain the understanding of as many listeners as possible, you will need to determine their familiarity with the problem and their technical knowledge, if that is relevant. You will also have to decide if there are any misperceptions you must correct. In Chapter 5, we saw Carol Stephenson, previously CEO of the Stentor Resource Centre, tell her audience of engineers, "I recognize that many of you may be unfamiliar with the Canadian regulatory and business environment. So I thought I'd begin with a brief chronology of key milestones."[22] One purpose of her speech was to present the strategies developed by Canadian telephone companies to gain a share of the wireless telecommunications market. A wise speaker knows that awareness leads to understanding, and then, it is hoped, to agreement.

State the problem clearly.   Your audience's level of knowledge will determine how you should explain the problem. Many business problems are complex: responsible speakers express them in ways their audiences can easily grasp without simplifying the issues, and thereby possibly misrepresenting the concerns. Rick George, president and CEO of Suncor, a major energy producer, spoke about how his company will be environmentally responsible while expanding its oil-sands production, goals that might seem inconsistent to his audience, the Vancouver Board of Trade. His challenge is to put the interrelated problems of environmental responsibility and economic growth clearly:

> ... In this case, we are faced with the risk of negative effects on the earth's climate caused by increasing amounts of carbon dioxide and other greenhouse gases being released into the atmosphere. These emissions are the result of important human activities: Keeping ourselves warm. Getting from one place to another. Producing the goods and services that are so fundamental to our economy and to our society.
>
> As you know, there has been a lot of rhetoric around this issue .... On one hand, the concern advanced by some is the possibility of catastrophic results if the climate changes due to excessive greenhouse gas emissions. And on the other hand, the concern is one of economic disaster, as industrialized nations limit growth and development in order to meet unrealistic emission reduction targets.[23]

George highlights the relevance of the problem to his audience by spotlighting the everyday need for fuel. He also expresses the concerns about the environment and the economy clearly by using the transitions "on one hand" and "on the other hand," thus setting up the two sides of the argument in a way his audience can easily grasp. George's message is that Suncor has developed a strategy that will satisfy both environmental and business concerns. He shows how his company intends to be environmentally responsible and at the same time grow as a company. The lessons we can learn from George's approach are these:

1. When dealing with complex problems, remember to take your time when discussing them.

2. Show the relevance of the problem to your audience.

3. Use transitions and other techniques, such as signposting, to guide your listeners.

Demonstrate Your Solution

Once you've made your audience aware of the problem, you should both describe and justify the actions taken to solve it.

Preview the steps leading to your decision. Solutions to problems can be complicated. It's necessary to keep your audience on track as you present your solutions. Using such guiding devices as internal previews will help you to lead your audience through your explanation. For example, as we've seen, Lyndon is faced with recommending whether his clients should sell their product in Canada. To help them understand how he arrived at his recommendation, he may decide first to refer to the separate phases of his research before discussing them in depth.

Show alternative choices. Often there is more than one way to solve a problem. While you may wish to discuss only the solution you have chosen, consider reviewing the ones you rejected. By showing their weaknesses, you further confirm that your decision is the best, and you earn your audience's confidence.

Offer your action plan. Many decisions are multi-faceted. A solution may involve several procedures or phases. Present them in an organized fashion, taking the time to elaborate on each one separately. Remember also to show the relationship between the steps of your decision or action plan, when appropriate. Lyndon, for example, may recommend a specific marketing plan to his clients for selling their product in Canada. The plan may include determining the target market, choosing the means of advertising the product, and setting up a distribution network, as well as setting a timeline for accomplishing each phase. A detailed plan will win consent from your audience more easily than a general one.

Show the benefits of your solution. We've seen throughout this chapter the importance of demonstrating the benefits of a strategy or process to your audiences. Your listeners will want to know how your decisions will help them. Will their jobs become more efficient? Will productivity improve? Will the value of a shareholder's investment increase? You must supply the answers to such questions.

Chapter Summary

Most all of your business presentations will be persuasive. To convince your audiences of the validity of your ideas and decisions, you must understand their needs and attitudes, show the relevance of your purpose to them, and choose the right overall strategy. As you develop your argument, you must be sensitive to its weaknesses, and deal with them openly in order to earn the trust of your listeners. By predicting their questions about the evidence and the logic of your arguments, you will have a good chance of persuading them to your point of view. And in all of your persuasive presentations, remember to highlight the benefits of your recommendations to your listeners. Business audiences always want to know how they can improve their earnings, productivity, or reputation.

So far in this book we've focused on words—on the texts of your speeches. In the next chapter, we'll look at another important component of business presentations: the visual support that complements your information and analyses.

Applications

1. Select a speech on a corporate Web site and analyze its persuasive elements. Is the argument convincing? What evidence does the speaker use to support the argument? Is the evidence sound?

2. Imagine you have to prepare remarks for the following situations. Would you use the direct or the indirect strategy? Give your reasons for your choice of strategy.

    a. telling employees that their company will relocate from Toronto, Ontario, to Fredericton, New Brunswick

    b. informing your audience of investors that their company did not meet its projected earnings for the year

    c. telling an audience of potential investors that your company's mutual funds are sound investments

3. How would you characterize the "right" tone and language for persuasive presentations? Why is assuming this tone important?

4. You have been asked to recommend a product such as a printer or fax machine for a friend. Choose two different models (they can be the same brand, or different brands), and develop a persuasive argument recommending one over the other.

5. Develop a motivational speech urging either your fellow workers or fellow students to volunteer two hours a week as a reading tutor in a local school. What strategies would you use to convince your audience?

6. What are the differences between oral proposals and written proposals? How do speakers adapt oral proposals for their audiences?

References

1. Shahid Hussain, "Re-engineering the Engineers —Telecommunications at the Crossroads" (delivered to the Engineering Institute of Canada, Vancouver, B.C., April 6, 1995). [www.bctel. com/library/845664481.html], September 4, 1997.

2. Cal Smiley, e-mail to author, August 11, 1998.

3. Bernard M. Michel, presentation delivered at 1998 annual general meeting (May 1, 1998). [www.cameco.com/investor/speeches/1998_annual.html].

4. Courtney Pratt, "Noranda: On the Leading Edge" (delivered in Toronto, Ontario, March 12, 1996). [www.noranda.ca/news/prattspeech.html], June 20, 1997.

5. Charles Coffey, "The Cost of Doing Nothing: A Call to Action" (delivered to the Royal Bank/CANDO Symposium, October 23, 1997). [www.royalbank.com/news/news/coffey_sp_eng. html], November 11, 1998.

6. Robert J. Sutherland, "The Benefits to Canadians of Building a Bank for the 21st Century" (delivered at the Annual Meeting of the Ontario Chamber of Commerce, May 3, 1998). [www.royalbank.com/news/news/19980506_sp.html], November 11, 1998.

7. Don Calder, "The Real News: How Change in Telecommunications is Benefiting Your Business" (delivered to the Vancouver Board of Trade Luncheon, Vancouver, B.C., May 27, 1998). Print copy courtesy of BC Telecom.

8. Matthew W. Barrett, "The Challenge of Change" (delivered to the International Financial Centre Vancouver 10th Anniversary Gala Celebration, Vancouver, B.C., October 24, 1998). www.bmo.ca/speech/bcmwb.htm], November 11, 1998.

9. Sutherland, "The Benefits to Canadians of Building a Bank for the 21st Century."

10. Carol M. Stephenson, "Stemming the Backlash: The Strategic Deployment of IT" (delivered to the Canadian Information Processing Society, Toronto, Ontario, May 14, 1998). [www.stentor.ca/bottom.cfm?/page_id=exsp24.html], October 29, 1998.

11. Stephenson, "Stemming the Backlash: The Strategic Deployment of IT."

12. Coffey, "The Cost of Doing Nothing: A Call to Action."

13. Barrett, "The Challenge of Change."

14. Stephenson, "Stemming the Backlash: The Strategic Deployment of IT."

15. Peter C. Godsoe, "Notes for Remarks to the Annual General Meeting," Ottawa, Ontario (January 27, 1998). [www.scotiabank.ca/speech5.htm], December 9, 1998.

16. Coffey, "The Cost of Doing Nothing: A Call to Action."

17. Peter C. Godsoe, "Remarks to B.C. Scotiabanker Tributes Dinner" (October 1, 1997). Print copy courtesy of Scotiabank.

18. Peter C. Godsoe, "Remarks to the Liberal Caucus Task Force on Financial Services," Ottawa, Ontario (June 16, 1998). [www.scotiabank.ca/speech6.html], December 9, 1998.

19. Coffey, "The Cost of Doing Nothing: A Call to Action."

20. Ibid.

21. Smiley, e-mail to author.

22. Carol M. Stephenson, "Opportunities in Broadband Services" (delivered to the Broadband Multimedia World Forum, International Engineering Consortium, Colorado Springs, Colorado, November 11, 1996). [www.stentor.ca/scripts/dbml.exe?template=/stentor/body. dbm&page_id=exsp2.html], August 29, 1997.

23. Richard L. George, "Responsible Growth: Suncor's Perspective on Global Climate Change" (delivered to the Vancouver Board of Trade, Vancouver, B.C., December 1, 1997). [www.suncor.com/05speeches/sp1197.html], April 29, 1998.

CHAPTER 7

Visual Support: Planning, Preparing, and Presenting

Although I've talked mostly about text in earlier chapters, planning visuals is very much a part of a business presentation. Effective business speakers pay attention to their visual support early in preparing their speech. As they gather data and frame their analyses, they think about the information they wish to present in visual form, and the best media to use for display. Early in the development of your presentation, you should consider the visual aids you will employ to present ideas and evidence to your listeners. Although the word "support" suggests that visuals play a secondary role, they are an element of a business presentation that can make it a success or a failure.

This chapter focuses on several topics. It will help you decide where to use visuals in your presentations and how to select the most effective graphics for communicating qualitative or quantitative information. It will discuss the standards of professionalism necessary for producing effective visuals and provide guidelines for incorporating them into your speeches. You will see that developing visual aids can be a creative and pleasant activity, but it is also time-consuming. (Mahima started preparing her visuals a full week before her presentation date, as her timeline in Figure 2–1 shows.) Don't let visuals become the last items you prepare before you deliver your speech.

The Need for Visual Support

Will all your business presentations require visual support? Think carefully about the purpose of your presentation and the needs of your audience. Remember that your listeners must fulfill a business-related function or make a business decision based on your speech; visual support will help them meet their goal. Remember also that your credibility is a factor in successful business communication; good visual aids enhance this personal quality. Let's review why visual support is typically an indispensable element of a business presentation—for the audience and for you, the speaker.

How Visual Support Helps Your Audience

Undoubtedly the main beneficiaries of your visual aids are your listeners. I'm sure you have sometimes found it difficult to listen to a speech with a consistent high level of attention and interest, but were stimulated by the visual support.

Visuals Help Keep Your Listeners Alert

At its simplest, visual support adds variety to a presentation. Listening to a speech involves only our sense of hearing; looking at visual aids employs our sense of sight. (Of course, multimedia presentations include not only video, but also sound.) Even a ten-minute presentation makes demands on your listeners' ability to concentrate; consider that your talk is only one component of their busy business day, and that your audience can be easily distracted by other concerns. Visuals are an alternative method of communication to the spoken word. As a diversion from your oral delivery, they help your listeners to renew their interest and to keep their focus.

Visuals Clarify and Reinforce Information

Another reason for using visual aids is that they emphasize key ideas and facts and clarify information. As you will soon see, a good deal of speech content lends itself to visual portrayal. Quantitative information, such as financial data and statistics, are "naturals" for visual aids, because it is very difficult for an audience to grasp and retain figures from an oral delivery only.

Visuals Make the Abstract Concrete

An entirely oral delivery of facts and analysis is somehow not completely "real," because the audience cannot "see" your information. Transparencies and handouts can transform verbal descriptions of products or locations, for example, into visible depictions, thus giving your audience a tangible sense of your material. If you need to review a process, a visual aid showing how that process works is much more effective than relying solely on language. However, keep in mind that visual support should never be gratuitous; an aid should be included because of an actual need for clarity, explanation, or reinforcement.

How Visuals Help You as a Business Speaker

Your audience isn't the only beneficiary of visual support; you are, too.

Visuals Enhance Your Credibility

I've already referred in this book to the idea of your "credibility" as a speaker: the quality that conveys your integrity and authority. Effective visuals show your preparation, your commitment to doing a thorough job, and your sincere desire to help your audience understand and retain your information. Imagine if the characters I introduced earlier, in Chapter 2, do not incorporate visual aids into their presentations. Mahima's audience of managers and executives may be overwhelmed by the comparative information she is presenting if she relies only on an oral delivery. Lyndon's listeners, recent immigrants to Canada, and Andrew's, novice investors, may not only have trouble grasping facts but may also doubt the validity of the information. Without visuals, the audience's esteem for the business speaker is diminished, and the speaker's position and reputation may suffer. For business speaking, visuals are essential for enhancing your image as a willing and complete communicator.

Visuals Help You Pace Your Speech

In Chapter 4, I discussed the importance of a moderate rate of speech. All speakers benefit by a judicious use of visual aids, because the act of displaying and interpreting them to the audience helps a speaker slow down and pause at intervals. Visuals will help you divide your presentation into separate, comprehensible segments.

Visuals Help Your Audience Understand You

This reason may seem obvious, but it is important to mention. What I mean here is that some ideas are hard to express in words only. Even outstanding speakers might have difficulty communicating complex ideas well. Effectively prepared aids will make you look— and sound—good: they save you having to exceed your own abilities (which you can't do).

Planning Your Visuals

Now that we've seen why visuals are an integral part of a business presentation, let's discuss planning them, the step preliminary to preparation. The main considerations at this stage are type, placement, and, to some extent, quantity.

Let's return again to our three characters from Chapter 2, Mahima, Lyndon, and Andrew. While doing their research and developing their discussions, they have decided that some information would be best presented in visual form for their audiences. For Mahima, separate tables comparing features of her selected notebook computers are potential visual aids. Lyndon might include in his presentation pictures showing competing products for his clients, as well as charts summarizing their specifications. Andrew may consider a line graph demonstrating the power of compound interest over time for registered savings plan (RSP) investments. These speakers would also prepare handouts summarizing key information for their audiences to examine at their leisure. Below, in the section on construction of graphic aids, I'll show some finished products that our fictional business people might create.

Using Your Outline for Placing Visuals

When your outline is relatively complete, review it thoroughly to determine where to place your visuals. We can use Radhika McDoom's outline for her speech about repetitive strain injury, Figure 3–4 in Chapter 3, as an example. She can prepare a transparency showing the title of her speech and her name for the beginning of her presentation. This type of visual aid alerts her listeners to her topic and helps to reinforce it in their minds. It also spotlights the speaker. Business communicators want their audiences to remember who they are, because a successful speech can generate more business for entrepreneurs, and more interesting assignments as well as opportunities for advancement for employees.

Radhika can follow her first visual with a brief bullet chart highlighting the main areas of her speech; this chart will preview her discussion for her audience. She might also create bullet charts summarizing the symptoms of repetitive strain injury and methods of prevention. Her speech offers a good opportunity for drawings to clarify information: a potential visual aid early in her speech might be a sketch of the wrist muscles and tendons, indicating the areas susceptible to repetitive strain injury, and another, at the end, showing a proper workstation setup with effective posture for computer use. Since Radhika's outline includes a description of exercises that alleviate muscle strain, a handout about them for the audience would also be appropriate.

Imagine listening to Radhika's speech without visual support. Would it be as effective? Imagine also how the audience might respond to Radhika as a business speaker. Would they respect her efforts without visuals? As you can see, examining your outline for potential visual aids will assist you in targeting areas suitable for graphic display and in developing visuals in an organized fashion.

Calculating the Number of Visuals

Planning your visual support means determining not only the kind of visual aid, but also how many you will use. Consider three elements when deciding on quantity: relevance, audience need, and time limit.

Ascertain the reason why the audience is attending your presentation, their level of knowledge about your topic, and their fluency in English. Stanley Jones, a professional speaker and consultant, notes that it is easier for people with limited fluency to follow written English than spoken English.[1] Hence, your analysis of your audience will help you determine whether you should use more aids such as bullet charts that announce topics or repeat main points. Furthermore, if your presentation transmits specialized information to a nonexpert audience, more visual aids will help them understand unfamiliar ideas.

However, while it is important to be considerate of all members of your audience, keep in mind that your presentation must rely predominantly on verbal, not visual, communication. The audience wants to hear your discussion and analysis, not look at numerous graphic aids. If you are to speak for 10 minutes, 10 visuals may well be too many. The audience will constantly be diverting their attention from you to your visual aids, and they may feel overwhelmed by a large quantity of visual information. A simple guideline is that the number of visuals should be about half of your speaking time in minutes, if you find you are creating a lot of visual support.

Rehearsing with your visual aids will help you determine the number you will finally use. While it is necessary to plan ahead, your decision on the quantity of visual aids may come late in the preparation process. You may find that preparing a business presentation is sometimes a difficult balancing act between the verbal and the visual. But as you refine your speech, remember that your visuals should play a supporting, not the central role—*you* are the starring actor.

Types of Visual Aids

Once you know what you want to show with visuals, and where to place them, you must plan which visuals to use. It is necessary to apply your discretion here, because only certain types of visual support are appropriate for certain types of information. You must also consider design features for your specific visuals, to ensure they have the intended effect on your audience. Generally speaking, visual support falls into four categories: charts, tables, illustrations, and objects.

Design Considerations

Some general design guidelines about visuals are in order before we examine their purposes and construction.

1. For overhead projections, be sure your font is sufficiently large. With word processing software, you can easily choose a font size that will show text clearly to your audience. Usually, a 14 point font works well with scalable fonts (see Figure 7–1). In selecting your typeface, choose one with a consistent thickness; variations can sometimes make the letter "B" look like the number "8" when projected onto the screen.[2]

2. Title each visual aid you display. Titles give your audience a clear idea of its content and will keep your audience on track. Make your titles concise; your listeners do not have time to read long titles, a distraction from you, the speaker.

Figure 7-1   Font Sizes

This is Times New Roman 10 point font.

This is Times New Roman 12 point font.

This is Times New Roman 14 point font.

This is Times New Roman 16 point font.

This is Times New Roman 18 point font.

3. Consider using lines to set off elements of your visual aid; for example, separate the title from the information. Figure 7–2 is one example. A restrained use of lines can add elegance to your graphics.

4. Use colour judiciously. Colour is beneficial because it adds interest to visual aids and helps your audience remember the information you communicate. When using a projector, you must consider that a dark background will prevent light from passing through the transparency, and your audience will be unable to see the information.[3] Furthermore, be restrained with your use of colour. More than two or three colours on one visual aid will create an over-elaborate appearance. Text is depicted most effectively in a dark colour, such as black, dark blue, or dark green. Use red or yellow for highlighting information.

5. Limit your use of clip-art. Presentation software includes clip-art libraries that can provide images suitable for many purposes, such as symbols that illustrate a theme, process, or product. You must have a good reason to include clip-art in your visual aid; otherwise you may have a cluttered graphic that will confuse your audience. And one reason for avoiding clip-art entirely is that it can have a canned, unoriginal look.

6. Create a consistent appearance for your visual aids. Using the same general design, font, and colours for each transparency will create a unified, professional package and will help to reinforce your ideas and maintain your audience's focus.

7. Keep your visual aids simple. Remember that you are communicating orally, not in writing. Many visual aids that are suitable for written reports, such as complicated

financial tables, are entirely unsuitable for oral reporting. Readers have as much time as they need to examine graphics in written reports. Your audience for your presentation has only one, rather brief, opportunity to examine each visual aid. Your visual support must communicate only the main point you are making. Extraneous information will distract or confuse your listeners.

Charts

Now that I've discussed some general design considerations, let's look at specific kinds of visual aids. Charts fall into two categories: those that represent text, or qualitative information, and those that transmit numerical relationships, or quantitative information. The following discussion does not cover all kinds of charts, just the ones most commonly used for oral presentations. These are also the simplest, the visuals that your audience can grasp quickly without the study required by more complicated graphics. You will find more elaborate charts in presentation software, but exercise discretion when using such images in your speeches.

Qualitative Charts

The qualitative charts we'll look at are bullet, organizational, and flow charts.

Bullet charts.   Bullet charts are the simplest kinds of visual aids to prepare. Their purpose is to help your listeners follow your speech easily: they list main points or key facts you want your audience to remember. At the beginning of her speech, for example, Mahima might show a bullet chart such as the one depicted in Figure 7–2 in order to help her listeners retain main topics.

Figure 7-2   Mahima's Bullet Chart

CRITERIA FOR COMPUTER NOTEBOOK PURCHASE

- Software capabilities
- Communication features
- Costs (including software and peripherals)
- Warranty and service contract

When creating a bullet chart, follow these guidelines:

1. Place no more than six words on each line.

2. Present no more than five points on one transparency.

3. Use parallel structure when listing points.

Parallel structure means that each point is presented with the same grammatical construction. For example, in Figure 7–3, all statements begin with the imperative form of the verb. I deliberately repeated the verb "make"; I could have changed the last point, for example, to "keep it simple," and still obeyed the rule of parallel construction. Figure 7–4 shows a bullet chart that violates the rule of parallel construction. Note that while the first two points begin with a subject and verb and are grammatical sentences, the third point begins with an adjective and is a statement. To be consistent, the third point should read, "Customers can make requests easily." Following the rule of parallelism is important because your phrases are consistent, and thus carry your audience along smoothly as they follow your statements. Mixed grammatical construction interrupts the flow, and thus diverts your listeners' attention.

Organizational charts.   An organizational chart depicts the chain of authority in a business. It is useful for describing the reporting structure or supervisory relationships; it gives an audience a sense of how a business operates. Site maps for Web sites are another kind of organizational chart, giving Web-page locations by category. Figures 7–5a and b portray an organizational chart: 7–5a illustrates the entire organizational structure, while 7–5b illustrates only one portion of the organization. When using an organizational chart for a visual aid, keep it simple: highlight only the segment necessary for your purpose, and omit unnecessary detail. You can distribute a fuller organizational chart as a handout.

Figure 7-3   Parallelism in a Bullet Chart

CREATING AN EFFECTIVE VISUAL AID

- Make it LARGE

- Make it short

- Make it simple

Figure 7-4   Bullet Chart That Violates the Rule of Parallel Construction

BENEFITS OF INTERNET BANKING

- Customers can bank day or night

- Customers can bank from their homes

- Easy to make requests

Figure 7-5a Organizational Chart

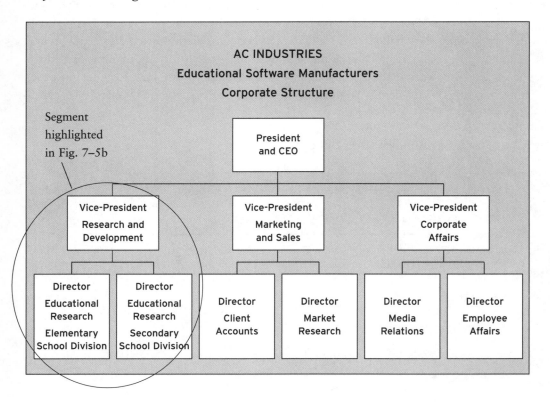

Figure 7-5b Partial Organizational Chart

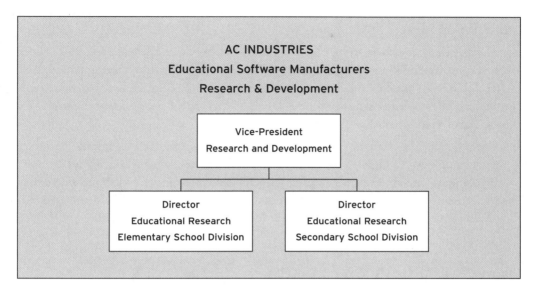

Flow chart. A flow chart explains how a process works by showing the separate stages. A decision-making process can be depicted in a simple flow chart, as shown in Figure 7–6. Flow charts are excellent for clarifying procedures for an audience, such as the steps to follow when troubleshooting a printer problem or the path for routing customer complaints.

Figure 7-6   Example of a Flow Chart

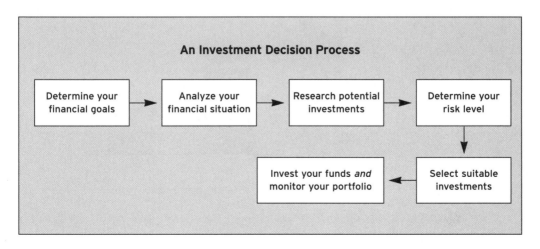

Quantitative Charts

Quantitative charts show numerical relationships. We'll consider bar, pie, and line charts in this section.

Bar charts. Use bar charts to highlight comparisons between a few data values. There are several different kinds of bar charts, such as single-bar, multiple, segmented, and bilateral. They all display a general, rather than a precise, comparison. However, you can insert the numerical figure, or data label, at the top of each bar, as Figure 7–7a shows. Each type of bar chart has its special purpose.

1. Use a single bar chart to compare a few distinct values of a measurable variable, such as money. As Figures 7–7a and 7–7b demonstrate, Andrew can use a bar chart to compare the difference in returns of an RSP investment based on when that investment is made. He will tell his audience that the chart is based on a $2000 annual investment, assuming 8 per cent interest, compounded annually.

Figure 7-7a Andrew's Vertical Bar Chart—with Data Labels

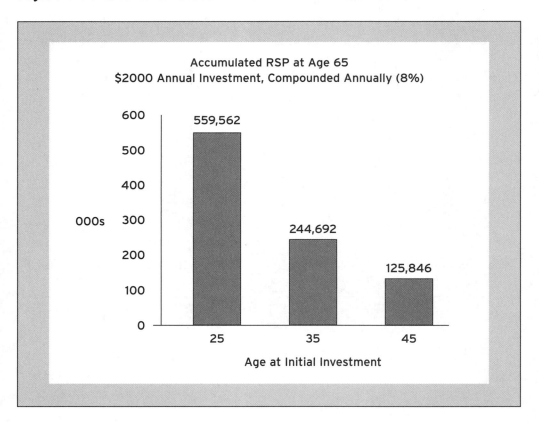

Note that both vertical bar charts and a horizontal bar chart (Figure 7–7c) based on the same information are provided. The difference between the two kinds of charts is the psychological effect: with the vertical chart, the height of the dominant value is emphasized; with the horizontal chart, the progress of the value is dominant ("look how far ahead the value is!").

2. Use a multiple bar chart to compare several sets of data measured against the same variable. In Figure 7–8, Andrew's chart compares the returns on a single amount ($2000) at two different interest rates for different times at which the amount is invested. When you use a multiple bar chart, you are making two kinds of comparisons; Andrew is comparing the amounts at different interest rates for each time, and at different times for each interest rate. Note that Andrew includes a legend to indicate what each bar represents. Because multiple bar charts are complex, an audience needs time to understand them. Prudent speakers limit the number of bar types—one guideline is to use no more than two—in a multiple bar chart.

Figure 7-7b Andrew's Vertical Bar Chart—without Data Labels

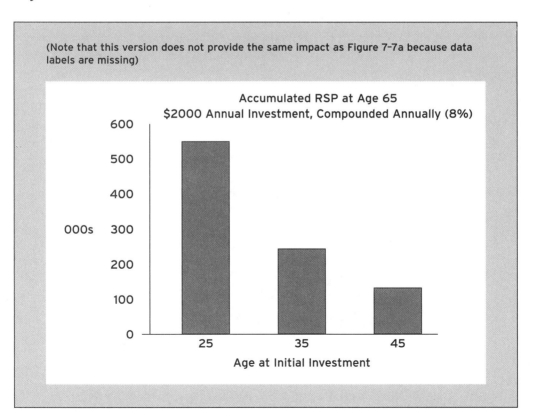

Figure 7-7c Andrew's Horizontal Bar Chart

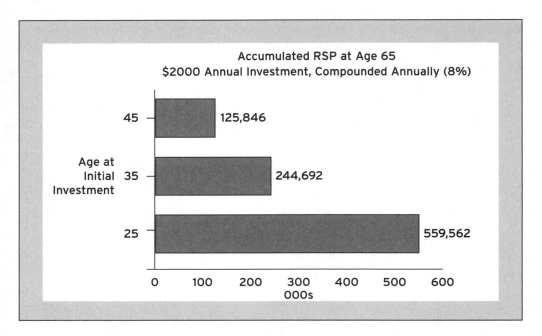

Figure 7-8 Andrew's Multiple Bar Chart

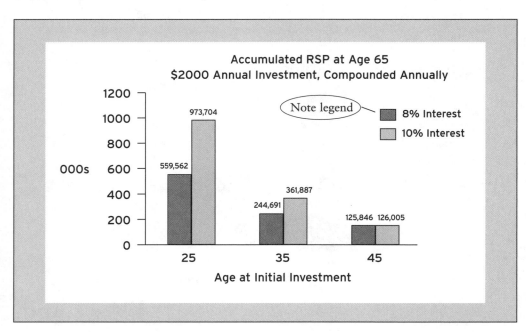

3. Use a segmented, or stacked bar chart, when you need to represent several components as parts of the whole. Here, in Figure 7–9, Andrew shows two different kinds of RSP mutual fund portfolios.

Figure 7-9   Andrew's Segmented Bar Chart

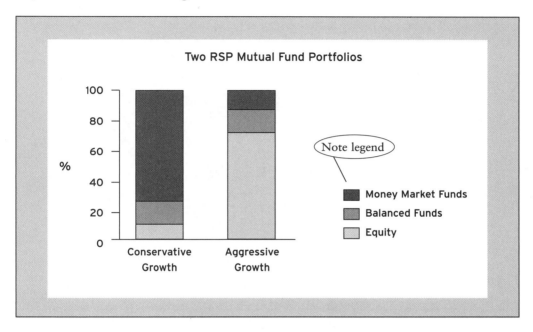

4. Bilateral bar charts (Figure 7–10) show positive and negative values. They are often used to show profit and loss. Here, Andrew is demonstrating a particular fund's performance.

Note that in these bar charts both the Y-axis and the X-axis are clearly labeled. Always label the axis if its meaning is not immediately clear.

Pie charts.   Pie charts represent the contribution of the parts to the whole. When preparing your pie chart, you must ensure that the segments add up to 100 per cent. Limit the number of slices you use: a pie chart with more than six parts is difficult for your audience to examine as a visual aid for a speech. Andrew might show his audience a particular kind of mutual fund portfolio (Figure 7–11). He has "exploded" one segment to which he wishes to draw particular attention. Label each slice in the pie, and, when appropriate, include in this graphic the numerical figure so that your audience can determine what the percentages represent. In principle a pie chart is similar to a segmented bar chart; compare Figure 7–11 with Figure 7–9 to note the similarities.

Figure 7-10 Andrew's Bilateral Bar Chart

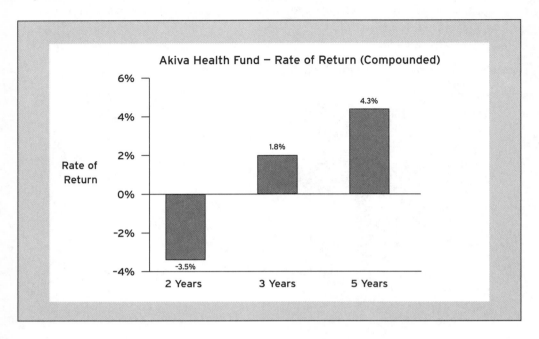

Figure 7-11 Andrew's Pie Chart

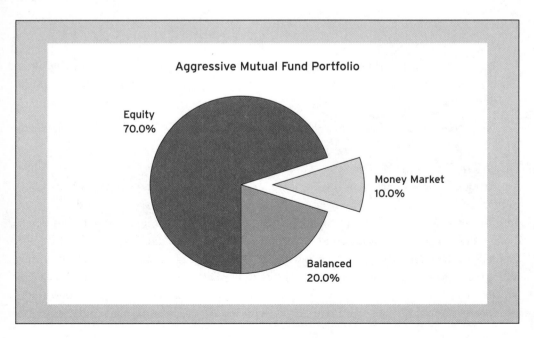

Figure 7-12 Andrew's Single-Line Chart

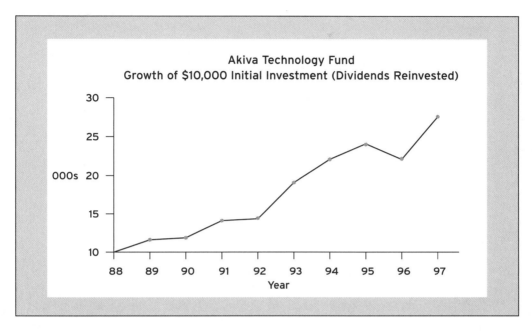

Line charts. Whereas bar charts stress comparison, line charts highlight a trend. The most common line charts are single line, multiple line, and volume charts.

1. Single line charts show the fluctuations of one item. Andrew can represent the growth of $10 000 in a mutual fund over a period of 10 years through a line chart (see Figure 7–12).

2. Multiple-line charts represent the fluctuations of more than one item. Andrew can demonstrate, for example, how $10 000 invested in the (fictitious) Akiva Technology Fund compares with the same amount invested in the Akiva Dividend Fund over a 10-year time period (see Figure 7–13). It is wise to limit the number of lines to three; otherwise, your audience will be studying your chart, rather than listening to you.

3. Volume charts are a form of stacked, or segmented, bar chart, except that one can compare the trends of the parts of a single entity. Andrew might use a volume chart, as shown in Figure 7–14, to show the growth of a $10 000 investment divided equally between two different mutual funds over 10 years.

Another consideration in creating line graphs is the spacing between points along an axis. As Figure 7–15 shows, equal distances along one axis that covers different increments in the data will misrepresent its fluctuations, and, consequently, mislead your audience. In

Figure 7-13 Andrew's Multiple-Line Chart

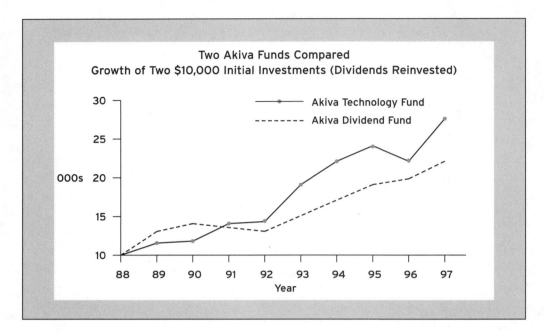

Figure 7-14 Andrew's Volume Chart

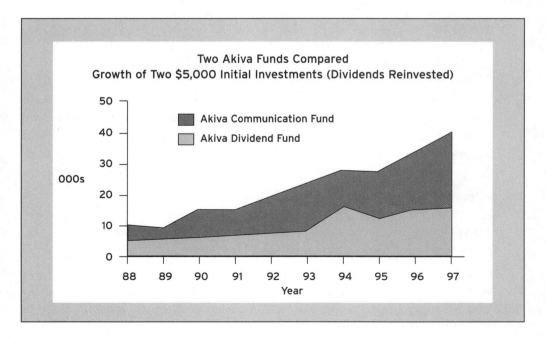

this example, the fund does not show a dip in 1996 because a three-year interval has been compressed to the same size as the one-year intervals (compare with Figure 7–12).

Tables

Tables do not portray numerical relationships pictorially. They display information in a columnar format and are often used to show exact figures. For example, as shown in Figure 7–16, Mahima would find a table handy for summarizing qualities of the two notebook computers under consideration, the Piglet and the Joey. Note the neat construction (Mahima uses a line to separate her column titles from her data, and the information is centred under the titles). When you create a table, be sure you have a logical rationale for its organization, such as a chronological or alphabetical arrangement of information, or ordering by degree of importance. Represent missing information by "n/a" (not available) rather than by leaving a blank space, which is ambiguous.

Illustrations and Videotapes

The category of illustrations includes diagrams, sketches, photographs, and maps. As mentioned earlier in this chapter, Radhika would find an anatomical drawing of the wrist area affected by carpal tunnel syndrome helpful in educating her audience about

Figure 7-15 Line Chart with Inconsistent Increments along X-Axis

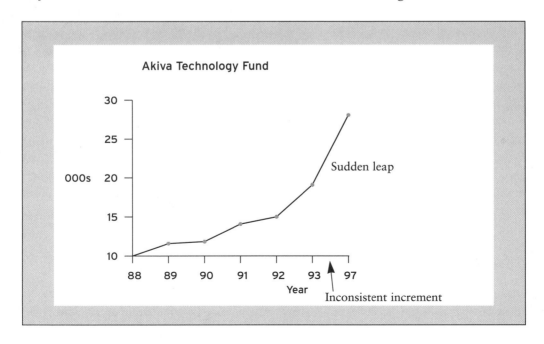

Figure 7-16 Mahima's Table, with Source Note

COMPARISON OF PIGLET AND JOEY NOTEBOOK COMPUTERS

	Piglet	Joey
Speed	300 MHz	233 MHz
Hard drive	4.3GB	3.2GB
RAM	64MB	32MB
Screen size	14.1"	13.3"

Source: Gary Aldheim, "The Newest Notebooks," *Today's Computers*, May 1998.

this medical problem. A speaker analyzing a location for a retail operation might create a simple map showing stores selling competing products. Such a map would show main intersections and perhaps use symbols to mark competitors. Do not photocopy detailed maps because the mass of information will obscure your main point. Your own simple map, drawn with a ruler and pen, will serve nicely.

Sometimes it's difficult to obtain a clear reproduction of a photograph you want to show to your audience. Also, the projection equipment might be inadequate, or the lighting in the room might alter the appearance of the image. You must balance the quality of the illustration against your need for clarifying information. Displaying a blurry or fuzzy picture will detract from your professionalism. You may find it better to omit inadequate visuals from your presentation rather than risk a poor reaction from your listeners.

You might want to use a segment from a videotape to illustrate a point in your speech—perhaps you have obtained a tape of a television advertisement you wish to incorporate into a marketing presentation. When using a videotape, be sure to have the part you are showing ready to play so that you don't waste time finding it. A videotape should be only a short segment of your presentation, perhaps 30 seconds to one minute for a 10-minute speech; otherwise the audience will lose their focus on you as well as on your purpose.

Objects

Objects—actual products or models, for example—are useful visual aids for showing an audience a three-dimensional item instead of a picture or for demonstrating how the item works. Mahima, for example, may wish to demonstrate the features of a state-of-the-art notebook computer for her audience, who will be making a purchase decision based on her information.

When giving a demonstration or showing an object, take the size of your audience into account. If you are speaking in a small boardroom, for example, your listeners may be able to see the object clearly. If you are speaking in a hall that accommodates 120 listeners, showing an object or giving a demonstration will defeat your purpose, as only people sitting close to you will be able to see, and those at a distance will feel frustrated. Show objects only if your setting is a relatively intimate one.

Some Cautionary Words about Visual Aids

Now that I've reviewed the purposes and construction of different types of visual aids, I want to discuss two other matters: crediting your sources and using presentation software for image construction.

Acknowledging Your Sources

Visual aids are created from primary or secondary information, or from a combination of each. You can obtain primary data by administering a survey to a sample group or interviewing individuals, in other words, by doing firsthand, original research. For his marketing presentation, Lyndon may have questioned focus groups about his clients' potential product. You obtain secondary data by reading about the research completed by other people, published in journals, magazines, and books. Company documents are also in the category of secondary information. Mahima probably used secondary information by reviewing evaluations of notebook computers in computer magazines.

Citing secondary research.   Any secondary research that you use for creating your visual support must be cited on the visual aid itself, in a source note. Figure 7–16, a table showing some results of Mahima's work on notebook computers, includes a source note indicating she obtained her information from a computer magazine. Crediting your source material, whether you use it exactly, such as by copying a bar chart or line chart, or you adapt it to create your own chart, communicates very visibly and concisely your honesty as a researcher.

Citing primary research.   If your visual aid is based on material from primary research, you have two choices. You can use the designation, "Source: primary," on your visual aid. Alternatively, you can omit this source note altogether. Including the notation, however, clearly distinguishes to your audience your original research from the research of others. Drawing attention to your efforts will earn the recognition of your listeners.

Violating copyright.   Be very careful when using the work of others. If you make a photocopy, scan a computer file, or hand-copy a visual aid from a secondary source, you may be using that document illegally if you show it to your audience or distribute it as a handout without securing permission. Similarly, making an audiotape or videotape may also require permission. Check if you need consent from the author, the publisher, or both.

Electronic Manipulation of Images

Modern software gives us great power over images when creating visual aids. With it we can highlight selected information graphically, for example, or make revisions to visual support quickly if we find new data to add to a bar or line chart. But the benefits of electronics can be undermined by unethical or imprudent use.

Using scanned images.   One innovation modern software has introduced is the ability to scan photographs, drawings, or text onto a computer disk. Using photo-editing software, you can manipulate an image and produce a visual aid that does not replicate the original exactly. For example, a builder might be tempted to erase features from a photograph of a landscape, or add elements, if he or she believes it would help to persuade the audience to invest in a venture. A person's appearance in a photograph can be changed, making an individual look more or less attractive. It can be very easy to deceive your audience through manipulating a scanned image. If you do make any changes to the original graphic, it is imperative that you advise your audience of electronic sleight of hand.

Using three-dimensional effects.   Modern software also gives us the opportunity to create three-dimensional images when preparing charts. Quantitative charts are often used to communicate financial trends and results. Business audiences make decisions based on this information, and visual representations can influence their actions. A business speaker's integrity is shown through the accuracy of his or her quantitative charts.

Three-dimensional effects could misrepresent data. Figure 7–17 shows a three-dimensional version of the bilateral bar chart depicted in Figure 7–10. Note that although both bar charts show profit and loss, in the three-dimensional chart the cube effect makes the bars appear higher than they actually are. (The data labels are missing from this version to clarify the distortion, but even with them the 3-D effect can be misleading.) The two-dimensional bar chart presents a more visually faithful depiction of the data. Compare the three-dimensional pie chart in Figure 7–18 with its two-dimensional counterpart in Figure 7–11, also to note the three-dimensional effect on pie charts.

Don't be seduced by the special effects offered by presentation software if they might misrepresent or conceal your information in some way. Your ethical obligation as a business speaker is to communicate your information fairly and accurately to your audiences. They expect you to use integrity in all elements of your speech, the visual content as well as the oral.

Figure 7-17   Three-Dimensional Version of Andrew's Bilateral Bar Chart

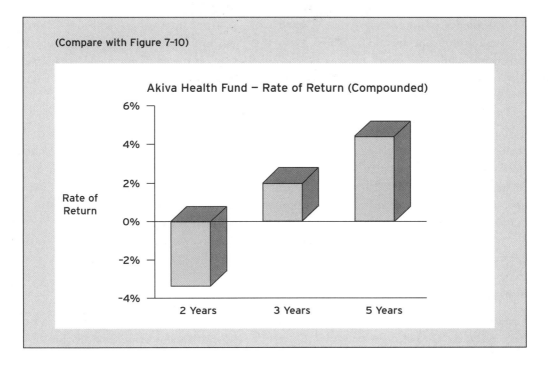

Figure 7-18   Three-Dimensional Version of Andrew's Pie Chart

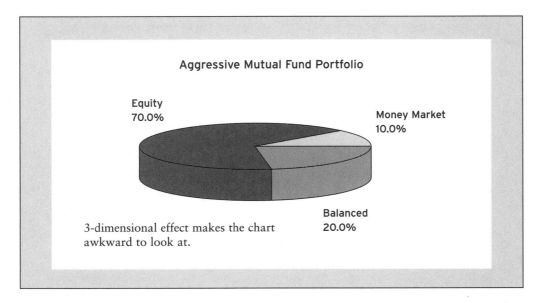

Presentation Media

Your audience will appreciate all the hard work you put into your visual aids if you choose the appropriate medium for displaying them and interact with your graphics effectively while you speak. In this section we'll examine the different media available for showing visuals and techniques for smoothly integrating visual support into your presentations. Figure 7–19 summarizes information about these media.

Before computers became commonplace, presentation media consisted of such devices as chalkboards and whiteboards, flipcharts, transparencies projected onto a screen, and handouts. Today, business speakers can create software-generated slide shows that not only display graphic aids but also enhance them with sound. I'm not suggesting that manual means of presenting visual support are obsolete; indeed, overhead transparencies are still the most popular method of communicating visual information.[4] But, as a business speaker, you probably will have the opportunity, if you don't already, to use computer-driven equipment for displaying your graphic aids. We'll consider both the old and the new means below.

Manual Presentation Methods

Manual presentation methods are the ones you've probably worked with most frequently; they are also the type that you may be most confident using. For any presen-

Figure 7-19 Assessment of Presentation Media

	Size of Audience	Clarity of Projection	Versatility*	Operation
Chalkboard/Whiteboard	Small	Fair	Poor	Basic
Flipchart	Small	Fair	Poor	Basic
Slides (35mm)	Small to Large	Good to Excellent	Fair	Intermediate
Transparencies	Small to Medium	Good	Fair	Basic
Electronic Whiteboard	Small	Excellent	Good	Advanced
Computerized Projection	Small to Large	Good to Excellent	Excellent	Advanced

*Versatility: Capable of displaying a variety of charts clearly as well as different kinds of electronic support, such as multimedia, animated graphics, and Web sites.

tation, it's important to match the method of delivery to two elements: the kind of graphic aid you are showing and the size of your audience.

Chalkboards and Whiteboards

Chalkboards and whiteboards are useful only in a small environment, because the information can only be seen comfortably from close up. Chalkboards, which generate a good deal of dust and must be frequently cleaned with a damp sponge to obtain a fresh surface, are rarely found in boardrooms. Whiteboards, which are quickly wiped clean with a dry eraser, are often furnished. Use chalkboards and whiteboards for spontaneous explanations or quick notations. They are not appropriate for prepared information such as bar or line charts because it is impractical to draw them ahead of time on these media. Furthermore, it is difficult to do so neatly. Mahima might use a whiteboard to write a technical term unfamiliar to her audience. She might also use it to show on the spot the volume purchase prices of the two different notebook computers, if her audience requests this information.

When using either a chalkboard or a whiteboard, try to talk to your audience whenever possible, not to the board. Write your notes on the board silently, and then, facing your audience, explain the information. Write large and legibly, and try to maintain as much eye contact with your listeners as possible; otherwise, they will be looking at your back for an extended time, and rapport will be weakened.

Flipcharts

Flipcharts are large pads of paper that sit on an easel. They too are a common feature in boardrooms. You can prepare a flipchart ahead of time by writing the points you wish to make, and then, during your delivery, turn over each page as you arrive at the relevant part in your speech. You can also use a flipchart for brief, spontaneous notations. Because you can only fit two or three words comfortably on a line, flipcharts are not useful for long bulleted points or for bar or line charts. Avoid using flipcharts for calculating figures: their dimensions, 90 cm high by 60 cm wide, will force you write in a cramped style. Use the larger whiteboard instead. Like the chalkboard and whiteboard, flipcharts are useful only in an intimate environment where everyone can see your visual aid easily.

Posterboards

Posterboard, made from thin, stiff cardboard, is usually 60 cm by 90 cm. It can be placed on an easel for audience viewing. Treat it as you would a flipchart—write very little on it, and write large. You may find it easier to prepare a number of pages on a flipchart than on several posterboards if you intend to use them to show a sequence of points. Posterboards are often used at trade shows or conferences where companies display their products; in these instances, posterboards contain a simple arrangement of text and picture, and invite close-up examination.

Transparencies and Slides

Transparencies, also called foils, and 35mm slides are two methods of presenting visual aids to a sizable audience because the information can be enlarged. A suitable screen size for a room seating 120 people is two by three metres. Both transparencies and slides easily accommodate all kinds of graphic aids, not just text aids such as bullet charts. Slides produced from photographs will offer much better colour resolution than transparencies.

There are several guidelines regarding transparencies and slides. Be sure you have organized them ahead of time to coordinate with your speech. It is confusing to your audience—and embarrassing for you—if a slide or transparency is out of order. You will be using up valuable speaking time setting things right and your audience will suspect you are unprepared. Another tip is to have a fresh bulb in the projector so that you do not experience an unpleasant surprise. In addition, turn off the projector when you are not using it; a bright light on a white screen is hard on your audience's eyes. Try to keep the lighting in the room balanced so that your audience can see you, the speaker, and your visual aid.

One nice feature of transparencies is that you can overlay them for an intended effect, such as showing the current trend in a product's earnings, and then, with an overlay, showing the projected trend for a time period in the future. When using slides and transparencies, be sure your body does not block your listeners' sightlines. Chapter 4 showed proper placement of the screen for different environments.

To emphasize points on a transparency or slide, you will find it best to use a pointer—laser or telescopic—to highlight specific elements on the screen. Transparencies also invite the interaction of the speaker. Using a felt-tipped marker, you can circle or underline specific elements you want your audience to note. Once again, remember to speak *to* your audience, not to the visual aid. Make your point about the visual aid, direct your audience to the element you want them to notice, then turn off the projector.

Handouts

Handouts are vital means of providing visual aids for business audiences because your listeners can study them at their leisure. Often, business speakers will prepare a bound or stapled package of the visual images used in the presentation plus additional detailed material. When preparing handouts, be sure to have a title page indicating the title of the presentation and its date. If it is a joint presentation, include the names of your partners and their positions and affiliations. If someone who is not speaking helped you prepare your material, acknowledge that person on the title page or on a separate page in the handout—your audience will notice your gracious gesture. Be sure to provide space on the handout for notes.

You must decide when to distribute your handout. If you want your audience to consult material in a handout while you speak, distribution before the presentation is appropriate: Mahima might feel that her listeners, executives and managers, would benefit from looking at the specifications and costs while she discusses them. Otherwise, save handouts for the end of your speech.

High-Tech Presentation Media

High-tech, or computer-driven, methods for delivering visual support offer business speakers extraordinary versatility and creativity. These media are becoming more and more common in both large and small businesses, and afford exciting opportunities when effectively used.

Electronic Whiteboards

Electronic whiteboards look like conventional whiteboards and are about the same dimensions, about 1.5 metres wide by 1 metre high. However, as a high-tech alternative, electronic whiteboards are more powerful, as they can be used both for writing and for projecting visual aids.

Products like the "SMART board" ™ (**www.smarttech.com**) provide a touch-sensitive screen. Speakers can use this whiteboard as they would a conventional one by writing on it with the stylus or markers (in various colours) supplied by the manufacturer. Unlike conventional whiteboards, however, with this device text and images can be saved to a computer file, including any marks made with the stylus during the presentation. Speakers can print out the material with their annotations as handouts during a break, or access the information in the future, be it for review, adaptation, or electronic transmission via e-mail.

Speakers using an electronic whiteboard as a projection screen can display a slide show prepared with presentation software. Using the electronic whiteboard also as a touch screen, the speaker can circle or otherwise highlight specific elements in the visual aid with a stylus or marker. The electronic whiteboard can display any software application, so, for example, speakers can create a "what-if" scenario using a spreadsheet if it is called for.

Presentation Software

I've already referred to presentation software in this chapter, in my discussions of clip-art and of the ethical problems with electronic manipulation. At this point, I want to focus more specifically on presentation software as a medium for creating and displaying graphic aids.

You can use presentation software for creating a single transparency or a complete electronic slide show. When integrating a slide show into a speech, speakers link their computer to an LCD (liquid crystal display) panel placed on top of a projector, or directly to a compatible projector. They can then project the visual aids onto a large screen. We can imagine that Andrew prepared an electronic slide show for his presentation, probably held in a large hotel meeting room or on-site corporate auditorium, on RSP investments. For a very small audience, such as two or three people grouped around a table, speakers sometimes rely on their notebook computer screen. Lyndon, for example, might do this with his clients when he makes his market presentation.

Many modern presentation software products offer the business speaker powerful tools for preparing visual support. This software supplies templates that automatically arrange your information, and offers a wide choice of designs, some tailored for specific industries. You can select colours and play with the size of your graphic, using on-screen palettes and rulers to help you achieve the look you want. Using modern presentation software, you can also insert sound effects and animated figures from among the many your package provides. An added benefit of some of these products is that you can insert speaking notes on your screen (but not elsewhere), thus assisting a polished delivery. Some products offer "rehearse modes," which monitor the amount of time it takes to project a single screen or to deliver your entire presentation. Look at computer magazines for reviews of current products on the market.

When you are delivering your speech, presentation software provides many interesting options. A sound cue, such as an arpeggio (a rising musical scale), between major sections in the speech body can signal a change of topic to your audience. You can fade in and fade out of bullet charts, move bars up the y-axis slowly or quickly to denote increasing revenue, or zoom in on a particular function in an organizational chart. With the magic of computer technology, you could have fun, and so could your audience.

But do they want to? And should you have fun? As with any presentation aid, you must use judgment. Remember that your audience is listening to your presentation in order to make a business decision that could profit them in some way. A frivolous—and inexpert—use of computer-assisted support can distract your audience from your message and weaken your argument as well as your image as a serious business speaker. Be alert to your purpose and to your audience. Don't become infatuated with electronic toys; you may be able to do a job as effectively, if not more so, with old-fashioned transparencies as you could with high-tech techniques.

Chapter Summary

Visual support is often an essential element of a business presentation. The pictures help you to tell your story, to inform your audience, and to persuade them. With visual support, your listeners will retain more of your information and raise their impression of you as a business speaker.

To portray the ideas and numerical relationships accurately, you must select the graphic to suit your material: brief bullet charts for text, bar charts for comparison, line charts for trends, and pie charts to show the relationship of the parts to the whole. You can also use objects, videotapes, and illustrations, but be sure they are visible to your entire audience.

While electronic media are overtaking traditional ones such as transparencies, the same rules hold true for both. You should never have to say you're sorry. If your visual aid isn't simple and neat, don't apologize for it; you shouldn't have used it in the first place. Don't overdo the number of visual aids: be sensitive to the needs of your audience, but don't overwhelm them with graphics. Presentation software offers exciting opportunities for creativity, but also poses the danger of overdoing the showy techniques. Remember that you, not your visual support, are the centre of attention.

Enjoy preparing your visual aids. They exercise your creativity and intelligence.

Applications

1. Distinguish between the applications of bar, line, and pie charts.

2. What is the ethical dimension of visual aids?

3. Create visual aids for the following:

   a. the cost of your groceries over the last six months

   b. the cost of your groceries compared with that of a friend's over the last six months

   c. the allocation of your monthly budget

   d. the cost of three different brands of desktop computers with identical features

   e. the main points for a presentation based on a speech you developed for exercise 3 in Chapter 5, or exercises 4 or 6 in Chapter 6

4. What are good design features for bullet charts? For other types of visual aids?

5. What special considerations concern a speaker when presenting visual aids?

6. What are the benefits of technology for preparing and presenting visual aids? Their potential problems?

References

1. H. Stanley Jones, "Speaking at an International Congress," *Association Management* 45 (August 1993), 85.

2. See Lisa D. Mason, "Design Issues for Producing Effective Multimedia Presentations," *Technical Communication*, 44, no. 1 (1997), 68.

3. See Mason, 68.

4. Reported in Kathryn Alesandrini, "Producing Effective Presentations," *Computer Shopper* 17, no. 4 (1997), 2. [www5.zdnet.com/cshopper/content/9704/cshop0010.html#3], January 20, 1998.

CHAPTER 8

Groupwork: Meetings and Telemeetings

So far in this book the spotlight has been focused on you as a presenter. We've pictured you standing in front of an audience, delivering a speech, demonstrating your best platform manner, and using visual support to enhance your presentation. Now let's put you in a different position, sitting at a table with your colleagues, where you are solving a problem, sharing information, or planning a new stage in a long-term project. Rather than presenting, you are now working collaboratively, as a member of a group.

Groupwork is a mainstay of the Canadian workplace. When people work together with a positive and organized approach, collaboration offers many benefits. In this chapter we'll focus mainly on group meetings in a business environment: we'll discuss the mechanics of meetings, such as setting the agenda and tracking the discussion, and the creative side, offering some suggestions to assist problem-solving. Along the way you'll find some tips to encourage productive interaction.

As the chapter title states, small-group meetings are not the only topic here. Because more and more Canadian organizations use teleconferencing— via computer, telephone, or video—to hold dispersed meetings, we'll also examine the benefits, as well as the obstacles, modern technology offers for groupwork.

The Team Culture and the Canadian Workplace

With the prevalence of teamwork in Canadian business, good meeting skills are an important requirement for productive collaboration. As Carol Stephenson, currently COO of Bell Satellite Services, said in a 1997 speech about leadership, "more and more individuals are working together in teams. The old command-and-control hierarchies are breaking down." She notes that "Canadians have an advantage in the team-based environment. Studies have shown that as managers we Canadians tend to be more cooperative than, say, our counterparts south of the border."[1]

A 1994 Conference Board of Canada study surveyed 109 Canadian firms from a variety of industries about the change from hierarchical organizations, where decisions are made by individuals, to team environments, where groups have greater responsibility. The survey found that half of the companies questioned viewed team-building as a key management skill, and more than 40 per cent cited teamwork as an important skill for nonmanagerial workers.[2] Carol Stephenson reported that the Stentor Resource Centre, an alliance of Canadian telecommunication companies disbanded in December 1998, maintained skills inventory and performance databases to help team leaders choose project participants.[3] Rick George, Suncor's president and CEO, told educators at Calgary's Mount Royal College that graduates "will need to work independently, inter-dependently, and as part of teams, depending on the task at hand."[4] At work you may participate on small or large teams; a Stentor project on electronic cash had a team of 300 workers dispersed among four cities.[5] Figure 8–1 shows three common types of business teams.

The Benefits of Teamwork

Teamwork has taken a strong hold in the Canadian workplace for good reason.

Economic Advantages

Teams help to reduce organizational costs and improve performance. Norcen Energy Resources, a Noranda Resources company, grouped employees into teams of about 10 and gave them decision-making responsibilities as part of their organizational "flattening." A human resources team member remarked that "Norcen's head office was able to address challenges efficiently and cost-effectively thanks to the team approach."[6]

Improved Outcomes

Another benefit of teamwork is the "magic" of group collaboration. You will find that working with employees who have different expertise and experience often creates results of higher quality than if the job were completed by one person. A Norcen team leader credited the collegial approach as an "incubator for new ideas. There is so much input."[7]

Improved Morale and Commitment

Working closely with others on the same project can also improve the quality of work life. Groupwork is a social activity: employees interact closely and gain satisfaction when they solve problems together and receive the praise of their peers and supervisors. A positive group atmosphere enriches what can be the daily grind of work.

Figure 8-1   Types of Teams

Project Teams

Bring together people with different skills

Complete a task from start to finish

Membership is fluid—individuals join and leave as project demands

Teams can be large or small

Self-Managed Teams

Administer all aspects of a project, including budget, personnel, and coordination with other organizational groups

Granted ability to make their own decisions by upper management

Self-Directed Teams (also called "work teams")

Common in the manufacturing and service sector

Focused on a particular function, such as quality-assurance teams that test and certify products before they leave a factory, or teams that specialize in one stage of the assembly process

Have less autonomy, or freedom, for making decisions than self-managed teams

Source: See Patricia Booth, *Challenge and Change: Embracing the Team Concept*, The Conference Board of Canada, Report 123-94 (Ottawa, 1994), 6.

More Opportunities for Learning

Because group members bring to their encounters with each other their special expertise and knowledge, they have opportunities for shared learning. They pick up tips on how to accomplish a job or deal with a problem more effectively. At Stentor, team project experience was one way employees informally acquired knowledge that they applied to new team situations, or used to target an area for more training.[8]

Conflicts of Opinion

Yes, disagreements can be positive for groupwork. Dissenting opinion is very beneficial because it steers members away from groupthink, when people accept a dominant view without questioning it, and stimulates new and creative ways of examining a problem. The difficulty with conflicting opinion is in trying to reach an agreement that is satisfactory to all group members. The absence of a true consensus is a fact of organizational life. Yet conflicting opinions do indeed inspire fresh viewpoints.

The Problems of Teamwork

While many employees like teamwork, they don't, in fact, like meetings, the most common medium for team members to solve problems, plan tasks, and review progress. Canada Post managers cited meetings as "the most irritating part of their jobs."[9]

Getting off Track

One danger of group meetings is that people become sidetracked from the job at hand, and the meeting develops into a social occasion. The managers at Canada Post complained about people arriving late, and then indulging in social chitchat.[10] Consequently, time is wasted, a new meeting needs to be scheduled, and productivity is undermined.

Groupthink

When group members avoid conflict or allow themselves to be pressured into accepting a majority opinion, groupthink can set in. Because of shyness or an unwillingness to confront outspoken participants, individuals sometimes find themselves agreeing to a decision they suspect is a wrong one. In organizations, groupthink can lead to financial, production, or health and safety problems.

Freeriders

Another problem with groupwork is that some members may not contribute their full share to the group effort. Each participant in a group or team has distinct responsibilities; employees feel resentful when they see fellow-workers taking advantage of the group framework by letting others shoulder the burden of the work. Dealing with unproductive members, often called "freeriders," can poison a positive group atmosphere.

Meetings: A Primer

Now that a context for groupwork is set, let's examine how to make meetings productive. I don't want to suggest that all meetings are handled in the same way. Different meetings have different purposes, and different ways of proceeding. People gather at work to analyze a problem, to plan a project, or to share information. They may meet frequently, perhaps every two weeks, to catch up on news, or, sporadically, only when a situation requires collaborative effort.

Meetings may be exclusively internal, solely among the organization's employees, or they may include external people, such as clients. Meetings vary in formality. An internal gathering may be quite casual, perhaps taking place in the cafeteria over lunch, while one that includes outsiders may be more formal, arranged for a boardroom. Not all meetings have a formal chairperson, nor do they abide by strict time limits, nor do they all have a designated meeting recorder. The circumstances and the people dictate how the discussion is managed.

Planning for Meetings

Despite the wide variety in business meetings, I want to consider two of the traditional, or more formal, elements of meetings: the agenda and the chairperson's role. Then we'll consider techniques that enhance analysis and problem-solving.

Setting the Agenda

To be productive, all meetings, including informal ones, must have a purpose. People need to know why the meeting is being held and how to prepare for it. Many meetings require an agenda. Let's imagine that Andrew works with a team that plans public seminars on their bank's products. Figure 8–2 shows an agenda Andrew's supervisor might write for a planning meeting. As you can see, the agenda gives participants the time and place of the meeting, its purpose, and items to be covered. Note also the suggested time limit, which warns participants to be prepared and focused. Circulate the agenda with enough lead-time; your colleagues are busy and need to schedule the event. If you cannot attend a meeting, inform the convenor as soon as possible so that another time can be arranged.

Choosing Participants

A productive meeting includes the key people. Be sure you contact them when choosing attendees; otherwise, your group will miss important information or meaningful perspectives on your task. If, as a participant, you believe someone should attend because his or her contributions are valuable, tell the convenor.

Preparing

When you receive the agenda, think carefully about the meeting's purpose. Prepare with it in mind, and your part will be constructive.

Plan your remarks.   Prepare your input early on. Make notes, and take them with you. If you foresee any obstacles to your suggestions, develop your case ahead of time so that you can respond readily to challenges. Perhaps you will need to photocopy information for other participants that they would require for reference. Sometimes the agenda allocates specific time limits for discussion items; focused preparation will help you cover your material within these restrictions.

Psych up.   Your attitude might also need some work. Perhaps you have attended meetings with something of a closed mind. You may have suspected the value of a co-worker's contribution, or felt negatively about the meeting itself, believing it takes time away from more important duties. Despite these attitudes, however, it is your responsibility to attend meetings with a positive outlook, so that the climate will be constructive.

Figure 8-2 Example of a Meeting Agenda

MEMORANDUM

To: Andrew Obolafia, Financial Products

            Miriam Saring, Event Planning

            David Maxwell, Art Department

From: John Arthur, Manager, Customer Services *JA*

Date: June 3, 1999

Subject: Planning Meeting for Educational Seminars

Here is the agenda for our planning meeting on June 17. The topic is our winter 2000 educational seminars. Please give some thought to the items before the meeting and bring any information we might need to consult. We'll meet in the boardroom at 10. Let's try to complete our discussion within an hour. If you have a scheduling problem, contact me at x56.

AGENDA

1.   Andrew's presentation on seminar topics

2.   Scheduling, venues, facilities

3.   Artwork–visual support, publications

And you must play by the rules. For example, if you exceed your time limit for your remarks, respect the timekeeper's admonitions.

Managing the Discussion

A clear agenda and effective preparation are two elements of productive meetings. The other element is proper meeting management. The meeting leader plays an important role. Of course, you may attend meetings that don't have a designated leader. Often, groups that have worked together for a long time share the chair's job; that is, different members assume the different functions, as each sees fit. We'll look at these functions, whether they are performed by one person or cooperatively.

The Leader's Job

Usually, the convenor chairs the meeting, but sometimes he or she might ask someone else to fulfill this role, perhaps a team member with specialized knowledge if the meeting requires his or her guidance. The leader's job requires alertness and sensitivity. If you have never led a meeting, you may yet be chosen to do so: some groups rotate the chair's job for frequent meetings.

Be warned that chairs who assume the roles of minute-taker and time-keeper in addition to guiding the meeting will likely have trouble following the discussion and asking pertinent questions. If you chair a meeting, ask others to take on these duties; you can even bring in outsiders if it is felt that all members must be fully involved.

So, what do good chairpersons do?

Effective chairs set the tone. Although team members know each other through daily work, a few pleasantries, such as welcoming participants and thanking them for appearing, help to create a comfortable atmosphere. Such comments also formally, yet tactfully, signal the beginning of the meeting, should people be socializing while waiting for it to begin.

Effective chairs encourage participation. Although the fundamental goal of meetings is to combine efforts for a better outcome, there are people who need to be prodded to speak. Perhaps they feel reservations about expressing an unpopular idea, or are shy. A good chair notices the silent members, and asks them for their comments. Quiet people often have an idea that crystallizes the discussion, or brings out a problem no one else has seen.

Effective chairs control dominators. Good chairing means letting people have their say, but maintaining an open atmosphere can be difficult if some members talk for too long. If there is not a designated time-keeper, the chair must interrupt and ask them to jump ahead to their main ideas.

Effective chairs track the discussion. The benefit of group interaction is that the blend of many viewpoints brings new perspectives to issues. An effective leader notes who has spoken, and who has not, as they seek input.

Tracking also means the chairperson should periodically ask the meeting recorder to summarize the discussion so far in order to keep the group focused. Summaries remind members of the points already covered, ensure that what someone said was accurately noted, and spur further thinking. Be sure to end the meeting with a general summary of what was achieved. A final summary helps participants plan for the next meeting and gives a feeling of closure to the current one. If the meeting concludes in an open-ended fashion, participants may walk away unsure about what was accomplished.

Effective chairs suppress socializing.   It's tempting for participants to make remarks to their neighbours in meetings, but doing so is distracting. A glance at the transgressors may be enough; if not, simply calling them by name or asking the person currently speaking to stop will get their attention.

The Recorder's Job

People usually take their own notes at meetings, but often meetings also require an official recorder. Minutes are important documents because they give everyone a solid idea of what was achieved and help participants to coordinate work between meetings.

If you accept the duties of meeting recorder, you will need to follow the discussion carefully, and to decide what to record. Try to focus on the remarks that relate to the meeting's purpose and on the important details, not the digressions. If you missed something, ask the speaker to repeat the comment. Your record is a document for future consultation, not only by those present, but also by other people, such as the executives who need to keep abreast of your team's activities. So ask questions if you feel the conversation is confusing, and urge speakers to slow down if you can't follow them.

Figure 8–3 shows minutes from Andrew's planning meeting. Note that these minutes include "action" comments that list participants' responsibilities. Not all meetings designate tasks; some occur so that members can update each other on current activities. For meetings that do need to record responsibilities, however, action statements helps keep a project on track by showing who is doing what. Finally, note that these minutes include an item about the next meeting, giving group members the opportunity to plan ahead.

As a meeting recorder, you should distribute the minutes as soon as possible, either by paper copy or e-mail.

Two Elements of Problem Solving

The most demanding kinds of meetings are those that solve problems and make decisions. Over the course of weeks or months, a project team, for example, will deal with many issues. To resolve them, they need to pinpoint the problem clearly and then to develop practical solutions. Problem definition and brainstorming are two methods many productive groups employ in the problem-solving process.

Figure 8-3 Example of Meeting Minutes

MINUTES OF MEETING OF JUNE 17, 1999, 10:00 a.m.

Present: Andrew Obolafia, Financial Products
            Miriam Saring, Event Planning
            David Maxwell, Art Department
            John Arthur, Manager, Customer Services
            Eleanor Mentz, P.A., Meeting recorder

1. Andrew Abolofia reviewed his ideas for the presentations he believes should be delivered in 2000. He discussed forecasts by Bill Gunning, a bank economist, for winter 2000. Andrew believes his presentations should focus on RSP contributions and mutual funds as an investment option. Andrew would like to give GICs secondary consideration in his presentations.

2. John Arthur suggested that Andrew start working on two separate presentations, one about RSPs themselves, and the other about mutual funds.

   ACTION: Andrew will prepare two outlines for the next meeting, one on RSPs, the other on mutual funds, for discussion.

3. Miriam Saring discussed the venues for last year's educational seminars. She noted that at two of the three locations (the branch at Laurier Ave. and Steele St., and the Finchurst Hotel) attendance was very low. She suggested that these locations be re-evaluated, and, in light of the findings, perhaps new ones be found.

   ACTION: Miriam will prepare a report on attendance at these locations for the team.

4. David Maxwell reported that the look of the visual aids will be updated this year. He has investigated new presentation software on the market, and would like to see the use of multimedia. He showed examples of last year's promotional material, and mock-ups of a new look he would like to see used.

5. John noted that the issue of poor attendance was a serious one. He suggested that Miriam prepare a presentation on the problem to be given at a meeting in about two weeks, to executive staff.

   ACTION: Miriam will prepare a presentation on the attendance problem, to be given the week of July 1.

6. The meeting ended at 11:15 a.m.

Defining the Problem

Carefully defining the problem under consideration should be the first step for arriving at an effective decision. Let's imagine that Andrew and his group are told that attendance at his local bank's financial seminars is low. They are asked to suggest ways of attracting more people. Communication experts suggest that groups should phrase problems as questions in order to focus the problem. Andrew's group might ask, "How can we improve attendance at our bank's public seminars?"

Problem definition, however, does not end at formulating the question. Look at the problem from as many angles as possible in order to determine its possible causes and its implications.[11] Andrew's group would need to do research to obtain such information. They would need to agree on how far back they should go in their research. They would consider whether they should limit their research to only their district, or compare their bank to branches in other cities or provinces, or throughout Canada. They might need to look at presentation outlines for the seminars and at promotional material, and to speak to presenters.

The group's entire first meeting might be devoted to problem definition, that is, determining how to explore the problem. The meeting might conclude with delegating responsibilities for gathering data, and the group might not meet perhaps until a month later, when the findings had been written up as reports and studied by the team's members. A thorough definition of the problem will help the group work more productively.

Brainstorming

Brainstorming is a technique that helps to generate ideas. With this method participants voice possible problem solutions, including seemingly outlandish ones. Then, after the brainstorming session is completed, the solutions are discussed. We can speculate that Andrew's group brainstormed during their first meeting when they tried to define the problem. Let's also imagine that Andrew's group brainstormed to generate possible reasons for poor seminar attendance, producing the following list:

- weather
- poor presentations
- poor advertising
- no free gifts
- no coupons
- bad time of year
- conflicting scheduling with competitors
- bad locations for seminars
- downturn in stock market

The following guidelines will enhance your group's brainstorming sessions.

Keep remarks concise.   Note that the solutions Andrew's team generated are expressed as short phrases. During their discussion of the ideas, the group will be able to fill out their thoughts, and respond to questions and comments. One ingredient of effective brainstorming is speed because it pressures group members to think in a concentrated fashion. Conciseness expedites the process.

Avoid judgments.   Commentary during the brainstorming segment of a meeting is ill-advised. Once people begin evaluating an idea, even by saying, "That's good," they can lose their momentum. People might start to digress, and judgmental comments can silence some participants, who might think that their ideas aren't worthy. The point of brainstorming is to pressure participants to express their ideas freely. Maintaining the pressure keeps generating suggestions.

Consider anonymity.   The nature of your group's members determines how comfortable they feel about expressing their ideas openly. If you believe that some members feel uncomfortable about identifying themselves with their ideas, consider ways to ensure some anonymity; pool writing and electronic support are two methods, described below.

Push past pauses.   It has been shown that the quiet periods during brainstorming sessions, when people are frustrated and feel that they have exhausted all possibilities, are often, in fact, the times when the most valuable ideas come up.[12] Take a lesson here, and don't stop just because people feel further brainstorming is fruitless.

Delegate note-taking.   As I've said, it's very difficult for a group member both to brainstorm and record all the ideas. Bring in someone outside the group to do the scribe's job.

Consider written brainstorming.   To facilitate the brainstorming process, your group might want to try these alternatives to vocal expression:

1. **Time-limited brainstorming.** This technique requires that group members write down their thoughts within a strictly imposed time limit, perhaps five or seven minutes. The pressure forces people to think hard, with the result that they come up with a variety of ideas. At the end of the time limit, people take turns reading out their suggestions, and discussion follows.

2. **Pool writing.** Here members sit at a table, write their ideas on paper, and place the sheets in the centre of the table. They then take a sheet from the pile and add their own comments.[13]

3. **Electronic brainstorming.** Groupware—software that supports collaborative work—facilitates computerized brainstorming.[14] The benefits of this method are speed, anonymity, and a complete and accurate record of the ideas generated. Typing their ideas at computer terminals, people can work quickly. Everything that is written is saved. No one knows who said what (unless someone confesses), so participants feel

more comfortable about contributing anything on their minds, even the most outrageous ideas. And, when the brainstorming segment is over, everyone can enjoy the convenience of viewing the entire list of ideas on his or her computer screen.

Further Steps in Problem Solving

Defining the problem and brainstorming for solutions are two steps in analyzing problems. After brainstorming, your group should evaluate the results of the brainstorming session. Your scribe or a group member should write the ideas in a place all participants can see, such as a whiteboard, so that your discussion can flow efficiently. Reduce the list by noting duplicate ideas, and rank the items according to criteria your group establishes; they may include practicality and cost. In future meetings you will work further on the criteria for a good solution. Turning to Andrew's group as an example, perhaps they answer the question, "How can we improve attendance at our bank's public seminars?" with the following suggestions:

- wider advertising, such as in community newspapers and foreign-language newspapers
- presentations with less technical content
- more use of visual aids in presentations
- promotional material in several languages provided at seminars

Andrew's team would recommend that these criteria be applied to future financial seminars. The work of Andrew's group, however, does not end with their recommendations. After their suggestions are implemented, they must determine the effectiveness of the solution. They will see if the number of people attending the seminars rises, if comment cards reveal positive or negative comments about presentation clarity, and if promotional material is taken home. When working on problems, your group must always evaluate the solution after implementation.

Telemeetings

Meetings bring people to a single location for group work. Teleconferences allow dispersed meetings; from distant places, be they within one city or around the world, people can collaborate in "real time." The number of products on the market testifies to the growing popularity of teleconferencing systems; large businesses are embracing this communication medium because it saves travel costs and travel time.

But when choosing a teleconferencing system as a substitute for face-to-face meetings, managers must consider if it will provide the same meeting experience as live, personal encounters, where spontaneous interaction can spark creative thought. They will need to determine if the teleconferencing medium will enhance productivity or compromise it. We'll look at the features of three types of electronic meeting setups—groupware, audioconferencing, and videoconferencing—and consider their applications for groupwork.

Electronic Meeting Systems: Some Mechanics

Figure 8–4 lists the three electronic meeting technologies and a few of their characteristics. Groupware, obviously, is an electronic medium requiring the use of written, not oral, communication. Groupware supplies frameworks for many tasks meetings accomplish, including problem definition, brainstorming, ranking ideas, and decision making.[15] Employees log on to their group meeting via a computer network and follow the pre-arranged structure for the job at hand. A meeting leader posts questions and remarks to guide the group, who keyboard their comments. Participants' computer screens can be arranged with a public window so that group members can see everyone's contributions, and a private window for entering and editing individual messages.[16]

Figure 8-4 Comparative Table of Electronic Meeting Systems

	Groupware	Audioconferencing	Videoconferencing
Communication medium	Written word (text on computer screen)	Voice	Voice and video
Level of anonymity	Potential for full anonymity	Limited anonymity (vocal recognition)	Full personal recognition
Required user skills	Good keyboarding skills	Good speaking skills	Good speaking skills, Composed "platform" manner
Level of social interaction	No social interaction	Limited social interaction	Limited social interaction

State-of-the-art audioconferencing equipment includes highly sensitive speakerphones that can pick up sound in rooms of six square metres and larger, thereby permitting a number of participants to communicate with colleagues at remote sites. You can log on to a corporate website, such as the Bank of Montreal's (**www.bmo.ca**) or Rogers Communications' (**www.rogers.com**), to hear a recorded audioconference as well as download a transcript of the proceedings.

Three kinds of videoconferencing systems—installed boardroom systems, rollabout or movable systems, and both desktop and notebook computer systems—allow groups to participate in visual meetings. With the large systems, a voice-tracking camera, mounted on top of a television monitor, automatically focuses on the speaker and will ignore extraneous noise. Modern technology allows a single monitor screen to be split among transmissions from separate sites, displaying two or more people simultaneously, or to show one person or a group of people. A single television or computer monitor can display video, sound, and graphics at the same time, with one window on the screen showing the speaker, and another, visual support.

Tips for Electronic Meetings

One element that distinguishes electronic meetings from face-to-face meetings is the stringent time limit. Like the traditional, face-to-face meetings described earlier in this chapter, electronic meetings are also arranged ahead of time and have a pre-determined end. Yet, as one study showed, awareness of the time factor is heightened for teleconferences because individual schedules, the equipment, and the facilities for conducting these meetings are more complex to synchronize. [17]

Regulating Tools

Because of the complexity of teleconferencing, the mechanisms that regulate meetings—the meeting leader, the recorder, the agenda, the minutes—are seen as having greater importance. Research has shown that in electronic meetings leaders must be more attentive to focussing the discussion and moving it along, and to coordinating tasks between meetings; in other words, in these high-tech encounters leaders should give more direction than in face-to-face ones. Research has also stressed the importance of distributing documents, such as agenda and minutes, to participants well beforehand, so that they can plan for the meeting more effectively.[18]

Personal Preparation

People who have participated in electronically-mediated groupwork also maintain that documents and visuals must be ready beforehand for fax or modem transmission, so that participants at other sites are not waiting for supporting material. If you take part in an electronic meeting, have your notes at your fingertips and your designated tasks completed. If you lead a teleconference, you must be familiar with the technology. Needless to say, you must check that the teleconferencing equipment is entirely functional; if technical difficulties delay or abort the planned meeting, everyone's time and effort is wasted.

Communication Skills

Successful teleconferencing also demands that participants know how to interact with the medium itself. For example, a groupware meeting requires typing in comments. How good are your keyboarding skills? Can you type quickly enough to input your ideas, and to respond quickly to those of others? How effective are your written communication skills? Will you be frustrated working with this medium, and then pull back from contributing?

For accurate communication in an audioconference, you must speak at an accessible pace, as you would during a formal presentation. Although most modern equipment does not "clip" voices and suppress echoes, it is still important to articulate clearly so that your listeners do not misunderstand you. Because the newest speakerphones can pick up many sounds, control private conversations, fingers drumming on tabletops, and pen-clicking. Avoid making distracting noises; practice self-control.

Videoconferencing also requires self-possession. Your image is transmitted on a computer screen or television monitor, so you must restrict unnecessary gestures. Your image will be magnified if remote sites use installed or rollabout television monitors, so mannerisms and facial expression will be heightened if the videocamera is focused only on you. Practice good platform manner when videoconferencing, as you would for a formal presentation.

Teleconferencing Choices

The selection of a specific type of teleconferencing system for a business meeting depends on a number of factors: the meeting's purpose, the user-friendliness of the technology, and the participants' comfort with communicating through the system. To what extent do electronic meeting systems reproduce the atmosphere of face-to-face meetings, discussed earlier in this chapter? Do these electronic systems replicate the experience of live meetings? Does the teleconferencing encounter supersede a real-life one?

Face-to-face communication is considered a "rich" communication medium because it transmits a broad range of visual and verbal cues. Computer-mediated communication is termed a "lean" communication medium because the cues are limited to printed text. With audioconferencing, listeners can pick up many cues from word choice, tone of voice, emphasis given to words and phrases, and volume. For its part, videoconferencing offers both visual and verbal signals because you both see and hear the speaker. But it too does not completely replicate a face-to-face encounter because the range of the videocamera may limit the visual signals that we would pick up in a live situation. Videoconferencing also cannot completely transmit the "social presence" of the participants, that is, the feeling of their actual presence.[19] With videoconferencing, we communicate with people at a remove from real life. Some might feel there is an element of artificiality because the experience is not "live."

Experience has proven the value of teleconferencing systems as well as their shortcomings. Some employees see computer-mediated systems as a way of equalizing participation in meetings because these systems offer anonymity and the means to express one's ideas freely, without interruption.[20] Group-decision support systems provide tools for problem analysis that help produce effective decisions. And in one study, respondents expressed their preference for computer-mediated meetings because they felt more comfortable with written communication than with oral communication. For many people, groupware is a very satisfying method of electronic groupwork.[21]

Nonetheless, some people may feel dissatisfaction because they cannot contribute vocally during computer-mediated meetings.[22] And it's been shown that such meeting systems are not as useful for solving complex problems as face-to-face meetings.[23] With audioconferencing, it's been found that combining this technology with permitting individuals to view presentations and documents on their computer screens while participating in the meeting, improves communication during an audioconference.[24]

Videoconferencing is useful for many activities, such as sharing and reviewing information, developing proposals, and planning projects. But for intercultural communication, for example, videoconferencing has its limits. Fares Salloum, senior vice-president, International Operations, GTE Service Corporation, says that to build successful partnerships in Pacific Rim countries, "You need relationships with the people you are doing business with. And you need to understand the environment you are working in …. The real connection must be made face to face."[25] For global business teams, face-to-face meetings are important for establishing trust; after an interpersonal basis is formed, teleconferencing is an effective method for continuing tasks.[26] In the words of Kenneth Chapman, a Toronto-based account executive for a Winnipeg printing firm, "Sometimes you just can't beat human contact."[27]

Chapter Summary

This chapter covered groupwork in the business environment. Collaborative effort is the modern way for Canadian organizations to share information, plan projects, solve problems, and make decisions. But, as with business presentations, working within a structure helps to create clearer and more effective communication, and better outcomes. For traditional, face-to-face meetings, the meeting leader, meeting recorder, agenda, and minutes give order to the task at hand. With developments in technology, teleconferencing offers exciting choices for collaborative work, but the efficiencies of costs and time must be weighed against the suitability of the technology for the job.

Collaborative work requires commitment to the purpose and the process. It also demands good "people skills"—the ability to listen, to interact in an appropriate manner, and to understand your co-workers. In the next chapter, we'll look at interpersonal communication, another requirement for success in the business environment.

Applications

1.   What are the "dangers" of groupwork? The benefits?

2.   Recall meetings you have attended, either at work or at school. Were they effective or ineffective? Did the group achieve its goals? How would you have liked them to be different?

3.   Form a group with two or three people and define the following problems:

     a.   how to improve customer service at a local retail store

     b.   how to improve advertisement of a product or service of your choice

     c.   how to persuade your co-workers or fellow students to volunteer some time each week at a local agency for the elderly

4.   In a brainstorming session, generate ideas for solving the above problems. Were your definitions thorough? Did you look at the various dimensions of the problems?

5.   What are the advantages and the disadvantages of the different types of brainstorming techniques described in this chapter?

6.   What are the advantages of telemeetings over face-to-face meetings? What are the disadvantages?

References

1. Carol M. Stephenson, "The New Art of Leadership" (delivered to the London Business Hall of Fame, Junior Achievement Awards, London, Ontario, October 17, 1997). [www.stentor.ca/bottom.cfm?page_id=exsp17.html], April 13, 1998.

2. Patricia Booth, *Challenge and Change: Embracing the Team Concept*, The Conference Board of Canada, Report 123-94 (Ottawa, Ontario, 1994), 6.

3. Carol M. Stephenson, "Learning for Life" (delivered to the PLAR Symposium, Montreal, Quebec, October 6, 1997). [www.stentor.ca/bottom.cfm?page_id=exsp18.html], April 13, 1998.

4. Richard L. George, "Sharing Common Ground—The Business of Education and the Education of Business" (delivered at Mount Royal College, President's Breakfast, Calgary, Alberta, September 16, 1997). [www.suncor.com/05speeches/sp0997.html], April 29, 1998.

5. Stephenson, "Learning for Life."

6. Noranda 1996 Annual Report, 23.

7. Noranda 1996 Annual Report, 23.

8. Stephenson, "Learning for Life."

9. Caroline Byrne, "We've Got to Start Meeting Like This," *Globe and Mail*, May 5, 1997, B8.

10. Ibid.

11. For a concise discussion of the problem-solving process, see Michael Osborn and Suzanne Osborn, *Public Speaking*, 3rd ed. (Boston: Houghton Mifflin, 1997), A4–A10. For a fuller discussion, see Gay Lumsden and Donald Lumsden, *Communicating in Groups and Teams: Sharing Leadership*, 2nd ed. (Belmont, California: Wadsworth, 1997), 214–237.

12. Lumsden and Lumsden, *Communicating in Groups and Teams*, 205.

13. See Milam Aiken, et al., "The Use of Two Electronic Idea Generation Techniques in Strategy Planning Meetings," *Journal of Business Communication* 34, no. 4 (October 1997), 370–382.

14. See Gail Kay, "Effective Meetings through Electronic Brainstorming," *Management Quarterly* 35, no. 4 (1994), 15–26.

15. See Mary Munter, "Meeting Technology: From Low-Tech to High Tech," *Business Communication Quarterly* 61, no. 2 (June 1998), 80–87; Bharat A. Jain and Douglas N. Ross, "Assessing the Impact of Integrated Group Support Systems on the Performance of Teams," *American Business Review* 16, no. 1 (January 1998), [proquest.umi.com], June 29, 1998; Simon S.K. Lam, "The Effects of Group Decision Support Systems and Task Structures on Group Communication and Decision Quality," *Journal of Management Information Systems* 13, no. 4 (Spring 1997), [proquest.umi.com], June 29, 1998; and Susan Rebstock Williams and Rick L. Wilson, "Group Support Systems, Power, and Influence in an Organization: A Field Study," *Decision Sciences* 28, no. 4 (Fall 1997), [proquest.umi.com], June 29, 1998.

16. See Lam, "Effects of Group Decision Support Systems," 7.

17. Paul Hart, Lynne Svenning, and John Ruchinskas, "From Face-to-Face Meeting to Video Teleconferencing: Potential Shifts in the Meeting Genre," *Management Communication Quarterly* 8, no. 4 (May 1995), 397, 401–402.

18. See Paul Hart, et al., "From Face-to-Face Meeting to Video Teleconferencing," 403–404; and Charlene Marmer Solomon, "Global Teams: The Ultimate Collaboration," *Personnel Journal* 74, no. 9 (September 1995), 6, [proquest.umi.com], April 29, 1998.

19. See Laku Chidambaram and Beth Jones, "Impact of Communication Medium and Computer Support on Group Perceptions and Performance: A Comparison of Face-to-Face and Dispersed Meetings," *MIS Quarterly* 17, no. 4 (1993), 465–491.

20. See Williams and Wilson, "Group Support Systems," 14–15.

21. See Kay, "Effective Meetings through Electronic Brainstorming," 15–25; Williams and Wilson, "Group Support Systems, Power, and Influence," 14–15; and Jain and Ross, "Assessing the Impact," 6.

22. Chidambaram and Jones, "Impact of Communication Medium," 477.

23. Jain and Ross, "Assessing the Impact," 7.

24. Chidambaram and Jones, "Impact of Communication Medium and Computer Support," 479–480.

25. Fares F. Salloum, "Getting Connected in the 'Pacific Century'" (delivered to the University of British Columbia Bridging the Pacific Conference '97, Vancouver, B.C., January 24, 1997). [www.bctel.com/library/pacific.html], September 4, 1997.

26. Solomon, "Global Teams: The Ultimate Collaboration," 6.

27. Kenneth Chapman, e-mail to author, June 17, 1998.

Interpersonal Communication on the Job: Listening, Interviewing, and Dealing with Disagreement

Interpersonal communication—or speaking one-to-one—what we do every day as an employee, manager, or entrepreneur. Does it require forethought or preparation, as business presentations and meetings do? Is it acceptable to speak and behave at work as we do at home? I'm sure you agree there is a difference between our private conduct and our business conduct. At home, or when we are socializing with friends, most of us are freer with our language, our tone of voice, and our gestures. At work, we are more conscious of what we say and how we say it. In other words, on the job we practise certain ways of speaking and acting so that we get along with our colleagues and sustain a productive and satisfying work environment. James Meek, senior vice-president and country head of Scotiabank's Peru office, says, "more and more [business] success comes mostly because of an organization's people and how well they work together. People are the only real competitive advantage."[1]

As we saw in Chapter 1, employers seek workers with effective interpersonal communication skills, or, to use Meek's term, "social intelligence." Employers value these skills because a business prospers when its people know how to create a professional atmosphere, both within and without; that is, among employees, and with suppliers, clients, or customers. As two of our topics, I've selected interviewing for information and dealing with disagreement. But first, we'll examine the most important and basic of interpersonal skills, listening.

Listening

In a speech titled "The Importance of Communication When Changing Corporate Culture," Paul Tellier of Canadian National Railway says, "Listening—not talking—is the first step of communication."[2] Suncor's Rick George notes, "If you want positive change to happen you have to involve people, and listen to their concerns, and, most importantly, listen to their ideas."[3]

Effective listening contributed to Carol Stephenson's success as a plant manager at a Toronto phone switching centre early in her career. She was the first female to hold this position, supervising 60 men, most of them engineers or technicians. Her boss told her it was "no job for a woman." But by "carefully listening," she learned " ... their real beef ... was that they had always been over-managed. They knew their job well, and resented the succession of managers who tried to impose the obvious on them." Her solution was to let them work independently as long as they maintained their high performance levels; she became the "resource person ... [to] be there to respond to their needs and requests." Stephenson says the outcome was a "win-win" situation; because she listened to their concerns, she understood their abilities and frustrations and had the confidence to give them a high degree of autonomy.[4]

These are the words and experiences of three of Canada's business leaders, but the need for effective listening is not reserved for company executives communicating with their employees. As we saw in the last chapter, the teamwork culture of the Canadian workplace means that more employees have management responsibilities: as team members, they plan tasks, solve problems, and make decisions. They also teach and learn from each other. Listening is one skill that helps teams work effectively as a unit and makes individuals feel valued and respected.

The Two Types of Listening

Let's eavesdrop on the following conversation between one of our fictional characters, Mahima, and her supervisor—we'll call him Jim.

Mahima:	[*Knocks on Jim's door, although it is open*] Jim, I'd like to speak to you for a couple of minutes.
Jim:	[*Keeps his eyes focused on his computer screen*] Sure, Mahima, sit down. [*Jim gestures to a chair across his desk*]
Mahima:	Jim, you remember that program we're designing for the marketing department. I'm trying to find out exactly what they want, and I'm having a bit of trouble pinpointing their needs.

Jim:	[*Looking at some papers on his desk*] Oh, yeah ...
Mahima:	They can't seem to define their scope, and they aren't exact about what they plan to do with the program. Perhaps if you can give me some pointers based on your past experience, I can help them find out what their needs are.
Jim:	[*Checking his watch*] Well, if they know what they want ...
Mahima:	[*Raises her eyebrows*] Um, Jim, I said they are having a hard time deciding that. What strategies can you suggest for me? Should we all have another meeting?
	[*Computer beeps, signalling e-mail message*]
Jim:	[*Looking at his computer screen*] Well, Mahima, can we discuss this later?

Obviously, Mahima did not get the help she expected, and, we can imagine, left his office feeling frustrated. How can this interaction be improved?

Social Listening: Creating a Receptive Environment

Listening is both a social and an analytical activity. When employees come to talk with a peer or supervisor, they come with specific expectations: that the listener will make the speaker feel welcome, encourage communication, and appraise the message fairly.

You may consider it odd that you need to prepare to listen to a co-worker, since we think of listening as an everyday, routine activity. But just as you develop a plan and an attitude for a presentation or meeting, so you should work on a receptive manner and mindset for listening, whether it's to answer a brief question or to deal with a larger concern. Effective listeners follow certain guidelines.

Delay the session if you are busy.   The first rule of good listening is to make sure you have the time. As the scenario shows, Jim was probably feeling pressured with work when Mahima knocked on his door. In his predicament, it was probably instinctive to put his needs ahead of hers. To help Mahima, Jim should have realized he couldn't give her his undivided attention, and postponed the meeting. He could have said, "Mahima, I'm sorry, but I've got a deadline to meet. Let's set up a time tomorrow morning, if possible. We can talk freely then." Such a comment would justify the delay and maintain a good working relationship with her. Remember, it is better to concentrate on the speaker entirely than to be distracted from the conversation. The problem won't be solved if your attention is diverted, and the negative impression you make will last for some time.

Welcome your colleagues.   When co-workers come to speak with you, let them know you are eager to listen to them. We saw Jim acknowledge Mahima's desire to consult with him. Sometimes, however, you should go a little further. If Jim sensed that she seemed nervous, he could have said, "Hello, Mahima, it's good to see you. Sit down. What do you want me to help you with?" Showing your willingness to listen encourages your colleagues to describe their concerns thoroughly.

Avoid distractions.   The foundation of effective listening is to focus completely on the speaker. By setting aside your work, you show you want to listen. Avoid looking at your e-mail and reports on your desk. If your phone rings, tell callers you'll contact them later. If the conversation demands it, use voice mail to answer your calls for the time being.

Maintain silence.   Don't interrupt the speaker. We often pause as we speak in order to gather our thoughts. These pauses do not mean we have finished what we want to say. If your co-worker stops speaking, wait before you talk.

Ensure the speaker is the centre of attention.   You may know people who make themselves the focus of a conversation, although it is you who have come to them with a concern. Don't be tempted to switch the spotlight onto yourself, by using the occasion to express your own ideas or problems. Your role is to listen, to receive information, and to help the speaker.

Make eye contact.   Looking at your audience is an essential element for establishing rapport during your business presentations; when listening, eye contact is vital both for connecting with the speaker and for absorbing the fullest meaning of the message. Eye contact tells your colleagues you are giving them your undivided attention. It might also help them relax and talk more openly, because they will feel you recognize the importance of their concerns.

Give a feeling of closure to the encounter.   When you finish talking with your co-workers, be sure to ask if you have answered their questions. Paraphrase their concerns and your responses, thank them for seeing you, and offer to be available for follow-up. Jim might say, "O.K., Mahima, as I see it, the marketing team probably hasn't really thought through their needs. Why don't you walk them through a possible program to give them a framework, and I'll speak to their director. Contact me early next week, and we'll take it from there. Thanks for filling me in."

Active Listening: Analyzing the Message

Listening is not just hearing the message, but making the effort to understand the speaker as fully as possible. James Meek says, "successful communicators ... listen to what people are saying—or more precisely—communicating."[5] That is, as a listener, you have to be sensitive to both the words and the nonverbal messages.

Ask questions.   If you are confused about something the speaker has said, ask for clarification. Your accurate understanding of the speaker's concerns are crucial for providing an appropriate solution. So at suitable breaks in the conversation, review any statements that puzzle you.

Take notes.   You cannot rely completely on your memory. Jot down the important ideas and facts.

Listen objectively.   Set your biases aside. If a speaker refers critically to a co-worker or uses disrespectful language, don't let such comments interfere with your effort to understand the issues.

Paraphrase the speaker's remarks.   From time to time restate, in your own words, what your co-worker has said to ensure that your understanding is accurate. Signal that you are summarizing remarks by saying, for example, "Now, if I understand you correctly …" or "I'd just like to see if I'm on track here." If you are listening to someone whose fluency in English is limited, try to restate the comments using simple vocabulary.

Use responsive comments and gestures.   To show your colleague you are listening, say "I see" or "yes, continue," from time to time. Many people naturally lean forward a bit and nod their heads to demonstrate attentiveness. Such remarks and gestures prod the speaker to talk. If you have ever spoken to people who don't signal that they are listening, you may remember that the experience is disquieting. Listeners like these appear highly judgmental—or tuned out.

Observe the speaker's mannerisms and tone of voice.   Speaking is only one element of communicating. Our "body language"—the way we gesture, our facial expressions—can reveal a good deal about our thoughts. For example, note that in the scenario Mahima raised her eyebrows when Jim misconstrued her problem; her expression probably signalled her exasperation. However, don't overdo interpreting mannerisms. Do people who keep their arms crossed in front of them show obstinacy or defensiveness—or is it a manner they assume when they are forming their thoughts? Tone of voice and speaking pace may reveal excitement or comfort, but are people who speak quickly always nervous? Try to take a "whole" view of your co-workers and see their mannerisms as part of their entire way of communicating, but avoid stereotyping body language.

Listen to the words, not the manner of speech.   Often we speak with people who have an accent, or have trouble using vocabulary precisely, or who speak ungrammatically. Look beyond accents and errors in usage to understand the message. As I said above, rephrasing the speaker's remarks in simple English will help the two of you to develop mutual understanding and trust.

Analyze vocabulary.   In Chapter 3 I discussed the denotation and the connotation of words, the denotation being the dictionary meanings, and the connotation the associations we have with them. Sometimes, in business as well as socially, we express what we really mean indirectly. For example, if we want to imply that a problem is extremely difficult to solve, we may say that the problem is a "challenge." To one person, hearing the word "challenge" might suggest that the problem will demand hard work, but that it can be solved. To another, the word "challenge" may mean that the problem cannot be solved at all. Mahima says to Jim that she's having "a bit of trouble" understanding the needs of the marketing group she is supposed to help. Mahima's phrase "a bit of trouble" may really mean that this team is giving her major problems! A good listener is sensitive to nuances of meaning, and to the distinctive way certain people may use language.

Serious listening is a hard job. There is much to judge and evaluate. A sensitive listener, however, is rewarded with trust, a key ingredient for a productive work environment.

Informational Interviewing

Whether you hold a management or a "front-line" position, one important interpersonal activity is interviewing. I want to focus on a common type: the information-gathering interview. I mean by this term an extended discussion such as the kind a financial manager might conduct to learn about the needs and attitudes of new clients. Applying a strategy for informational interviews and knowing the different ways to phrase questions will help you with this task.

Targeting Questions

As I've said throughout the book, preparation is key in any business interaction. When setting up an interview you should decide on the two or three general areas for discussion and develop questions for them. You may not be able to cover everything in a single session. You don't have to follow your script in the meeting if the answers inspire a line of questioning that you didn't predict, but it's important to enter the interview with a structure.

Arranging the Meeting: Some Practical Considerations

For informational interviewing, the scheduling and the venue are important initial considerations. Lyndon, our fictional consultant, needs information from his clients about the product they wish to sell in Canada for his marketing study. Mahima, our computer specialist, needs information from the marketing group in her company in order to design a computer program that meets their needs. Both Lyndon and Mahima will contact the people they must question to arrange the time and venue of the meeting. As a consultant, Lyndon would probably visit his clients at their business or home. As an in-house specialist, Mahima would arrange a meeting with the marketing team in their offices or in a boardroom, where a whiteboard will permit Mahima to diagram their requirements. Noting their remarks publicly will clarify them for herself as well as for the team. In other words, when deciding where to interview your sources, choose the spot that is best for them to answer your questions. This is where they will be most comfortable and will have access to the data and people they might need to consult in the course of the discussion.

If you are holding an interview in your office, decide on the seating arrangements. If your respondents sit across from you at your desk, the discussion will feel more formal, and might influence its flow. If you sit facing each other without a barrier in between, the meeting will probably seem more casual and spontaneous.

It's important to arrange the length of the interview when setting it up. An interview that is too long—perhaps more than one hour—may tire both you and your respondents, possibly resulting in incomplete answers to your questions as the interview progresses. You should also do your best to ensure that the venue is quiet and free of interruptions, so that you can carry on your work efficiently.

Another consideration is recording the information. Usually taking notes on a notebook computer or by hand is sufficient. You can enlist a scribe, as you might in a meeting. If the occasion requires it, ask your respondents if they feel comfortable having the conversation tape-recorded; often, people forget they are being recorded when they become involved in answering your questions. An audio record will provide an accurate transcript of the meeting. But don't rely completely on electronics. Have paper and pen handy to track the conversation and to note answers you wish to pursue more thoroughly.

Introducing the Interview

Although your respondents know why you need to gather information from them, it's still important to begin with some introductory remarks about the interview. Your comments will help place your interviewees at ease and will help them focus on the meeting.

When introducing the interview, review the purpose of the meeting. Preview what information you wish to obtain, and why you need it. For example, Lyndon might tell his clients that their meeting will help him understand their product, their perceptions of its competition, and their financial situation for marketing it. Mahima might tell her respondents that she needs to learn what they hope her computer program will do and about their experience with specific kinds of software.

You can also tell your listeners the approximate number of questions you will ask, so that they have a sense of the extent of the interview. The more information they have about structural matters, the more they will relax and focus on helping you.

Concluding the Interview

Concluding the interview effectively is as important as introducing it. Never end the interview abruptly; review the significant facts, thank your respondents for their help, and mention that you will follow up with more questions, if necessary. In some situations, you may want to send your respondents a memo summarizing the information you obtained so that they can check it for accuracy or make additions.

If the amount of time for the interview was inadequate, schedule another meeting to continue the discussion. And always remember to thank your respondents for their help.

Types of Questions

The success of an information-gathering interview is based not only on cordial relations, but also on knowing how to phrase your questions so that you receive the information you are seeking. Different kinds of questions elicit different kinds of responses.

Your information-gathering tasks will require you to speak to people with different levels of knowledge regarding the subject matter. Orient your questions toward the expertise of your respondents. When interviewing clients for information, financial and technical professionals, for example, should avoid using acronyms and jargon. They should take the time to explain any technical terms their respondents may not understand.

Some of your questions may need to be prefaced by explanations if you are speaking with a layperson. On the other hand, if you are gathering information from people who have more specialized knowledge than you, don't pretend you understand everything they say. Be honest and ask the respondent to explain technical terms and jargon that are unclear.

Open Questions

An open question seeks general information. For example, Lyndon might say to his clients, "Tell me about this product you want to sell in Canada." The answer will give Lyndon both an idea of the product and of his clients' perception of it, that is, what they see as its distinctive features and the order of their importance. An open question also gives the interviewer a base for asking more detailed questions. For example, if when discussing the qualities of their product, his clients say that it is "user friendly," Lyndon might pick up on that term in a succeeding question, and ask, "What do you mean by the product being 'user friendly'?" Open questions also allow the interviewer to "size up" respondents, that is, to evaluate their ability to communicate and to think logically, and their priorities.

As for Mahima, who will design a computer program for the marketing team, she might ask the following open question early in their meeting: "What do you want the program to do?" The answer to this question would tell Mahima whether or not her respondents have a clear understanding of their own needs. If they don't, Mahima will need to work on helping them determine what it is they want.

Open questions are very useful as the first questions in an interview, not only because they are a basis for other, more detailed questions, but also because they encourage respondents to open up to the interviewer.

Closed Questions

Closed questions seek specific information. Lyndon's question about the "user-friendliness" of his clients' product is a closed question because it focuses on a particular quality. Another closed question Lyndon might ask is, "What other products currently on the market in Canada are similar to yours?" Here Lyndon will learn if his clients are familiar with the Canadian market segment in which they intend to compete.

Mahima will also use closed questions when interviewing her respondents. Perhaps she will want to know what databases they work with or if team members have any programming experience. Answers to these concerns would help her determine the sophistication of the computer program she will design for them.

One type of closed question is that which seeks a "yes" or "no" answer, and little else. For example, Lyndon might ask his clients, "Will you raise money from family for manufacturing your product?" The answer to this question is either "yes" or "no," though his clients might elaborate on the viability of this financial source. Avoid such questions if you want the speaker to reflect at some length and to give a full response. Another way Lyndon might phrase this question is, "How will you raise the money to manufacture the product?" This form of the question will prompt his clients to give a more elaborate answer than the closed version.

Leading Questions

Leading questions direct the respondent, either intentionally or unintentionally, to a desired answer. For example, if Lyndon said to his clients, "Don't you think it's unrealistic to ask your family to loan you so much money for manufacturing your product?" he is suggesting that they should answer yes, it is unrealistic. Leading questions may influence the respondents to answer in ways they wouldn't if the questions were impartial. Your information consequently would not accurately reflect the beliefs and opinions of your respondents, and the integrity of your data would be impaired.

Ancillary Questions

Ancillary questions continue a line of questioning you have established. They permit you to probe deeper into your respondent's knowledge, attitudes, or feelings about the matter under discussion. Use ancillary questions when you want respondents to elaborate or clarify. For example, when Lyndon followed his open question about his clients' information with a focused, or closed, question about its "user-friendliness," he was also using an ancillary question, because it picked up on vagueness in the previous question. Lyndon can continue his line of questioning about the product's ease of use depending upon the answers he receives. If his clients mention the product's dimensions as being one factor, but don't mention the specific size, Lyndon can probe for concrete information: "You say the dimensions help to make the product easy to handle. Tell me, what are the specifications?"

Let's imagine the marketing team tells Mahima they have been "unhappy" with a previous computer program that was intended to help them analyze a product's sales. She would ask them what they mean by the term "unhappy" so that she can understand, in concrete terms, what they mean. For example, she would inquire if the program worked slowly, or if it was complicated, or if its functions were limited.

When using ancillary questions, be sure to keep your respondent on track. Repeat the key words in the question. For example, Mahima might say, "I understand your dissatisfaction with the limitations of the current program's problems with analyzing sales by district. But I'd like you to clarify this problem by giving me a specific example with one product."

Nonverbal and Vocal Cues in Informational Interviews

Don't forget that, as an interviewer, you are not only recording your respondents' answers but observing their mannerisms and vocal emphasis. If you sense through nervous gestures that respondents aren't as forthcoming as they might be, probe further. Don't highlight any awkwardness in their behaviour, however; be tactful. Perhaps Lyndon's clients aren't making direct eye contact with him when answering a question. Lyndon might say to his clients, "Is there anything else you might want to tell me about the possible shortcomings of your product?" if he senses they are uncomfortable about one of its features. A strident or high-pitched voice might signal defensiveness. Tactfully pursue the line of questioning to satisfy yourself that your respondents are giving you honest answers.

Mahima might note that her respondents feel insecure about their inability to use a computer database to its full potential. She might say, "I know it's sometimes difficult to learn all the features of a software product. Would you like to tell me about any problems you've encountered in learning this one?" Your diplomacy will encourage candid answers to your questions.

Dealing with Disagreement

Tact and understanding—these are two qualities required of employees at all levels to foster a collegial environment. But sometimes it's difficult to sustain such an atmosphere because of disagreement, be it over policies, procedures, plans, or people. Disagreement and conflict are common in business. As mentioned in Chapter 8, they can be highly beneficial because they thwart groupthink and can stimulate new directions of thought. If poorly managed, contention can create poor morale and weaken a company's performance. In this last section we'll explore ways to manage disagreement in the workplace.

Conflict at Work

I'm sure if you examine your place of employment you will quickly notice interpersonal problems. A management style, for example, might be insulting to workers; you recall Carol Stephenson's story, told early in this chapter, of the engineers and technicians who resented being overmanaged. For his part, Peter Spelliscy, senior vice-president at Suncor, comments that executives who "are overly involved in the day-to-day operations of a company ... can create a very intimidating and unproductive environment."[6]

Organizational change is another cause of disagreement: downsizing and restructuring are obvious occasions for conflict among employees and between employees and management. In a speech about Suncor's move "from downsizing to growth," Mike O'Brien comments that people "were frustrated and unhappy." The "whole organization was in a state of fear" during the process. "People didn't know what was going to happen next."[7] Anxiety over job security and the unknown both generate conflict. So does the introduction of new technology and new procedures.

Competition is a source of conflict. Spelliscy observes that during Suncor's downturn, "operating groups did not really talk with each other. There was such a strong sense of independence that no one knew or cared what anyone else was doing, so if someone was doing well, it didn't get shared."[8] Personality is another cause. I mentioned in Chapter 8 certain types of unproductive team members: freeriders, who don't do their share of the work, and dominators, who monopolize the discussion. And there is difference of opinion—the belief by one person, or a group, that an idea, strategy, or method is wrongheaded. In her speech "The New Art of Leadership," Carol Stephenson compares managing an alliance of Canadian telephone companies "with nine CEOs with equally strong and occasionally divergent views," to the family mealtimes of her youth, with their "ferocious debates."[9]

Maintaining Interpersonal Relationships

Morale and productivity, so interrelated in the workplace, require that differences be resolved. Not always, however, can they be settled to everyone's satisfaction. Even if you disagree with a policy or a decision, for example, it's important to realize that a fact of business life is compromise. You may believe your opinion is right; your evidence may support it thoroughly, but your arguments are dismissed. You might be a minority voice; the budget may not allow for your idea to be implemented; a superior, with the power to make the final decision, may not favour your approach—these are all possible reasons. There are ways to deal with conflict and disagreement so that interpersonal work relationships remain intact.

Develop the Right Attitude

As an employee, it's necessary to be committed to your group. A professional outlook will foster trust among members.

Develop mutual respect.   One characteristic of successful global business teams is that they respect each other. In one study, a respondent said that "team members are fun and challenging, we have no politics." Another said they appreciated the input of each member, and another that being aware of each member's limitations contributed to group productivity.[10] These qualities of global teams, where intercultural differences can pose obstacles, can be incorporated into any work group.

View disagreement as an opportunity for learning.   Avoid "ownership" of your ideas; distance yourself from them. Try to see how a fellow employee thinks, and remain open to other opinions. Be adaptable and flexible; your view is not the only one. Perhaps Jim, Mahima's superior, thinks database software from company X is the best purchase for the marketing team. He has more years in the company and more practical experience with assisting the firm's computer users. Yet Mahima, through research and a close understanding of the marketers, believes company Q's product will better serve their needs. Undoubtedly Mahima will need to convince Jim of her viewpoint, but Jim must also listen to her arguments, although she is less experienced than he.

Know how to give and take criticism.   Members of productive global teams challenged each other more than those on unproductive teams. It was shown that less productive groups tended to make more approving remarks about the topic under discussion; more productive groups were more critical, and the criticisms were valued.[11]

The lesson here is that criticism of an idea of yours is not a judgment of you as an individual. Instead, you should receive constructive criticism as a professional evaluation; view it as a better, or worse, solution to a problem you and your critic want to solve together. We can use Lyndon and his clients as an example. Perhaps Lyndon feels their aspirations for their new product in Canada are unrealistic, and communicates his reservations. His clients should hear his comments as an authority's opinion, as a way to help them succeed in the Canadian market, rather than fail. If they listen with the right attitude, they will appreciate Lyndon's remarks as sound advice.

Apply Effective Leadership

Effective leadership is not unique to CEOs and managers. As a team member, you also should exhibit the qualities of effective leaders.

Communicate clearly.   Again and again, Canadian business leaders stress the need for open communication. CN's Paul Tellier, who led the railway through major organizational change, says that CEOs "must be able to meet employees without an interlocutor. A CEO must explain in language everyone should understand."[12] Tellier's advice, of course, applies to all employees, not just chief executives. We saw in Chapters 3 and 6 techniques for speaking plainly. In interpersonal communication, as in presentations, transparency is key for achieving both the understanding and respect of your listeners, even if you disagree with each other.

Communicate through the appropriate channels.   There are many ways to send messages: verbally, through e-mail, in memos and letters, and indirectly, through an intermediary. Let's say Jim, Mahima's supervisor, has disappointing news for her; perhaps he feels she is too inexperienced to lead the design project for the marketing group, and replaces her. Should he tell her in person or in a memo? Delivering bad news personally takes strength, but it also has a greater chance of earning the respect of your colleagues.

Don't be sneaky.   Other leadership qualities Tellier cites are "no hidden agendas" and "no glossing over the bad news." He says that "Employees are willing to hear the bad news—even news about forthcoming layoffs—provided it's delivered honestly and directly."[13] Your own integrity is critical for maintaining trust, the foundation of interpersonal relationships.

Listen.   We've spent several pages discussing the importance of listening skills. You know their value.

Be timely.   One cause of disagreement and conflict is delay. People who don't meet their deadlines or furnish information when promised are viewed as untrustworthy and unreliable.

Recognize achievement.   Working with people has its ups and downs. Despite disagreements, it's important also to let people know if they've done a good job or have helped you in some way. When employees receive disappointing news or feel frustrated, they also remember the praise they received. Don't be tight with it. As a good supervisor, Jim might say to Mahima, "The presentation you did on the notebook computer purchase was highly praised. They all thought it was very professional." Should she receive bad news at another time, she may also recall her achievements.

Be tactful.   How you express criticism or disagreement goes a long way toward keeping a good relationship. In some situations it's fine to say, "You're wrong," or, "That's a dumb idea." But you have to know your audience. Some people find bluntness hard to take. Try to phrase your opinion in an impartial way. For example, if Jim thinks the computer program Mahima is designing for the marketing team is inadequate, he might say, "I want you to try it this way," and give guidelines, instead of, "That's inept." Be sensitive to the feelings of your colleagues.

Part of being tactful is also being even-tempered. If personal remarks are directed at you during a disagreement, don't respond in kind. Focus on the facts, on the business problem, not on the person.

Mediate.   Carol Stephenson observes that another leadership quality is "the ability to mediate or negotiate among conflicting groups. Alliances cannot be managed by an 'old-style' leader. These relationships would fall apart if one partner began issuing orders to the others."[14] Mediation means finding common ground between differing groups. Lyndon's clients, for example, might disagree on how to sell their product in Canada.

Lyndon might have each person voice or write down his and her ideas, and then they would discuss the results. Similar ideas would be a basis for agreement. Different approaches would to be defended and discussed, with Lyndon helping his clients decide which ones could be modified or sacrificed for their objectives. Highlighting the areas where opposing parties have similarities and can agree is critical to settling conflict, as well as determining which can be conceded.

It's important to maintain good relationships at work, because our business lives will be more pleasant as well as more productive. Sometimes, however, with difficult co-workers, people who are very stubborn and unable to compromise, little can be done. In such cases, morale may suffer, and seeking intervention from a higher level might be necessary. But always remember that communicating good will and a sincere desire to understand others' opinions and viewpoints will build a good interpersonal environment.

Chapter Summary

In this chapter we covered three important interpersonal skills for business: listening, interviewing for information, and dealing with disagreement. Listening is not a passive, but an active process. Effective listeners see beyond words to the person's feelings and attitudes. Good listeners are empathic, that is, they try to see the situation from the speaker's viewpoint, to comprehend the message as fully as possible. For their part, good interviewers must listen carefully and without bias as they gather information; their attentiveness will assist the questioning process, and help them acquire the data they need for the task at hand.

The final interpersonal skill we considered is dealing with disagreement. To create a positive atmosphere at work, it is essential to accept criticism and to manage conflict with the right attitude, that is, by communicating clearly, honestly, and tactfully. The teamwork culture of the modern Canadian workplace requires that employees at all levels apply these three interpersonal skills.

Interpersonal skills are one "skill set" that employers value. They are important not only in the workplace, but also in the job interview. In the next chapter we will focus on this vital area of business communication.

Applications

1. Why is listening the most important interpersonal skill?
2. Analyze recent conversations at work, applying the ideas in this chapter about

listening. Were these conversations satisfactory? What was beneficial about them? How could they have been improved?

3. What are the differences between social listening and active listening? Why are both important?

4. Set up an information-seeking interview with a friend that deals with one of his or her areas of expertise, applying the principles described in this chapter. Be sure to use open questions and ancillary questions.

5. What are the qualities of effective leadership? Why is it important for employees at all levels to be effective leaders?

6. Why is disagreement beneficial?

References

1. James T. Meek, draft of remarks delivered to the National Student Leaders' Orientation Conference, June 4, 1996, 6. Print copy courtesy of Scotiabank.

2. Paul M. Tellier, "The Importance of Communication When Changing Corporate Culture" (delivered to the Conference Board 1998 Corporate Communication Conference, Toronto, Ontario, February 19, 1998). [www.cn.ca/english/news/speeches/confboard.html], April 21, 1998.

3. Richard L. George, "Creating a Legacy of Excellence in Communications" (delivered at the Legacy Public Relations Scholarship Gala, Calgary, Alberta, October 17, 1997). [www.suncor.com/05speeches/sp1097.html], April 29, 1998.

4. Carol M. Stephenson, "The New Art of Leadership" (delivered to the London Business Hall of Fame, Junior Achievement Awards, London, Ontario, October 17, 1997). [www.stentor.ca/scripts/bottom.cfm?page_id=exsp.17.html], April 13, 1998.

5. Meek, 8.

6. Peter Spelliscy, "Moving from Survival to Expansion—Why Changing the Culture is Essential" (delivered to the Human Resources Association of Calgary 1996 Conference and Expo, Calgary, Alberta, April 4, 1996). [www.suncor.com/05speeches/sun07spa.html], June 23, 1997.

7. Mike O'Brien, "The Next Big Challenge: Moving from Downsizing to Growth" (delivered to the Ontario Club, Toronto, Ontario, November 28, 1996). [www.suncor.com/05speeches/sun07spc.html], June 23, 1997.

8. Spelliscy, "Moving From Survival to Expansion—Why Changing the Culture is Essential."

9. Stephenson, "The New Art of Leadership."

10. Quoted in Dianne M. Hofner Saphiere, "Productive Behaviors of Global Business Teams," *International Journal of Intercultural Relations* 20, no. 2 (1996), 247.

11. Saphiere, 245.

12. Tellier, "The Importance of Communication When Changing Corporate Culture."

13. Ibid.

14. Stephenson, "The New Art of Leadership."

CHAPTER 10

Employment Interviewing: Expectations and Performance

Your employment interviews are probably your most memorable business speaking events, whether you are pursuing your first job, a move within your present place of employment, or work in a new company. For those who approach employment interviews seriously (and some don't), these opportunities are preceded by a good deal of research and preparation. Within the one to two hours (or longer) of these question-answer sessions, job candidates not only discuss their skills and their work history, but also reveal themselves as communicators and as individuals who may (or may not) fit into the company culture. As we saw in Chapter 1, companies hire people who have not only the technical expertise to do the job, but also the ability to speak and write well and to interact effectively with co-workers.

Employers, of course, take job interviewing as seriously as you do. A Royal Bank study of 13 major Canadian corporations reveals some telling facts about the expense of recruitment. One organization, a small bank, spent $3266 in 1995 in hiring costs for each new employee. Another, a large bank, spends $6 million annually on recruiting.[1] Companies often interview more than five candidates for one position, notes a survey undertaken by the American Society for Personnel Administration.[2] And filling available positions can be a lengthy process. According to the Royal Bank study, employers may spend at least three months to find entry-level people, one to six months to hire mid-level managers, and at least three to six months to fill senior positions.[3]

The employment interview is the most critical event in an organization's hiring process. It's when the employer sees the person behind the résumé, and judges the job candidate's credibility and character. During the interview itself employers have particular expectations regarding a candidate's performance and knowledge of both the job and the company. As we discuss employment interviews, we'll focus on several components: pre-interview preparation; interview formats; interview behaviour; and, interview questions.

Pre-Interview Planning

Planning is key to a successful job interview. By successful, I mean, of course, you are offered the job. But remember that every job interview is an experience through which you can develop confidence and hone your interviewing skills, even if you aren't hired. That is, you can have a satisfying interview, and still be rejected. The reasons may be clear—perhaps you did not have the special combination of skills the company is seeking, or the years of experience ideally required. When you receive the bad news, the interviewer may tell you why the company chose another candidate. On the other hand, you may never learn why, even if you are perfectly qualified and your interview performance was a winner. Perhaps one of your interviewers had a "gut feeling" you wouldn't fit into the company culture. Or an internal candidate was already marked for the position, but the department was ordered by upper management to interview other applicants. So, although you may not get the job, you may still have a good interview: that is, you answered questions fully and articulately, your interviewers tried to make you feel comfortable, and you controlled your nervousness. In other words, you passed a personal milestone by meeting, or surpassing, your own standards for effective job interviews.

As you read through the following strategy for interview preparation, compare it to your own approach.

Step One: Self-Analysis

Let's suppose Mahima entered university straight from secondary school, and graduated with a degree in computer science. During her education she participated in clubs, helped to organize events, and played on her secondary school and university badminton teams. She worked part time at a local doughnut shop and was a camp counsellor in the summer. She also taught herself several programming languages and how to design her own Internet home page. She currently works as a technical specialist for her employer, a pharmaceutical firm, but would like to move into a different position. Her company has an opening in quality assurance in its information systems department.

For his part, Andrew, a bank's customer service representative, spent several years travelling and working at various jobs after secondary school, being undecided about his career goals. During this time he spent a year in college studying for a certificate in justice studies, thinking of becoming a police officer, but didn't complete his degree. He did become a Big Brother volunteer, and while working as a teller in a bank, took advantage of his company's educational support program to start a part-time university degree in accounting, which he completed. Sparked by an interest in finance, he then enrolled in a securities course to become certified to sell mutual funds for his bank. Like Mahima, he, too, hopes to move on in his career. He is looking for a customer service position with a mutual fund company.

I've developed these case histories for Mahima and Andrew to illustrate how to make an inventory of your experience and skills as a basis for your job search. Notice that I included education, employment, and volunteer experience, as well as personal interests in these stories. You see that Mahima followed a straight path from school to career, while Andrew didn't. Now, get out several sheets of paper, and make notes about your own history while we consider Mahima's and Andrew's. You will undoubtedly use some of your information in an employment interview.

Organizing Your Personal Analysis

As with most activities, approaching the task in a structured fashion helps to focus your thinking and saves a lot of unnecessary work. On separate pages write down the following headings: "education," "work experience," "computer skills," "unpaid experience," and, finally, "general work-related skills." The work-related skills are the most important area, so be sure to give them a lot of thought.

Always write your analysis; don't simply keep your thoughts in your head. For one thing, a written analysis forms a good basis for your résumé. For another, as you write, you will think of more details; the act of writing helps you remember.

Compiling Your Inventory

Now, begin your personal inventory. You should eventually transfer your notes from paper to a computer file so that you can update them easily, but keep a print version handy for quick reference as you prepare for job interviews.

Education.   Providing your educational experience is straightforward. List your secondary and post-secondary education, including accreditation courses. Don't limit yourself to your major program of study; include computer, liberal arts, and communication courses, written and oral. Andrew, for example, would include his year at college and his securities course as well as his university education. Also, list any awards or formal recognition you received.

Work experience.   Your work experience is another straightforward category. Subdivide it between part-time and full-time work to keep the list organized. Go back to your first job, and record all position titles and duties, as well as any special accomplishments, such as projects that improved profits or productivity. Let's say that Mahima attracted more customers to the doughnut shop where she worked by urging sponsorship of a junior hockey team. Try to be thorough.

Computer skills.   Computer skills are demanded almost everywhere. Suncor's president, Rick George, notes that at their Sarnia, Ontario refinery, "thanks to a company computer purchase and training program we have close to 100 per cent computer literacy. I think that's phenomenal, especially when you consider that a refinery is considered to be a blue collar workplace."[4] Write down the computer software with which you've worked, the hardware you've used, your experience with the Internet and e-mail, and any knowledge you've gained on your own. Mahima wrote that she used Java script to create her homepage.

Unpaid experience.   Perhaps you've done volunteer work, or belong to a club or social organization where you learned new skills, or applied current ones. Don't neglect this informal area of experience. It is as valuable as your paid experience to help you develop a thorough profile of your work history and knowledge. Mahima was involved in sports and clubs, and Andrew is a Big Brother; what skills do these activities suggest to you?

General work-related skills.   Work-related skills cover a broad field: competence in written, oral, and interpersonal communication; supervisory, teamwork, and meeting skills; organizational and time-management skills. These are the abilities that demonstrate you are capable of translating ideas into actions, participating in group projects, and working independently as well as guiding others. For many candidates, these are the qualities that win the job. Undoubtedly, the technical expertise must be present, but often employers are very willing to train new employees further if they demonstrate that they can work effectively with others as well as on their own.

Analyzing Your Inventory

Because general work-related skills are so critical, I want to focus on them here. Think carefully about your inventory to determine the extent of your work-related skills. Even if your formal work history is limited, you probably developed these skills informally, through unpaid experience. We can look at Mahima and Andrew to see how school and volunteer experience as well as recreational interests helped to form their competencies.

Mahima's education and experience show her skills. Her involvement in school athletics suggests that she can work effectively in a team environment, collaborating with others in order to reach a specific goal. Her ability to juggle part-time work and studies reveals her time-management skills. The fact that she was a camp counsellor suggests her ability to communicate interpersonally and to supervise others. Her self-taught computer skills reveal that she is highly motivated and disciplined, has initiative, and can work independently.

Andrew demonstrates similar competence to Mahima's. Although he took a nontraditional route to a career, spending time travelling and holding a series of short-term jobs, he demonstrates interpersonal and supervisory skills. His Big Brother activities are one example. He also shows time-management and organizational ability, having combined work and school successfully. His enrolment in a securities course suggests motivation and self-discipline—qualities that employers prize.

So when you examine your own background, don't neglect unpaid experience, school activities, or volunteer work. The ability to coordinate work and school, the development of self-taught skills, and participation in recreational activities signal to employers competence that can be transferred smoothly to the workplace.

Step Two: Document Preparation

After completing your skills inventory you should revise your résumé and work on other documentation needed for your job search. The inventory is your main source for updating your current résumé or creating a new one. Even if you already have a completed résumé, it's a good idea to consult books on résumé preparation. If you are a student, your school's career resource centre will have plenty of material. Look at electronic resources also: **www.careermosaic.com** and **www.workinfonet.com** are comprehensive career-related Web sites, and both the Royal Bank and the Canadian Imperial Bank of Commerce offer advice on résumés and cover letters in their sites (**www.royalbank.com** and **www.cibc.ca**). You should always check the Web site or contact the human resources department of any company to which you are applying to see if they prefer a particular résumé style.

Other documents to prepare include the cover letter, list of references, and samples of your work, created either in school or privately: these might include training manuals, Web pages, business plans, and reports. Be sure you take extra copies of your résumé and references to your job interview; you may need to consult them in the course of the conversation. Place work you might show your interviewers neatly in a folder or portfolio—good organization will broadcast your professionalism.

Step Three: Company Research

A favourite interview question is, "What do you know about the company?" A concrete answer always impresses the interviewer. Consider the following ways to learn about a company's vision, operations, employees, and culture.

1. **Career fairs.** Whether they are held at a school or convention centre, career fairs are an excellent opportunity for meeting a variety of employers in a specific industry. You will not only be able to pick up brochures, but also speak to company representatives. Talking with them in this congenial environment will help you develop your poise and self-confidence for interviews.

2. **Business directories.** Check out such references as the *Blue Book of Canadian Business*, *Dun and Bradstreet Key Business Directory*, and *The Globe and Mail Report on Business: Canada Company Handbook* at your local library.

3. **Periodical databases.** Up-to-date company information can be gathered through research in newspapers and magazines. Many public libraries have CD-ROM databases, such as *Canadian News Disc* and *Canadian Business and Current Affairs*. If you don't know how to execute a search, ask the librarian.

4. **Company documents.** To get a sense of a potential employer, call or e-mail the company to request information. For publicly-held organizations, or other organizations that produce them, you may obtain quarterly and annual reports. A careful reading of the annual report will reveal much about recent trends and developments, management's attitude toward its employees, community service programs, and the balance sheet.

5. **Company Web sites.** More and more companies are realizing the power of the Internet to promote themselves and to reach prospective employees. (At the Royal Bank Web site, you can take a quiz to help you target a suitable career with them; see **www.royalbank.com/english/hr/resources/quiz.html**.) If you don't have access to the Internet via a home computer, try the public library; many have terminals hooked up to an Internet service provider. You can use a search engine, such as **www.yahoo.ca**, to find a company site, or you can simply try typing in the company name, such as **www.suncor.ca**, and see what happens. A company Web site may include the latest news releases that announce product developments, appointments, and earnings.

Step Four: Interview Rehearsal

After you've gathered your information and documents for an interview, stage some mock interviews with the help of friends or family members. To help you visualize the experience, borrow videos on job interviews from public libraries or Human Resources Centre Canada. If you are a student, your school's career counsellors may offer practice interviews as part of their service. You can also try a virtual interview on the Internet: see **www.aboutwork.com/ace/virtual.html**. This chapter will later review the types of questions interviewers often ask.

To have a meaningful rehearsal, try the following.

1. **Set the stage for a mock interview.** Try to replicate the interview setting in order to give the rehearsal a sense of formality. Some interviews are held in a somewhat casual manner, with the job candidate sitting on a couch facing the interviewers across a coffee table or empty space. Other interviews, particularly panel interviews, take place in a boardroom or in an office with the interviewer at his or her desk. However you approach an interview rehearsal, pay attention to the setting, because it will affect your attitude toward the experience.

2. **Predict questions your interviewer will ask, but allow for spontaneity.** After completing this chapter, you will have a fairly good idea of the questions you might

be asked in a job interview. For your practice interview give your interviewer a list of questions. But also let your interviewer surprise you. In real interviews you may be asked unusual questions that the interviewer expects you to take seriously. The president of a market research firm likes to ask job candidates, "If you were a car, what kind would you be, and why?"[5]

3. **Dress and behave as you would at an interview.** It's tempting to wear casual clothes to practice interviews, but dressing as you would for a real one will heighten your sensitivity to the actual event. If you don't want to don your best outfit, that's understandable, but do dress appropriately. In your practice sessions be sure to follow the guidelines for appropriate interview behaviour; employers are as aware of your manners as your answers to their questions.

4. **Do a post-rehearsal analysis.** When the interview is completed, ask your interviewers to criticize your behaviour and responses. How was your handshake and eye contact? How was your posture? Did you answer the questions, or did you digress? Were your responses clear? A post mortem is essential to help you perform at your best. You might want to videotape your rehearsals, or appoint a silent observer to give you feedback afterward.

Interview Formats

You've submitted your résumé and cover letter, and received a phone call inviting you to an interview. You've researched the company, and undergone a couple of practice interviews to polish your performance. What kind of interview might you expect?

Depending on the position and the hiring policy, you may be subjected to two or even three interviews. The first might be a screening interview with a human resources staff member. If successful, you would be invited to an individual interview with the manager of the department where you would be working. To help ensure the right decision is made, a panel interview with other managers in the reporting structure might be arranged. For a job candidate, it is a daunting experience.

The One-on-One Interview

One-on-one is most the common type of job interview. Your interviewer has already consulted with his or her supervisor regarding the kind of person suited for the position, and perhaps collaborated on a list of questions. For a job candidate, the benefit of a one-on-one interview is that you might be more comfortable speaking with one person than with a group of interviewers. From the interviewer's point of view, one drawback is that he or she has the sole responsibility for the hiring decision, so if the choice turns out to be the wrong one, it may harm the manager's reputation. Another problem is that a single interviewer might overlook certain questions that should be asked; in a group interview, different people bring different concerns to the encounter, and examine the applicant on a greater variety of areas.

The Panel Interview

The panel interview, a conversation with three or four people, can be a more demanding and nerve-wracking encounter than the one-on-one meeting, because you must respond to different people with different personalities and ways of asking questions. But a panel interview can be a valuable experience for candidates: they can get a fuller picture of the company and its employees than by meeting one representative.

Sometimes the panel divides areas for questioning ahead of time so that the interview will run efficiently; a specialist in a particular field, for example, will focus on technical questions, and an administrator on managerial ones. After the interview, the panel will compare their notes to determine your ability to fill the job and to rank you with other candidates. One information systems manager considers panel interviews a mirror of real-life work situations where a technical expert has to meet with groups of users to determine their needs.[6] How well job candidates handle panel interviews can foretell how effectively they will deal with group situations on the job.

Electronic Interviews

Some organizations will hold initial interviews using voice response, interactive Internet, or computer response technologies. Communicating through these systems is not, of course, the same as the live encounters we've been considering. Corporations that use these technologies do so early in the recruitment process to screen candidates. With interactive voice systems, candidates answer questions over the telephone; with Internet-based recruitment, applicants complete on-line questionnaires. Applicants who meet predetermined criteria are contacted for more information and face-to-face interviews. (You can try a demonstration of an on-line interview at **demonet.aspentree.com/Screen1.asp**.)

Nike has used computer-assisted interviewing when hiring for their retail outlets. Applicants watch a video showing different customer-service scenarios and respond to a series of questions by keyboarding their answers. Responses are printed out after the computerized interview, giving managers information to use in the live interview held immediately afterward.[7]

Voice response, Internet-based, and computer-assisted interview technologies are becoming popular because these automated systems, tailored to the needs of the employer, take the place of managers manually sorting through numerous paper applications. The time and cost efficiencies are significant. Another benefit is that employers can cast their hiring nets across a broader population than with traditional interviewing. Furthermore, it is claimed that applicants are more truthful with a computer than with a live interviewer.[8]

The downside, however, is that electronic recruitment systems may reject gifted candidates if they do not meet certain predetermined criteria. Another problem is that electronic systems are insensitive to the nuances of manner and voice that a human interviewer will notice.[9]

Videoconferencing is another electronic interviewing medium. Manpower Canada has found it to be a cost-effective way to interview applicants at remote locations. Unlike other electronic recruitment systems, videoconferencing permits the interviewer to see job candidates, and consequently to take note of their behaviour. However, says Dan Williams, a professional recruiter, the "all-important" last interview, before the hiring decision is made, should be held face to face.[10]

Interview Behaviour

In Chapter 4 we saw how to establish rapport when delivering presentations. Undoubtedly, in job interviews, you must also be aware of how your manner and tone might affect your audience's perception of you. Employers regard job interviews not only as an occasion for judging whether you have the technical skills to fill the position. They will infer from your behaviour your ability to interact effectively with co-workers and to represent the company to customers and suppliers. In other words, how you carry yourself during your job interviews signals whether you will be a "team player" and whether you will enhance the firm's reputation with the public.

Those First Moments

First impressions are hard to erase, be they good or bad. Your interviewers will understand that you are nervous, but they will also expect you to project confidence. Let's imagine Andrew has arrived for his first interview at the bank where he now works, having applied for the position of teller. The job would require him to deal with the public in a way that shows he is both assured and competent. He has been waiting in the reception area for his appointment.

Interviewer: [*Comes out of her office*] Hello. I'm Francesca Delgardo. I will be speaking with you today, Mr. Abolafia. [*Holds out her hand*] I'm pleased to meet you.

Andrew: [*Stands up, makes eye contact, smiles*] Thank you, Ms. Delgardo. [*Shakes her hand*] It's nice to meet you too. [*Follows her into her office*]

Note the three basic elements of Andrew's response: he looks the interviewer in the eye; he smiles; and he shakes her hand. He shows that he knows how to greet someone in a businesslike manner, and that he is, probably, prepared for the interview. Although it may sound silly to suggest that you incorporate this "greeting" scenario into your interview rehearsals, consider doing so. Practice will accustom you to this element of business etiquette. Have your interviewers in these sessions tell you whether you made direct eye contact, and if your handshake was firm. (The Royal Bank says, "Never underestimate the power of a limp, floppy handshake to turn someone off before the interview has even begun."[11]) Have them also comment on your posture; a good stance is another sign of confidence and preparation.

Also note that Andrew repeats the name of his interviewer. When he was invited to the interview, he may have been told who his interviewer would be. Repeating the name, however, is important for two reasons: one, it shows that you recognize that person as an individual; and, two, nervousness can make us forget, so repeating the names of each interviewer you meet will help you remember them.

During the Interview

Andrew can continue the good impression he established with Ms. Delgardo by following these simple guidelines:

1. Don't sit down until your interviewer invites you to.

2. Don't slouch or cross your arms in front of yourself. You want to avoid projecting an image of sloppiness, or creating a barrier between you and your interviewer.

3. Maintain eye contact, and look interested and friendly.

Although in a panel interview you will be asked one question at a time, don't focus only on the person asking the question. Everyone is listening to your answer, and looking at each panelist will show your intent to communicate on an individual level. Again, remember that your interviewers are looking at you as a potential employee, one who will communicate effectively on the job, and not only as an applicant.

Pace, volume, and vocal mannerisms are other concerns. Speak at an accessible rate, and be aware of the loudness or softness of your voice. Try your best to control vocal mannerisms: the "uhs," "ahs," "ums" mentioned in Chapter 4. Don't tack phrases such as "you know" or "o.k." at the end of statements; they are meaningless, and can irritate your interviewers. Also avoid uptalking, that is, letting your voice rise at the end of statements; this habit projects a lack of confidence.

Departure

When the interview is over, stand and say thank you. If your interviewers extend their hands again, be sure your handshake is firm. As you leave, say good-bye to the receptionist; this small courtesy may be reported back to your prospective employer.

Controlling Nervousness

In Chapter 4, I suggested methods of controlling nervousness when delivering presentations. In many ways, the rules are the same for job interviews. Prepare thoroughly by learning about the job and the company, and by anticipating questions. Hold practice interviews, and try to visualize the interview itself, with you answering questions. Speaking with company representatives at job fairs whenever possible will help you break the ice.

During your practice interview try to control nervous mannerisms, such as looking at your watch or playing with your pen or jewellery, because they will detract from your performance during the actual event. One study of speaking anxiety during job interviews found that people with low anxiety were absorbed by the interview;[12] a positive attitude with good preparation will help you relax and even enjoy the experience.

Interview Questions

Employers are concerned with five basic areas when considering job applicants:

1. **Technical skills and workplace knowledge.** Can the applicant do the job effectively? How familiar is the applicant with the industry and with the company?

2. **Communication skills.** Can the applicant speak and write clearly?

3. **Interpersonal skills.** Can the applicant relate well to co-workers and to the public?

4. **Integrity.** Is the applicant trustworthy and ethical?

5. **Personal strengths.** Is the applicant motivated and disciplined? Is the applicant aware of his or her weaknesses as well as strengths?

Interviews are often designed to test whether the applicant succeeds in all these areas. To gather this information interviewers will use a variety of questions, some of which have been discussed in Chapter 9, such as open-ended and ancillary questions. The employment interviewer will also use behavioural interviewing, that is, finding out how you handled situations in your past work. The assumption is that your answer will predict your future performance. Another type of question is the scenario: the interviewer will describe a problem, and ask how you would solve it. Your interviewers will ask you both general questions and specific ones based on your education and work history.

When answering questions, offer concrete examples, but don't ramble, and don't give one-word answers. Often, an interviewer will ask a closed question, beginning, "Do you think that ...?" Just answering "yes" or "no" is inadequate; indeed, the meeting may come to a standstill. Always elaborate on your response. And, if you don't understand a question, ask for clarification. Doing so is certainly acceptable; and your interviewers will expect you to.

Something else to keep in mind when preparing for an interview is to have a clear definition of terms you use in your answers. Your interviewers may feel that a word or phrase needs elaboration, and will ask for further commentary. Analyze the vocabulary of your responses so that you will be well prepared.

My purpose here is to present sample questions, with strategies for responding. Use these questions as a starting point to predict questions for job interviews you will have. You can find many books of interview questions in libraries and bookstores, some directed toward specific industries.

Questions about Technical Skills and Workplace Knowledge

Let's say Mahima's employer had selected her for an interview because her résumé and application letter indicated she was qualified to fill the job. The interviewer wanted to learn about some factors the résumé may not have revealed: the extent of her skills, how effectively she has applied them, and how current her knowledge is. She might be asked the following questions:

Mahima, please describe how you keep up with trends in the field.

In her answer Mahima would discuss the ways she keeps current. Perhaps she reads technical magazines and journals. She might belong to a professional association and attend annual conventions, or take a course in night school. She should be concrete and detailed, mentioning the titles of the periodicals she reads and the name of her professional association. She might also mention a specific article about a new product.

One way interviewers discover a candidate's problem-solving skills is to present a scenario and ask how the problem would be resolved. You can probably think of several incidents at your job when you had to troubleshoot problems. Another approach an interviewer might take is,

Describe two recent technical problems you encountered in your job. How did you deal with them?

The prospective employer might ask Andrew this question at an interview for a customer-service position he is seeking at a mutual fund company. When answering questions such as these, do not name people with whom you work or criticize them. A personal quality employers value is discretion; be sure to apply yours in job interviews.

Another question you might encounter is,

What salary do you think is appropriate for this position?

Applicants are often taken aback by this question. However, it is important to learn the typical salary scales for the job. You can check on-line resources: see the "Wage and Salary Information" page at **www.careermosaic.com/cm/crc/crc18.html,** for example, which lists sources for different fields. Also ask the librarian to direct you to publications listing salary scales. When answering this question, indicate that you have investigated the topic.

And, at the end of the interview, you will probably be asked this favourite question:

Do you have any questions for us?

This is a perfect opportunity to demonstrate that you have investigated the company. Questions about training opportunities, challenges in the job for which you're applying, and the working environment are suitable areas. Let your interviewers know that you have read company material; they will notice your initiative.

Questions about Communication Skills

As you already know, communication skills are a universal qualification. Your interviewer will be judging your speaking skills by listening carefully to how you answer questions: do you use language precisely? are you clear? how effective is your grammar? Your interviewer may ask you to describe some significant reports or other documents you have written, or presentations you have delivered. Your interviewer may also ask how you communicate with people whose understanding of English is limited.

Let's say that Andrew is asked about presentations: we know that he delivered a presentation to novice investors about RSPs. He could discuss how he developed his presentation by indicating how he analyzed his audience, narrowed his topic, and developed an outline and visual aids. He might also discuss how he adapted his topic for a diverse audience, how he handled questions, and what he learned from delivering a speech.

If you have taken any communication courses in secondary school, college, or university, be sure to mention them when asked about your practical communication experience. You can also discuss any collaborative writing you did in your courses, such as group projects.

Questions about Interpersonal Skills

Interpersonal skills are another important area. How you manage conflict is one important concern of employers:

> Please describe a meeting in which participants disagreed, and tell what you did to help them come to a resolution.

Let's say Mahima is asked this question. Her answer must be tactful, yet sufficiently detailed to show her ability to deal with conflict. Perhaps she is asked this question in a panel interview: she says that she would "mediate" the conflict, but does not explain what she means by the term. Another interviewer might ask her to define it; if she is well-prepared, she will be able to do so smoothly.

For certain jobs, an interviewer would be concerned with the applicant's ability to deal with the public:

> Imagine that a customer calls with a complaint about his account statement. He believes that the company has made an error. But he has misread the statement. First, describe how you would deal with this problem. And, second, describe how you would handle the customer when he becomes belligerent.

If Andrew is asked this question, his challenge would be to explain how he would deal with the customer and maintain good will.

Questions about Integrity

Companies want to hire employees whom they can trust, and who will contribute to a positive workplace environment. Interviewers might ask you about any problems you encountered with fellow workers regarding misuse of company equipment or services, for example. Or, you might be presented with the following scenario:

> Imagine you are trying to persuade a customer to buy our product instead of a competitor's, although you know the competitor's would meet the customer's needs more effectively. What would you do in this situation?

Think carefully: do you place company profits over customers' needs, and risk losing them if customers realize the product does not live up to their expectations?

Questions about Personal Strengths

Questions about personal strengths might deal with your ability to handle stress and your work habits. A frequent interview question is,

> Tell me about two of your weakest areas.

Employers want an honest response, but it's important to tell your interviewer how you are overcoming your weaknesses. Your interviewers might also ask,

> Describe a time when you were unable to meet a deadline. How did you handle this?

Alternatively, they might select details from your résumé or application letter. Andrew might have been asked at his first interview at the bank,

I see that you are a Big Brother. How do you think this experience relates to working as a customer service representative?

Andrew would highlight the connections between his voluntary activity and assisting customers, perhaps commenting on the ability he developed to understand peoples' needs and to deal with them in a clear manner.

Chapter Summary

The employment interview is important for employers and for you. Employers want to feel confident in their hiring decisions, and, like most people, you want to have a job that will not only give you a livelihood but also a degree of fulfillment. A good deal hangs on the job interview, and it might seem unfair that so much preparation is focused on one, two, or three meetings with a potential employer. If you don't get the job, learn from the experience, and use it to help you prepare for your next interview. Stay focused and committed to the job search.

I hope this chapter has alerted you to some basic interview skills. Be sure you have a thorough understanding of your current skills, and target areas where you need improvement. Your documents—your résumé, job application letter, and samples of your work, where relevant—should be neat, attractive, and, certainly, correct in grammar and spelling. Do research on the company and industry, and have several practice interviews, trying to duplicate possible interview situations as much as possible. Predict the questions you might be asked, and formulate answers so that you can deliver your responses smoothly. And maintain a positive attitude—your interviewers will notice it. Good luck!

Applications

1. Compile an inventory of your work history, making it as complete as possible. Analyze this inventory to determine the extent and variety of your education and of your communication, management, and technological skills.

2. Choose one or two companies you might like to work for and do research on them, using as many of the resources mentioned in this chapter as you can.

3. Look through newspapers and trade magazines, or at your school's career centre, to find a job for which you might want to apply. You can also use an opportunity in

your workplace. Create a set of interview questions covering the areas discussed in this chapter, and your answers.

4. Ask a friend to play the role of interviewer for Application 3. Be sure your interviewer notes your behaviour during the interview. Discuss the areas in which you were competent, and those needing improvement.

5. Why is nonverbal communication important in job interviews?

References

1. Royal Bank Financial Group, "Recruitment Benchmark Survey: Executive Summary." [www.royalbank.com/english/hr/reality/bench/execsumm.html], June 17, 1998.

2. American Society for Personnel Administration, "The Employer's Perspective." [is.dal.ca/~hrd/intervie/emppers.htm], June 22, 1998

3. Royal Bank Financial Group, "Recruitment Benchmark Survey: Executive Summary."

4. Richard L. George, "Sharing Common Ground—The Business of Education and the Education of Business" (delivered at the Mount Royal College President's Breakfast, Calgary, Alberta, September 16, 1997). [www.suncor.com/05speeches/sp0997.html], April 29, 1998.

5. Vicki W. Kramer, "Job Interviews: Employers' Favorite Interview Questions." [www.kiwicare.com/fav_questions.htm], June 23, 1998.

6. Leilani Allen, "Taking a Team Approach to Filling Open Jobs." *Computerworld* 31, no. 48 (December 1, 1997), 2. [proquest.umi.com], June 11, 1998.

7. See Linda Thornburg, "Computer-Assisted Interviewing Shortens Hiring Cycle." *HR Magazine* 43, no. 2 (February 1998). [proquest.umi.com], June 11, 1998.

8. Thornburg, "Computer-Assisted Interviewing Shortens Hiring Cycle."

9. Ibid.

10. Greg Meckbach, "Your Next Job Interview Might be at Home." *Computing Canada*, 23, no. 16 (August 5, 1997), 2. [proquest.umi.com], June 11, 1998.

11. Royal Bank of Canada. "Career Tips." [www.royalbank.com/english/hr/hints/tips.html], June 17, 1998.

12. Joe Ayres et al. "Communication Apprehension and Employment Interviews." *Communication Education* 47, no. 1 (January 1998). [proquest.umi.com], June 11, 1998.

CHAPTER 11

Ceremonial Speaking: Mixing Business and Pleasure

Many Canadian companies take time out from the daily routine of work to honour employees and to celebrate achievements. These moments of recognition are important to businesses from a business viewpoint: they help to promote a company by drawing attention to its good works and good people, thereby raising its reputation in the eyes of the public and of its employees. Recognition ceremonies also help to foster morale and productivity, by showing not only that labour is compensated with regular paycheques, but also that individuals are valued. It can be argued that honours and celebrations represent business's desire to give meaning to work, by humanizing business.

A good ceremonial speech can go far in achieving its dual purpose: to promote the organization so that people will learn about it, and, it is hoped, buy its products and services, and to present the company's human face. Typically, for high-profile events such as public ceremonies that mark a company's contributions to social, educational, or research programs, high-level executives will say the necessary words. But there are times, such as retirement and award ceremonies, when employees not accustomed to delivering a ceremonial speech must express themselves to their peers. We'll look at ceremonial business speaking and the occasions that demand it.

Some Basic Rules for Ceremonial Business Speaking

Like any speeches, ceremonial ones should observe the basic structure of an introduction, a body, and a conclusion. They also follow three particular guidelines:

1. Lean Toward Brevity

I don't want to proscribe what would be considered a lengthy ceremonial speech of, say, 20 minutes, because some special occasions call for extended remarks. For example, the event may be linked to a business theme worth discussing, and your audience will benefit by listening to you develop it. But remember that ceremonial business speeches are usually delivered at social occasions; the atmosphere is relaxed, and the audience want to enjoy themselves. Part of the speaker's job is to sustain and to enhance the good feelings associated with the moment. If the speech is too long, the audience is likely to become restless and resistant. So if you feel the need to speak at some length, consider warning your audience. Note how Matthew Barrett, former CEO of the Bank of Montreal, alerts his audience at the University of Waterloo's graduation ceremonies to his protracted remarks:

> I ... very much appreciate the invitation to address this Convocation. I know that all of you who are graduating have two overriding interests right now—and neither of them is a speech. You are here, after all, to receive your degrees. And your parents, relatives, and friends who have come to share this happy occasion with you are equally looking forward to that moment. I understand that your job prospects are also uppermost in your mind. So I shall make my remarks brief, and I shall relate them to the outlook for job creation in Canada.[1]

While using humour to assure his audience that he understands they would rather receive their diplomas than listen to him ("... two overriding interests right now, and neither of them is a speech"), Barrett also justifies his serious subject by showing its relevance to the occasion ("I understand that your job prospects are also uppermost in your mind"). So if you want to develop a particular theme in a ceremonial speech, be aware of your audience's expectations, and lean toward brevity.

2. Make It Positive

Frequently, the ceremonial occasions associated with the workplace mark milestones in a business, employee achievements, or contributions the company has made to society. Good ceremonial speeches focus on positive qualities; they don't complain about low profits or cite shortcomings in performance. The speaker's goal is to foster in the audience a sense of community and pride.

Yet ceremonial speeches may include serious thoughts, as we just saw in the excerpt from Matthew Barrett's speech delivered at the University of Waterloo. For some events, such as special-occasion dinners, executives will discuss an important business-related topic—perhaps the company is under attack for high prices or for the nature of their practices—and they will explain company policies or correct misguided perceptions in their remarks.

But sensitive speakers are aware of their audience's reaction when sober thoughts intrude upon the celebration. Skillful ceremonial speakers both justify the serious theme and balance it with confidence and optimism. For example, in his speech delivered at a British Columbia Scotiabanker Associations Tributes dinner, an event honouring employees, the chairman and CEO, Peter Godsoe, defends the banking industry against such accusations as excessive profits, favourable tax rates, and the size of Canadian banks. He justifies his topic by telling his audience—his employees—"we all have a stake in how our bank is perceived—and we all have a stake in making sure that our bank continues to be successful."[2] After addressing the criticisms, he then discusses the many contributions of Canadian banks to Canadian society and to the Canadian economy. In other words, he balances the negative with the positive.

The "make it positive" rule also means concluding the speech on a positive note—be it an optimistic look toward the future or praise of employees. Celebrating the 50th Canadarm mission, David Masotti, president of Spar Space Systems, ends his remarks by reinforcing the Canadarm's scientific and business benefits: "Building on the heritage that Canadarm represents, we at Spar know that not only is just about anything possible … it is within arm's reach."[3] (Note how he plays on the word "arm.") A good ceremonial speech sends the audience off thinking favourably about the company and proud to be connected with it.

3. Make It Personal

While innovative products, high profits, and worthwhile social causes are often the motivations for ceremonial business events, speeches for these occasions usually celebrate people. To generate an upbeat feeling, it's important to praise the employees who contributed to the achievement, and to offer some stories that exemplify the effort. For example, at the Suncor Oil Sands 30th anniversary celebration, Mike Ashar, executive vice-president of Suncor Oil Sands, says,

> Many of those bold adventurers who came to Fort McMurray in the '60's are here with us today. You persevered through the fires, the freeze-ups, and when you went home to your trailers in the knee-high mud on Biggs Avenue, you couldn't even watch *Hockey Night in Canada*. Imagine—not even CBC television could reach into the frontier town of Fort McMurray![4]

Observe here how Ashar creates a vivid picture through detail ("the knee-high mud") and through humour—the deprivation of *Hockey Night in Canada*! Brief narratives such as these try to recreate personal events, so that the audience can understand the conditions behind the success.

Types of Ceremonial Business Speeches

While you should keep the principles just described in mind for any ceremonial speech you might deliver, remember that each special occasion calls for its own approach. We'll look at specific applications of the basic rules.

Speeches Celebrating Employee Achievement

Recognizing outstanding employees with awards and special events is one way business shows its appreciation. Pick up an annual report for any major Canadian corporation, and chances are you will see a section crediting the unusual effort of workers. Canadian National Railway's 1997 annual report, for example, devotes a page to the "President's Awards for Excellence," citing specific CN workers for exceptional service.[5] And many organizations, as we've seen with Scotiabank, hold special dinners as a way to thank employees for their performance. The speeches delivered at these occasions should be carefully shaped to emphasize accomplishments and to foster pride and self-esteem.

A good speech that celebrates employee achievement turns the spotlight on the individual. Begin by describing why the group has gathered together for the occasion, so that the audience understands its importance. If the celebration is connected with a specific award, give some facts about its history and meaning. Introduce the individual being recognized, give some background information, such as the years of service with the company and the positions held, and highlight the special achievements that earned this recognition. Remember to be concrete and specific, so that the audience clearly understands why the person is being celebrated and what his or her contributions mean to the company. Conclude by asking the audience to join in with applause while the award is given.

In instances when a company holds an event to show appreciation to a group as a whole, such as a regional sales team, but not to give awards to individuals, it's still important to single out particular people in the audience and to mention their accomplishments. For example, you might refer to "Andrew Abolafia, whose ideas for special customer events increased accounts at his branch by 20 per cent." Citing specifics, even briefly, adds the human touch to the event, and shows that management is aware of the many contributions by each employee.

If you receive an award, you must, of course, give an acceptance speech. Be sure to thank the presenter, comment on the award's importance, praise people who helped you, and show appreciation to the company. Upon receiving the CEO of the Year award in 1995, the Bank of Montreal's Matthew Barrett said,

Perhaps no recognition is more highly valued than recognition by your peers. Individuals who not only know you, but also know the road you have travelled because they have travelled it themselves. I am deeply grateful to them all.

. . .

This award honours individuals, but its real purpose is to remind Canadians of the importance of business enterprise to the success of a nation. Last, but in a very real sense first, I want to thank my colleagues at Bank of Montreal for everything we have accomplished together in the six years I have had the privilege of leading them. It has not always been easy, but I believe we have often shared a sense of real achievement, and the exhilaration of exploring new frontiers.[6]

Notice how graciously Barrett acknowledges others upon receiving this recognition, and extracts the greater meaning of the award—that it represents the contribution of business to Canada's prosperity.

Speeches Marking Retirement and Departure

Companies often mark the retirement of long-serving members or the departure of valued employees, especially those who are well-liked, whether they are going to other jobs or to pursue their education. Speeches delivered on such occasions are very similar to those granting awards. In these instances, after referring to the purpose of the gathering, give a brief account of the employee's history with the company, cite his or her special contributions and good relations with colleagues, and how you valued the individual's advice. You can include some humour, but be sure to be tactful. Embarrassing stories will mortify the person being recognized and reflect poorly on you, the speaker. If you know what the person's plans are, whether hobbies, travel, or volunteer work, mention them as you conclude with everyone's best wishes for the future.

You can easily adapt the approach for speeches marking retirement to remarks about people leaving the firm. Perhaps Andrew is moving from his bank to a new job at a mutual funds company. Since he has been a very pleasant and productive employee, his colleagues take him out to lunch. His manager's brief speech comments on Andrew's performance and personality, and ends with wishing him good luck in his new job.

Speeches Marking Company Milestones and Achievements

Companies celebrate special achievements, such as an anniversary of a product, financial success, or a major venture. During these occasions the accomplishment may take slight precedence over the people involved, but employees still play an important role in speeches of this sort. In Mike Ashar's speech celebrating the 30th anniversary of the

Suncor Oil Sands project, we saw acknowledgment of the personal effort it took for the venture to succeed.

Speeches marking company achievements open with positive remarks about the occasion. Ashar introduced Suncor's celebration by saying,

> The gathering here today reminds me of a saying—"Whatever you can do, or dream you can, begin it. Boldness has genius, power, and magic in it."
>
> A German philospher wrote these words more than 100 years ago. I think they are fitting words for a company that was built on dreams, by men and women who were bold enough to pursue them.
>
> The dream was pursued long before J. Howard Pew boldly invested a quarter billion dollars in Great Canadian Oil Sands in 1963. Long before the GCOS even existed. The dream has been alive as long as people have known there was a huge reserve of oil trapped in the sands of this region. The dream has been alive as long as entrepreneurs and scientists have searched for the magic formula that would release the oil from the sand. The dream has been alive as long as politicians and governments have recognized the potential for energy self-sufficiency.
>
> Today, we are celebrating the realization of that dream.[7]

Note how Ashar uses repetition—a technique discussed in Chapter 3—to highlight the achievement and to emphasize its significance.

Spar's David Masotti began his speech celebrating the 50th Canadarm mission somewhat differently from Ashar, with the following words:

> Thank you, and good afternoon ladies and gentlemen.
>
> I cannot tell you what a thrill it is for all of us at Spar to host this celebration. There are a number of people here today who invested buckets of blood, sweat, and tears in the years leading up to that first mission in November 1981. We owe those individuals—from Spar, from our many subcontractors, from the NRC, from the Canadian Space Agency, and from other organizations—a great debt for their dedication and determination in seeing their dream through to reality. Without them Canadarm could not have flown even once, let alone 50 times.[8]

Masotti's remarks are more direct than Ashar's, but they serve the same purpose of highlighting the significance of the occasion.

The strategy for ceremonial speeches that mark company milestones includes giving the background to the accomplishment; marking the contributions of employees, business partners, and various institutions involved in the project; describing the difficulties encountered along the way to success, as well as the triumphs; and noting the benefits to the company, and, where relevant, to the industry and to society. Masotti stirs pride in Spar's Canadarm by citing the economic implications of the space-age technology:

> Although Canadarm is a tremendous technological achievement, it has grown over the years to also become a business success. It represents approximately $500 million in export sales direct to the United States from Spar, much of which has in turn gone from Spar to our Canada-wide subcontractor team. Although the first Canadarm was a gift from the Government of Canada to the Government of the U.S., the Canadarm fleet grew with the shuttle fleet, eventually numbering five. That is not the end of the export revenues Canadarm represents, however. Ongoing maintenance and sustaining engineering support have added approximately $20 million annually.[9]

Sometimes, occasions marking company achievements feature several speakers, and the master of ceremonies must introduce them. The Canadarm mission celebration is one such event. Here, Magued Iskander, vice-president and general manager of Spar Space Systems, introduces the astronaut Colonel Chris Hadfield:

> Our next guest speaker accomplished several firsts. He was the first Canadian aboard the Russian MIR, the first Canadian mission specialist, and the first Canadian to operate the Canadarm. Next year, on the 100th mission of the space shuttle program, Canadian Space Agency astronaut Col. Chris Hadfield will be involved in another first—the delivery and installation of the Canadian space station remote manipulator. We are proud to have Col. Hadfield join us today to share his experiences. Ladies and gentlemen, Col. Hadfield ...[10]

Good introductions of featured speakers note their significant accomplishments, including the most recent. Instead of offering general praise, let the speaker's achievements speak for themselves.

Speeches Announcing Community Service Programs

Through community service—donations to charitable causes or to medical research, sponsorship of youth sports teams, or employee volunteer projects such as literacy programs—Canadian companies "give back" to Canadian society. In the words of Tony Comper, CEO of the Bank of Montreal,

> ... social responsibility is not something any of us has tended to associate with big business; it has not loomed as a priority. But that is changing too—quickly and profoundly—right across corporate North America. The well-being of the wider community is becoming a business priority.[11]

These "social responsibility" speeches are somewhat different from the ceremonial speeches we've already seen. First, they may be delivered at professional gatherings such as conferences as well as on social occasions. And, instead of highlighting people, they focus on a "need" and on the company's plans for alleviating it. However, if the speech emphasizes the company's generosity for its own sake, the organization risks projecting a self-serving image; that is, the appearance that the only reason the company made the contribution was to promote itself. While a company's financial donations and community programs undoubtedly raise its public profile, the primary purposes of a speech explaining the endeavour are to improve recognition of the need for help and to encourage similar acts.

Of course, a major corporation must deal with the fact that its generosity is indeed self-serving. The best way to brave such honest accusations is to be forthcoming. In his speech delivered to the Learning Partnership Conference in Toronto, a gathering attended by educators and businesspeople, Comper admits,

> one of the main reasons the Bank of Montreal is interested in The Learning Partnership is nothing more or less than our own self-interest. By contributing to a system that equips more and more people for the new corporate culture and for the new global economy we improve our chances of employing such people at the Bank of Montreal. And because such people inevitably attract like-minded customers, we end up increasing our competitive advantage.[12]

Comper also confesses, "While we are not at all interested in selling RSPs to eight-year-olds, we do hope that when the time comes, they will recall how, back in Grade 3, Bank of Montreal was the good guy. And, of course, we do hope that in the here-and-now their parents will also think fondly of us."[13] Such openness can certainly charm an audience, disarming their cynicism by confronting it.

A speech announcing a company's good works should describe what the company is doing to address the need for help, be it a financial donation, a donation of products such as computers to local schools, or an employee volunteer program. In a speech given at the Suncor Oil Sands Discovery Centre community open house, Mike Ashar introduced a new air monitoring network, and explained Suncor's corporate commitment to a clean environment. He discussed the history of environmental problems, and noted that Suncor's programs "reduced sulphur dioxide emissions by 75 per cent from 1990 levels."[14]

When appropriate, the speech should give some background to the cause and highlight significant elements in its history. The speech should, of course, stress the need for the company's contribution. Comper says the Bank of Montreal wants to become a "partner" with public education because "We see the education of children—and their personal development—as overwhelmingly critical needs that we can help address." Providing facts undoubtedly raises awareness of the cause itself. Comper remarks,

> Between 1991 and 1993, jobs for university graduates increased by 308,000, a gain of 17% over 1990, and jobs for people with college diplomas or trade certificates increased by 170,000, a gain of 5%. At the same time, jobs for high school dropouts fell by a whopping 651,000, a decline of nearly 20% ... It has become a crisis in young people's confidence .... Many are simply disengaging from the system—not just the education system, but the whole system ....

If the supportive role of business in learning partnerships does little else and
I know it will do much else, it will send a signal to the next generation that yes,
there are good answers out there, and that we have people from all walks of life
working together to find them.

An effective conclusion to a speech announcing a company's community-service
effort can reaffirm the need, and look with hope to the future. Comper says to his audience at the Learning Partnership Conference,

My Bank of Montreal colleagues hope to come away from today's workshops with
concrete partnership ideas to follow up on promptly in their own communities. It is
my personal hope that a great many of the educators, businesspeople, and parents
gathered here today share our sense of urgency.[15]

Remember that you can reinforce a serious message better with simple words than
with elaborate ones.

Chapter Summary

Ceremonial business speeches are given on special occasions, outside the daily routine
of work. They celebrate the good times in business, when companies achieve success,
and the employees, the people whose accomplishments create it. These speeches are also
given on occasions that announce a company's service to the community, whether it is a
financial donation to an important cause or a volunteer program. Because of their positive content, ceremonial speeches may appear easier to compose than the more strictly
business-oriented presentations discussed earlier. However, ceremonial business speeches
demand sensitivity to the audience and to the occasion in order to be memorable.

Applications

1. What are the general characteristics of ceremonial speaking? Why is it important to
    follow these rules?

2. How does ceremonial speaking differ from the types of presentations discussed in
    Chapters 5 and 6 in terms of language and style? How is it similar?

3. Imagine that you are a speechwriter in a company that has donated $2 million
    toward cancer research at a major hospital in your area. Write a speech that the
    CEO would deliver at a luncheon marking the generosity of individual and corpo-
    rate donors. When delivered, the speech should be about four minutes long.

4. Why are corporations concerned about being good corporate citizens? What is the ethical dimension to corporate community service?

References

1. Matthew W. Barrett, "Notes for Remarks delivered at the University of Waterloo Convocation," Waterloo, Ontario, (October 22, 1994). [www.bmo.ca/speech/8447.htm], August 21, 1998.

2. Peter C. Godsoe, "Remarks delivered to the B.C. Scotiabanker Associations Tributes Dinner" (October 1, 1997). Print copy courtesy of Scotiabank.

3. David F. Masotti, "Remarks delivered at the 50th Canadarm Mission Celebration," Brampton, Ontario (June 18, 1998). [www.spar.ca/corp/masotti.htm], August 19, 1998.

4. Mike Ashar, "Remarks delivered at the Suncor Oil Sands 30th Anniversary Celebration and Opening of Suncor Bridge" (September 7, 1997). [www.suncor.com/05speeches/sp0697. html], April 29, 1998.

5. See Canadian National Railway Company, *1997 Annual Report*, 16.

6. Matthew W. Barrett, "Remarks on receiving the CEO of the Year Award," Ottawa, Ontario (November 8,1995). [www/bmo.ca/speech/ceo.htm], August 21, 1998.

7. Ashar, "Suncor Oil Sands 30th Anniversary Celebration and Opening of Suncor Bridge."

8. Masotti, "50th Canadarm Mission Celebration."

9. Ibid.

10. Magued Iskander, "Remarks delivered at the 50th Canadarm Mission Celebration," Brampton, Ontario (June 18, 1998). [www.spar.ca/corp/miskan.htm], July 14, 1998.

11. F. Anthony Comper, "Notes for Remarks delivered to 'Breakthrough and Beyond '94' The Learning Partnership Conference," Toronto, Ontario (April 16, 1994). [www.bmo.ca/speech/4782.htm], August 24, 1998.

12. Comper, "Remarks delivered to 'Breakthrough and Beyond '94.'"

13. Ibid.

14. Mike Ashar, "Remarks delivered to the Community Open House: Regional Air Quality Coordinating Committee and Southern Wood Buffalo Monitoring Zone," Oil Sands Discovery Centre, Regional Municipality of Wood Buffalo, Alberta (March 25, 1998). [www.suncor.com/05speeches/sp0298. html], August 24, 1998.

15. Comper, "Remarks delivered to 'Breakthrough and Beyond '94.'"

Index

Accents, 72
Acronyms, 102
Active voice, 45–46
Agenda
    for meetings, 165, 166
    for training, 95–97
Allan, Deborah, 34–35, 38–39, 44, 47–48,
    89–90, 93
Analogy, 103
Anxiety, public speaking. *See* Stage fright
Argument, 120–21
    challenges to, 120
    status quo, 121–22
    weaknesses of, 120–21
Ashar, Mike, 212, 214–15, 217
Attention-getters, 36–38
    humour, 37–38
    paraphrases, 38
    questions, 38
    quotations, 38
Audience
    and controlling stage fright, 61
    and motivational speaking, 122–24
    and oral proposals, 126–27
    and oral reports, 83
    and referential remarks, 21
    and training, 94
    and visual support, 134
    audience profile, 18–20
    defining, 17–20
    external, 18
    for persuasive speaking, 111–12
    for speeches justifying decisions and
        actions, 127–28
    identification with issues, 117
    internal, 18
    mixed, 21
    needs, 117–18
    nontechnical, 20
    primary, 21–22

secondary, 21–22
shadow, 21–22

Baillie, Charles, 42, 44–45
Barrett, Matthew, 8, 115–16, 120, 211,
    213–14
Benefits
    different from features, 118–19
    in proposals, 127
    in speeches justifying decisions and
        actions, 129
    of business speaking skills, 10–11
    of visual support, 133–34
Body language
    and listening, 183
    nonverbal cues in informational
        interviewing, 188
    See also Movement and mannerisms
Body of speech, 40–50
    See also Language; Popular culture;
        Previews, internal; Sentences; Summaries,
        internal; Transitions
Brainstorming, 170–72
    electronic, 171–72
    pool-writing, 171
    time-limited, 171
Bullet charts
    for non-native speakers of English, 135–36
Business speaking
    and professionalism, 9
    and public speaking, 7–8
    benefits of, 10–11

Calder, Don, 115
Carter, Lisa, 9
Ceremonial business speaking
    introducing speakers, 216
    rules, 211–12
    speeches announcing community service
        programs, 216–218

speeches celebrating employee achievement, 213–14

speeches marking company milestones and achievements, 214–16

speeches marking retirement and departure, 214

Chapman, Kenneth, 176

Charts, 138–49

bar, 142–43, 144

bi-lateral, 145–46, 152–53

bullet, 135–36

flow, 141

multiple bar, 143–44

multiple line, 147–48

organizational, 139–41

pie, 145–46, 152–53

segmented (stacked), 145

single line, 147, 149

volume, 147–48

Chrominska, Sylvia, 93

Clip-art, 137

Closings. *See* Conclusions

Coffey, Charles, 114–15, 119, 123, 124

Colour

and visual support, 137

Comper, Tony, 216, 217, 218

Conclusions, 38–40

for motivational speeches, 124

for speeches justifying decisions and actions, 129

mistakes in, 40

summarizing, 38–39

Concreteness, 119

Conflict

and interpersonal relationships, 190

and teams, 163

in the workplace, 189

Connotation, 46

Copyright, violating, 151–52

Credibility

and expert testimony, 119–20

and persuasive speaking, 116

and training, 104–105

and visual support, 134

Definition

defining for common understanding, 102

defining the new, 101–102

Denotation, 46

Description, 103

Detail, 85–88

and concreteness, 88

and numbers, 88

interpreting, 87

selecting, 86–87

Direct strategy, 112–13

Disagreement. *See* Conflict

Diversity, 7

Downsizing, 6

Electronic interviews, 201–202

Electronic meetings. *See* Telemeetings

Employee forums, 6

Employment

and oral communication skills, 2–4

interviews. *See* Job interviews

Ennis, Pam, 61–62, 64

Enunciating, 71

Ethics, 10

and communicating information accurately and objectively, 86

and crediting sources, 85

and detail, 85

and research, 85

Nortel code of ethics, 10

See also Copyright, violating; Presentation software

Evidence, 85, 88–90, 119–120

Exercising, 61–62

Expert testimony, 119–20

Eye contact

and listening, 182

and vocal variety, 70

for presentations, 62–63

Face-to-face communication, 175–76

Facts. *See* Detail

Falcao, Glenn, 102

Font

in bullet charts, 136–37

in scripts, 72–73
in speaking notes, 76
Freeriders, 164

George, Rick, 37–38, 47, 128, 162, 180
Gestures. *See* Movement and mannerisms
Godsoe, Peter, 35–36, 39, 42, 43, 121, 123,
    212
Groupthink, 164

Handouts
    as visual support, 156
    for training sessions, 97
Humour, 37–38
Hussain, Shahid, 110

Identification, 117
Idioms, 47
Illustrations, 149–50
Indirect strategy, 113–14
Information
    selecting for oral reports, 84
Informational business speaking
    and persuasive business speaking, 82–83
    see also Overviews; Progress reports;
        Proposals, oral; Reports, oral; Training
Interpersonal relationships, 189–92
Interviewing, informational, 184–88
    arranging the interview, 184–85
    nonverbal and vocal cues, 188
    targeting questions, 184
    types of questions, 186–88
Introductions, 32–38
    attention-getters, 36–38
    for motivational speaking, 122–24
    full, 34–35
    previewing key ideas, 33
    stating purpose, 33
    succinct, 35–36
    using humour, 37–38
Iskander, Magued, 216

Jackson, Christopher, 9
Job interviews
    behaviour, 202–204

company research, 198–99
document preparation, 198
formats, 200–201
nervousness, 204
personal inventory, 196–98
pre-interview planning, 195–200
questions, 204–208
rehearsal, 199–200
self-analysis, 195–96
Key points, 25–29
    determining, 25–26
    developing, 26–29
    in conclusions, 38
    previewing in introductions, 33
Key-word outlines, 74–76, 77
King Lear, 68

Language
    active voice, 45–46
    and training, 105
    for persuasive speaking, 114–16
    idioms, 47
    level of, 46
    needless fillers, 69–70
    repetition, 48
    unbiased, 47–48
Leadership, 190–92
Listening, 180–84
    active, 182–84
    social, 181–82

McDoom, Radhika, 50, 135
MacNaughton, John, 20–21, 103
Management, delayering, 5
Maps, 150
Masotti, David, 212, 215
Mayberry, John, 5, 46, 47, 88, 102
Meek, James, 179
Meetings, 164–72
    agenda, 165, 166
    brainstorming, 170–72
    leader's duties, 167–68
    managing discussion, 167–68
    minutes, 168, 169
    planning, 165–67

problem definition, 170
problem-solving, 168–72
recorder's duties, 168
See also Telemeetings
Michel, Bernard, 21, 113
Minutes, 168, 169
Mothersill, Gillian, 9
Motivational speaking, 122–24
    adapting strategy to audience, 122–24
    understanding climate for, 122
Movement and mannerisms, 63–65

Needless fillers, 69–70
Needs, 117–18
Noise, 22–23
    causes of, 22–23
    controlling, 23
Notes
    and font, 76
    and white space, 76
    marking transitions and pauses, 76
    speaking, 76, 78–79
    tracking, 79
    using cover sheet, 79
    see also Outlines; Scripts

Objective. *See* Purpose
Objects, 150–51
O'Brien, Mike, 47, 49, 189
Open communication, 6
Openings. *See* Introductions
Oral communication skills
    research about need, 4
Oral reports
    and written communication, 57
    and written reports, 21–22, 83–84
Organization
    chronological, 91
    of overviews, 91–92
    procedural, 91–92
    topical, 91
Osborne, R. W., 25
Outlines
    creating, 74–76
    for planning visual support, 135

key-word, 74–76, 77
outline systems, 74–76
preparation, 50–53
sentence, 76
stage directions in, 74, 77
Overviews, 90–92
    organization of, 91–92

Pace, 67–68
    and visual support, 134
Parallel structure
    in bullet charts, 139
Paraphrases
    in introduction, 37
Partners, presenting with, 65
Patterson, Lynn, 103
Persuasive speaking
    and informational speaking, 82–83
    audience for, 111–12
    benefits vs. features, 118–19
    direct strategy, 112–13
    expert testimony, 119–20
    identification with issues, 117
    indirect strategy, 113–14
    language and tone, 114–16
    motivational speaking, 122–242
    questions of argument, 120–21
    questions of evidence, 119–20
    questions of personal value, 116–19
Photographs, 150
Pitch, 71
Poetry
    and vocal delivery, 68
Popular culture
    references to in business speaking, 47
Pratt, Courtney, 38, 44, 113
Preparation, 15–17
    organizing yourself, 15–16
    outline, 50–53
    timeline, 16–17
Presentation media, 154–58
    chalkboards, 155
    electronic whiteboards, 157
    flipcharts, 155
    handouts, 156

posterboards, 155
presentation software, 157–58
slides (35mm), 156
transparencies, 156
whiteboards, 155
Presentation software, 157–58
scanned images, 152
three-dimensional effects, 152–53
Presentations
energizing, 61–65
formal, 14
with partners, 65
Previews
in introductions, 33
internal, 43–44
Problems
evaluating, 172
expressing in speeches justifying decisions
and actions, 128–29
problem definition, 170
special audience-related, 20–21
Professionalism, 9
Progress reports, 92
Pronouns, 45
Proposals, oral, 125–127
and written proposals, 125–126
content, 126–27
Proposals, written
and oral proposals, 125–26
content, 125–26
Public speaking
and business speaking, 7–8
anxiety *See* Stage fright
Purpose
formulating, 23–29
for training, 94
in introduction, 33
See also Key points

Question-answer sessions, 66–67
Questions
ancillary, 187–88
and listening, 182
as attention-getters, 38
as transitions, 42–43

at job interviews, 204–208
closed, 187
leading, 187
of argument, 120–21
of evidence, 119–20
of personal value, 116–19
open, 186
Quotations
in introduction, 37

Rapport. *See* Movement and mannerisms;
Vocal delivery
Repetition, 48
Reports, written
and oral communication, 57
and oral reports, 21–22, 83–84
Research
and credibility, 116
and persuasive speaking, 111–12
for job interviews, 198–99
primary, 151
secondary, 151
Room arrangements
for presentations, 60
for training, 98–100
Royal Bank study of employee recruitment,
194

Salloum, Fares, 45–46, 49, 176
Scripts, 72–74
Sentence outlines, 76
Sentences
topic, 49
variety in, 49–50
Service attitude, 6
Signposting, 44–45
Smiley, Cal, 111, 126
Sources,
crediting, 88–90
in visual support, 151–52
Speeches justifying decisions and actions,
127–29
action plan, 129
benefits in, 129
demonstrating solution, 129

problem overview, 127–28
Spelliscy, Peter, 42–43, 47, 48, 57, 102, 189
Stage fright, 57–61
    controlling, 58–61
    reasons for, 57–58
    See also Job interviews, nervousness
Stephenson, Carol, 8, 37, 41, 43–44, 91,
    117–18, 118–19, 121, 128, 161–62, 180,
    189, 191
Stewart, Gayle, 48, 104
Summaries
    conclusions in, 38–39
    internal, 44
Sutherland, Robert, 115, 117
Swartz, Mark, 9

Tables, 149–50
Teams
    composition of, 5
    skills needed for, 5
    team culture and the Canadian
        workplace, 161–62
    types, 163
Teamwork, 5
    benefits, 162–63
    duties of team members, 5
    problems, 164
Technical support, 5
    skills needed for, 5
Technical terminology, 101–104
    acronyms, 102
    analogy, 103
    defining for common understanding, 102
    defining the new, 101–102
    description, 103
Teleconferencing. See Telemeetings
Telemeetings, 172–76
    choice of system, 175–76
    meeting systems, 173–74
    tips for, 174–75
Tellier, Paul, 87, 180, 190, 191
Time management, 29–30
    correlating content to time, 30
    determining time limit, 29

for training, 97
    timeline, 16
Titles
    of visual support, 136
Tone, 71
    and persuasive speaking, 114–15
    uptalking, 70
Training, 93–107
    agenda, 95–96
    atmosphere, 105
    difficult people, 106
    facilitating, 106
    handouts, 97
    hands-on sessions, 97
need for, 93
    organizing material, 94–97
    presentation techniques, 105
    time management, 97
    types of, 93
    venue preparation, 98–100
    See also Technical terminology
Transitions, 41–43
    questions as, 42–43
    showing contrast, 42
    statements as, 41–42
Transliteration, 71

Uptalking, 70

Variety
    and vocal delivery, 70–71
Venue planning sheet, 24
Videotapes, 150
Visual support
    and non-native speakers of English, 135–36
    benefits of, 133–34
    bullet charts, 135–36
    calculating number of visuals, 135–36
    charts, 138–49
    clip-art, 137
    design considerations, 136–38
    electronic manipulation of images, 152–53
    handouts for training, 97
    illustrations, 149–50

inconsistent increments in line charts, 147, 149

maps, 150

objects, 150–51

parallel structure in bullet charts, 139

photographs, 150

planning, 134–36

presentation media, 154–58

sources, crediting, 151–52

tables, 149–50

titles, 136

using outline for, 135

videotapes, 150

Vocal cues in informational interviewing, 188

Vocal delivery, 67–72

controlling pace, 67–68

controlling pitch and tone, 71

enunciating, 71

injecting variety, 70–71

preventing needless fillers, 69–70

reading poetry, 68

uptalking, 70

volume, 71

Volume, 71

Wilson, L. R., 101–102